Image of Istanbul
Impact of ECOC 2010 on the c

TRANSNATIONAL PRESS LONDON

Books by TPL

Image of Istanbul: Impact of ECOC 2010 on the city image

Conflict, Insecurity, and Mobility

Family and Human Capital in Turkish Migration

Göç ve Uyum

Little Turkey in Great Britain

Overeducated and Over Here

Politics and Law in Turkish Migration

Turkish Migration, Identity and Integration

Turkish Migration Policy

Journals by TPL

Border Crossing

Göç Dergisi

International Economics Letters

Journal of Gypsy Studies

Kurdish Studies

Migration Letters

Remittances Review

Transnational Marketing Journal

To my father
Prof. Dr. Hasan Zafer Doğan

Image of Istanbul

Impact of ECoC 2010 on the City Image

Evinç Doğan

TRANSNATIONAL PRESS LONDON
2016

IMAGE OF ISTANBUL: IMPACT OF ECOC 2010 ON THE CITY IMAGE

Evinç Doğan

First Published in 2016 by TRANSNATIONAL PRESS LONDON in the Ukinted Kingdom, 12 Ridgeway Gardens, London, N6 5XR, UK. www.tplondon.com

Paperback

ISBN: 978-1-910781-26-5

Cover Photo: Evinç Doğan

Cover Design: Nihal Yazgan @ nihalidea.com

Contents

List of Tables

List of Figures

List of Abbreviations

A.Ş.: Anonim Şirket
AKM: Atatürk Kültür Merkezi
AKP: Adalet ve Kalkınma Partisi
AMA: American Marketing Association
CDA: Critical Discourse Analysis
CoC: Cities of Culture
EACA: The European Association of Communications Agencies
EC: European Commission
ECCM: European Cultural Capitals and Months
ECoC: European Capital of Culture
EU: European Union
FIA: Fédération Internationale de l'Automobile
GaWC: Globalization and World Cities
IBB: Istanbul Büyükşehir Belediyesi
IKSV: Istanbul Kültür ve Sanat Vakfı
IMC: Integrated Marketing Communication
IOC: International Olympic Committee
ITU: Istanbul Technical University
MTM: Medya Takip Merkezi
NISI MASA: European Network of Young Cinema
OED: Oxford English Dictionary
PPP: Public Private Partnership
PR: Public Relations
SSM: Sabancı Üniversitesi Sakıp Sabancı Müzesi
T.C.: Türkiye Cumhuriyeti
TCC: Transnational Capitalist Class
TMSK: Turkish Music State Conservatory
TOKI: Toplu Konut İdaresi
TOSFED: Turkish Automobile Sports Federation
WRC: World Rally Championship

Acknowledgements

This book is based on the doctoral research and revised and written while being supported by the Scientific and Technological Research Council of Turkey (TUBITAK) under the programme TUBITAK BIDEB 2219 – International Postdoctoral Research Scholarship for author's post-doctoral research at the University of Belgrade in Serbia. I would also like to thank Mrs. Yavuz, who was Head of Tourism & Promotion Directory of Istanbul 2010 Agency for providing the original digital copies of posters.

About the Author

Evinç Doğan obtained her PhD in Management and Development of Cultural Heritage from IMT Institute for Advanced Studies Lucca (Italy). She holds MSc in History of Architecture from Istanbul Technical University and BA in Tourism Management from Bogazici University. She has been a visiting post-doctoral fellow at Bocconi University, ASK Center, resident research fellow at Istanbul Studies Centre, Kadir Has University, and visiting PhD fellow at the Regent's Centre for Transnational Studies (RCTS), Regent's University London. Currently, she is a post-doctoral research fellow at University of Belgrade (Serbia). Doğan's research interests include place marketing, city branding, cultural heritage, tourism, and visual culture.

Introduction

The mega-events are useful to spread the word about the city. Yet the meaning is created through imaging the city and positioning this image in the minds of the people. In this sense, the mega-events may be used as forms of advertising for city marketing and branding, where the signification is not only about production of meaning but also staging of the meaning. The cities hosting mega-events can be turned into the protagonists of the spectacle by showcasing their cultural products as well as cultural being. Thus, what staged there are the city, its image as well as the events. The ways in which the city and its image are influenced and perhaps modified in the process of a mega-event, where the meaning is expressed, disseminated while also being staged is the subject of this book.

The first chapter of this book sets the theoretical approach for understanding and dissecting the city image. Thus, the object here is the city image. It moves from wider through narrower definition of concepts through which the city and its image are discussed in a relationship to different approaches and contexts determining the focus area of the study. In the second chapter city marketing is explained by the spectacles' mechanisms, acting as marketing and branding tools to communicate the city image.

The third chapter draws the contextual framework in an exploratory reading of stages in the development of the city and its image through myths, politics and discourses. The impact of the spectacle (or interchangeably mega-event of Istanbul 2010) on the image-making process for the city is explored. Istanbul "took the stage" as one of the three European Capital of Culture (ECoC) cities, where the urban spaces have become the theatre décor while the inhabitants and the visitors have become the spectators of the event. Istanbul 2010 is chosen as an example of a mega-event. Communication strategy was reported to be one of the strong points for Istanbul's ECoC application (Rampton et al., 2011:67). Therefore, the image-making is analysed as part of the marketing communication strategy.

The concept of city image in a marketing and advertising perspective is a component of city brand. The language of signs is the main instrument used in understanding the discourses and the image of Istanbul as reflected on the posters of Istanbul 2010. The analytical framework is based on the city image making process, which was one of the objectives of the cultural programme of Istanbul 2010. The sample of Istanbul 2010 posters through their form and content is described in chapter four. In the fifth chapter, I deal with the question of the ways in which ECoC 2010 impacted on the city image of Istanbul, a component of the city brand. Further questions raised include the ways in which the city brand created, ECoC's relevance to the brand of

Istanbul, distinctive features of Istanbul used in branding the city, branded components linked to Istanbul image, and the existing images of Istanbul prior to ECoC.

I focus on the "How" question, and therefore the visual meanings and messages behind this image-making process are examined by analysing the posters used in marketing communication. Advertisements and posters are not simply visual displays to be looked at, but they generate discourses aimed at communicating the brand (Oswald, 2012: 35).

Branding and image making are recognized as part of the strategic goals of Istanbul 2010. "Enhancement of the city image" (Palmer, 2004: 17) is set as a part and parcel of the objectives of ECoC Programme. This also explains the reason why the case of ECoC is chosen to investigate a mega event's impact on Istanbul's image. The case of Istanbul 2010 is discussed in terms of both its temporality and its sustainable effects on the city image. The link between the urban transformation projects, cultural and artistic events and promotional discourses are investigated within this framework.

The study focuses on the urban representations with an aim to identify shared imaginary and the variability in meaning. It is essential to have a multiple perspective approach in order to develop understanding of symbolic meanings created through branding strategies. Therefore, it is needed to strive for conscious pluralism to generate as many different meanings as possible. This suggests an interpretive research based on critical approach to the collected data rather than being largely concerned with the conceptual domain of theory testing.

As the researcher, my role is to throw a light on the process of (re)creating and positioning the city image in the minds of the people by deconstructing the images and messages used on posters of Istanbul 2010 events. The posters are the reflective materials where one can trace the evidence to unravel the attempts, intentions, or steps - conscious or implicit - that might have influenced the city image. Therefore, I have chosen to employ mixed qualitative methods for analysing visual data. The interpretation is based on certain degree of subjective knowledge of the cultural codes and shared meanings among the society. The high degree of complexity in this process is reflected on the findings. Clarity and justification around process and practice of method is vital for better understanding and possibility of application of the analytical model for future projects. This effort can, hopefully be recognized as a valuable contribution, which can be applied to further studies in this field.

Chapter 1: Understanding and dissecting the city image

What is the city in terms of lived space vs. imagined space?

The imagined city as the space of representation and fantasy in the literary texts intersects with the real city as the lived space (Bridge & Watson, 2000). This intersection determines how the city is signified, perceived and experienced (Stevenson, 2003).

Calvino (1997 [1972]) portrays cities as imaginary spaces and forms a playground for cognitive imaging of the city. Without the narrator's imagination cities cannot exist, so that they are invisible. Pike (1981: 126-127) claims "word-city exists not in space but in narrative time". The oldest literary texts in the history one can ever think of, such as Gilgamesh or Iliad, could not have been imagined without the cities they are about. Yet, the imagined city, with all its "illusions, myths, aspirations and nightmares" becomes real; as real as the city located on the maps, in statistics and in architecture (Raban, 1974: 2). Abbas (2003: 143) comments about the play between the city and the image:

> *"We learn more about the image through the city than about the city through the image. That is why so many images of the city tell us so little about the city itself."*

So, why produce all this work on the city image? The answer lies in the fact that the city is not our product but the city image is. Is it possible to name the city as a product at all? Yes, the city is product of human existence and lived experience. This is an approach to the city as a lived space. On the other hand, branding approaches to the city as an imagined space and aims to influence people's perceptions of the city image. Therefore, branding is recognized as a form of communication to convince people to buy images circulating in the market. Yet, people remain free to buy or not to buy, as they remain free whether to look at those images, or to look the other way, or not to look at all (MacCannell 2001: 24). My concern here is not the end result, but the overall process of communicating the city image.

The city and its image are open to different readings. Since, understanding the city image requires firstly understanding the city, it is essential to define the city in different contexts.

Mumford (2007: 87) defining the city as a social institution says *"A city is a geographic plexus, an economic organization, an institutional process, a theatre of social action, and an aesthetic symbol of collective unity."*[1] In this

---

[1] "What's a City" has first appeared as a text in Architectural Record, LXXXII (November, 1937).

theatre, the roles of actors and spectators are interchangeable. The city is dynamic. It is created and recreated in the ever-changing social, cultural, political and economic conditions as its function, meaning and use change. Lefebvre (1991: 121) explains the *"raison d'etre"* of the spaces by a certain order and also a certain disorder of do's and don'ts associated with the power. The space is produced and reproduced (Lefebvre, 1991). Space is a product of the society, which also transforms the society itself.

Lefebvre (2003 [1970]: 57) describes the relationship between the city and its image by suggesting the image as the social object in contrast to the city itself:

> *"The concept of the city no longer corresponds to a social object [...] However, the city has a historical existence that is impossible to ignore. Small and midsize cities will be around for some time. An image or representation of the city can perpetuate itself, survive its conditions, inspire an ideology and urbanist projects. In other words, the "real" sociological "object" is an image and an ideology!"*

In this context, Kipfer et al. (2008: 292) comment on Lefebvre's understanding of the city image, by focusing on differences and contrasts in the city:

> *"The city can be defined as a place in which differences know, recognize, test, confirm, or offset one another: space–time distances are replaced by contradictions, contrasts, superimpositions, and juxtapositions of different realities."*

Lefebvre (1991) employs a conceptual triad in explaining the "production of space". In this framework "spatial practices" refer to perceived space, "representations of space" denote the conceived space and "representational spaces" address the lived space (Lefebvre, 1991). I concentrate on the "representations of space" in an attempt to identify what is lived and what is perceived by means of what is conceived. Accordingly, the first part -city of signs- describes how the city is conceived through signs and codes, which are tied to the representations imposed by the flows and the networks binding cities. The second part –city image– is about how the city is perceived through the visual signs that are communicating the city image. City of spectacle, as the final part of this chapter, rests upon the theatre metaphor in defining the city both as a lived space and as a stage. The concept of spectacle addresses the mega-event as a marketing tool for showcasing the city and its image.

City of Signs

City of signs tells about the representation and communication process in recognizing signs as means of mediation. According to Ledrut (1986: 223) "the city is a symbol, and there is symbolization of the city, but it is in the image itself, apprehended through and by discourse [...]". Cities are complex systems of representations, in which space and time are imagined as well as experienced through signs - written words, painting, photographic images, maps and signals, filmic narratives, choreographic movements, installations and events, buildings and places (Borden et al., 2001: 14-15). These selective representations (re)shape the metaphors and narratives, which are widely used to describe the experience of urban living.

Real city vs. represented city:

Calvino (1997 [1972]) underlines the distinction between the city in its real form and its representation. Short (1999: 38) describes different ways of representing cities as the acts of urban representation: "the naming of cities, the mapping of cities and the written and spoken descriptions of cities". These acts intend to communicate selected representations with their intended meanings.

The cityscapes are central to the global culture industry as "architecture and urbanism become less a question of objects and volumes while urban space becomes a space of urban intensities" (Lash & Lury, 2007: 15). Koolhaas et al. (2002) claims that architecture becomes increasingly surfaces of communication, intensities, and events. Tschumi (1991) expresses these intensities by "event-architecture", which is placed in the contemporary culture. Architecture can be seen as a form of representation with all the meanings created through culture, economy and branding of cities. Mega-projects require mega-budgets, in which the economic capital is transformed into symbolic capital (Bourdieu, 1977: 121). The notion of representation and sign value draws us closer to the debate on the global cities and power mechanisms. Globalization process was initially linked to the process of "internationalization of capital" (Palloix, 1975), and then to the transnationalization through "the rise of global cultural flows and deteriorating signs, meanings and identities" (Amin & Thrift, 1994: 4). Therefore, it does not only refer to the flows of goods and capital but also to the process of creating the sign value and the symbolic meaning through an exchange in the urban networks. Jacobs (1969, 1984) defines the livable city where she highlights mechanisms of production, consumption and distribution through her concept of city generic processes. She argues that rapid, explosive economic growth is provided by the city network formation.

What she has described about economic arrangements and networks in the 1960s, is visible in the processes of today's global city.

World city vs. global city:

Sassen (1991) coined the term "global city" with respect to the centrality of cities in the global economy. The term "advocates a shift of attention to the advanced servicing of worldwide production," and takes "power" central to the world economy system (Derudder, 2006: 2034). According to Friedman's (1986) "world city hypothesis", cities are identified as "global players" in terms of concentration of international institutions, banks and the headquarters of transnational corporations (Thornley, 1999: 3). As it can be seen, "world city" is used widely in the literature as a synonym to "global city", although world city literature has been characterized by "theoretical sophistication and empirical poverty" (Taylor, 2004: 33). Derudder (2006) posits that Friedmann's formulation takes multinational corporations as the key agents of world city system whereas Sassen emphasizes production side in the global economic system. Table 1 summarizes the distinction between the world city and the global city by comparing the two.

Table 1. "Taxonomy of main theoretical approaches"

	World cities	Global cities
Key author	Friedmann	Sassen
Function	Power	Advanced servicing
Key agents	Multinational corporations	Producer service firms
Structure of the network	Reproduces tripolar spatial inequality in the capitalist world-system	New geography of centrality and marginality cutting across existing core/periphery patterns
Territorial basis	Metropolitan region	Traditional CBD (Central Business District) or a grid of intense business activity

Source: Derudder (2006).

Friedmann (1986) and Sassen (1991) shared a common interest to explore the new geography of the world economy. They have sought for nodal points to connect "geographically dispersed production units" (Friedmann 1986: 71), as well as "locations for the governance of cross-border economic activities" (Sassen 1991: 3). In this framework, while the global interconnectivity becomes inevitable in the pursuit of "global-scale competitive efficiency", the strategies become more responsive to country-level operations (Sirkeci, 2013a: 25). Sassen (2000: 33) defines a transnational urban system wherein "cities are crucial nodes in the cross-border network of financial centres". This kind of transnational structure is different from the dominant cities in the world system by definition and by operation means. The global cities in the transnational urban system are not

Table 2. Largest Urban Areas in the World/ Megacities

Rank	Geography	Urban Area	Population	Density	Land (km²)	Density
1	Japan	Tokyo-Yokohama	37,126,000	11,300	8,547	4,300
2	Indonesia	Jakarta	26,063,000	24,200	2,784	9,400
3	South Korea	Seoul-Incheon	22,547,000	27,000	2,163	10,400
4	India	Delhi, DL-HR-UP	22,242,000	29,700	1,943	11,500
5	Philippines	Manila	21,951,000	39,900	1,425	15,400
6	China	Shanghai, SHG	20,860,000	15,500	3,497	6,000
7	United States	New York, NY-NJ-CT	20,464,000	4,600	11,642	1,800
8	Brazil	Sao Paulo	20,186,000	16,500	3,173	6,400
9	Mexico	Mexico City	19,463,000	24,600	2,046	9,500
10	Egypt	Cairo	17,816,000	27,000	1,709	10,400
11	China	Beijing, BJ	17,311,000	12,800	3,497	5,000
12	Japan	Osaka-Kobe-Kyoto	17,011,000	13,700	3,212	5,300
13	India	Mumbai, MAH	16,910,000	80,100	546	30,900
14	China	Guangzhou-Foshan, GD	16,827,000	13,700	3,173	5,300
15	Russia	Moscow	15,512,000	9,100	4,403	3,500
16	Bangladesh	Dhaka	15,414,000	115,000	347	44,400
17	United States	Los Angeles, CA	14,900,000	6,100	6,299	2,400
18	India	Kolkota, WB	14,374,000	30,900	1,204	11,900
19	Pakistan	Karachi	14,198,000	47,300	777	18,300
20	Argentina	Buenos Aires	13,639,000	13,400	2,642	5,200
21	Turkey	Istanbul	13,576,000	25,100	1,399	9,700
22	Brazil	Rio de Janeiro	12,043,000	15,400	2,020	6,000
23	China	Shenzhen, GD	11,885,000	17,600	1,748	6,800
24	Nigeria	Lagos	11,547,000	33,000	907	12,700
25	France	Paris	10,755,000	9,800	2,844	3,800

Source: Cox (2012).

necessarily historical capital cities such as Rome or Cairo and they are not in competition with one another (Robinson, 2009: 18). According to Sassen (2000: 41-44):

> *"The implantation of global processes seems to have contributed to increasing the separation, or disarticulation, between cities and sectors within cities that are articulated with the global economy and those that are not. Some cities become part of transnational networks, whereas others become unhinged from the main centres of economic growth in their regions or nations."*

GaWC (Globalization and World Cities) Study Group and Network founded by Loughborough University established research for an "analysis of detailed empirical data in constructing a global urban hierarchy" and produced an inventory known as "GaWC Inventory of World Cities" (Beaverstock et al., 1999). McAdams (2007) notes that that many of these cities are large cities, but not among the mega-cities that count over ten million population (see Table 2). When looked at the geographical and demographic features of the mega-cities, there are two issues to be raised. First is the issue regarding the size, and second is the economic development level.

The major condition to be identified as a global city is the function of economic coordination of complex activities at a global scale. Moreover, to be able to form such global interactions, cities need to establish infrastructure and specialized services in order to "organize production, exchange and consumption in their economies" (Bourdeau-Lepage & Huriot, 2005). However, most of the cities listed in the Table 2 are controversial examples that have high population but low development level. Istanbul is listed as the 21st on the list according to the population size exceeding thirteen million. The European cities are less in number on the list, because their size is small although their economic performances are large. Thus, size is not the only and the major condition. The global functions of the megacities are closely related to the "less measurable human elements", as the city should be able to create sufficient diversity, skills and information externalities (Bourdeau-Lepage & Huriot, 2006: 5,8).

Transnational network of cities:

Since the early 1990s, the network of cities expanded through the growing number of cities "that either are global cities or have global city functions" (Sassen, 1991: 347-8). New geographies of centrality emerged and linked major financial centres into an integrated system, which expanded the network of global cities from the North to the South. In this context, there has been a shift in the definition of the network of cities as well as in the notion of the term. Transnational network of cities and transnational urban systems entered into the literature as a result of this shift "characterized by world market orientations and significant concentrations of company headquarters..." (Robinson, 2009: 17). Transnational networks of cities operate on the "global flows of money, information, and people" (Robinson, 2009: 12). Parnreiter (2010) remarks the transnationality of the cities as the "sites of transnational practices, contexts of transnational network formation, socially structured settings for social interaction, and mediators of the power, meaning, and effects of transnational flows from above as well as from below".

Establishing networks between the cities, through programmes such as ECoC and Twin Towns or Sister Cities, is crucial for the spread of information and facilitating mobilities. In 1991, Network of European Cultural Capitals and Months (ECCM) is created to enable "dissemination of information" (Varbanova, 2009: 3). The images of cities become inevitably transnational in this network through mega-events such as ECoC. One of the operational objectives of the ECoC Programme is stated as "facilitating international exchanges and create international networking structures" through "individuals and organisations on exchanges and transnational activities" (Rampton et al., 2011: 8). In the report (Rampton et al., 2011: 82); the role ECoC is stressed in establishing collaborations with other cities across Europe:

"For example, the "41°-29° Istanbul Network" brought together fifteen European cities to create opportunities for intercultural co-operation between young artists; in recognition of its contribution to world peace, mobility of young artists, development of culture, and intercultural dialogue, the Network was awarded the "European Culture Award" by the Kultur Forum Europa. The agency also provided support for 36 of Istanbul's 39 municipalities to implement transnational cultural projects in collaboration with their sister cities in Europe and elsewhere in the world. For many of these municipalities, the projects were the first time that they had undertaken such transnational activity of a cultural nature."

These processes are linked to the formation of transnational class in the global political economy (Gill, 1990) and the new vocabularies brought by its context. Globalization reshapes the economic activities and organizes the production and consumption mechanisms according to the orders of the capitalist system (Sassen, 2007). Culture is commodified in "globalizing cities and the cities capitalize a globalizing culture" (Short, 2012: 50). Thus, globalization is associated with the capitalist system, which gave birth to new social forms such as transnational class and network society (Robinson, 2009: 5). These two social forms are crucial in the global system theory, which is based on transnational practices across the national boundaries. The city systems are part of the global system theory. The networks facilitate the communication and economic transactions as they "account for the transactions binding global cities" (Sassen, 1991: 171-2).

Homogenization and uniform urban representation:

Sklair (2006: 24) defines the building blocks of global system theory in the sphere of culture-ideology of consumerism, which is shaped by transnational corporation, transnational practices, and still-evolving transnational capitalist class (TCC). According to his theory, iconic architecture is exemplified "as a prime strategy of urban intervention" by the different fractions of TCC (Sklair, 2005: 498). Thus, iconic architecture is a part of city image through the orders of spectacle. The examples of iconic architecture resemble to each other by the homogenizing effect of forces shaping them as "they belong to an international property market" (Presas, 2005: 4). The threat of globalization as a matter of homogenization leads to a paradox in city branding in terms of iconic architecture. Crampton and Krygier (2006: 17) comment on the contemporary architectures that convey the global mind-set of consumption of culture and consumption of images leading to the dissipation of the historical context and identity. Wilk (1995: 117) formulates this in the form of social re-organization of the diversity, what he calls as "structures of common difference" to fit into the web of global cities through a uniform presentation.

The commodification of culture produces "symbolic meanings and associations increasingly determining economic value of goods" (Short, 2012: 48). Cultures of cities are subjected to commodification while the images of cities are exploited, reinvented or recreated in order to "sell the place as a destination product for tourists or investment." (Page and Hall, 2003: 309). The effect of standardization in the culture industry brought by the capitalistic order introduced the terms such as McDonaldization (Ritzer, 2000) and Disneyfication of urban space (Sorkin, 1992; Bryman, 1999; Eeckhout, 2001), which stand out for the commodification, homogenization and rationalization of time and space (Gotham & Krier, 2008: 172). The flow of ideas, symbols, goods and capital creates homogeny in consumption habits through time and space compression. When we evaluate consumption habits in the context of consumption culture, we can infer that "culturally led redevelopment schemes" reduce cultural products into visual representations

(Miles, 2005: 899) and create "a landscape of visual consumption" (Zukin, 1991: 230).

Nevertheless, the processes behind the homogenization of cultures and spaces are different from the consumer markets and the global entertainment industry (Sassen, 1991: 347-8). Globalization makes the cities resemble to each other and leads to homogenization of culture both in terms of their images, identities and cultures. National identity is diminishing while the transnationalism is rising and the order of capital asks for commercialization of culture (Canclini, 2001: 90).

The city imaging visualizes homogenized spaces where the message would be banal as they only talk about what is already known. The symbols, the urban representations are the references of perception, but when they resemble to each other, the context is lost. Homogeneity can be explained by the globalization effect as well as the "sharpness of the image", which is described by "vividness and integrated physical setting" of the image (Lynch, 1960: 4). The social role of the sharp images is related to the collective experiences, which also explains shared meanings. Cities cannot be imagined as ghost towns of corporate towers belong to international business and finance firms (Sassen, 2007: 23). Cities do not exist without its people. That is why, in opposition to the homogenization of the urban forms and urban space, big metropolises emphasize the diversity and multiculturalism in their image. The key to branding cities is recognizing the "city's complexity and heterogeneity" (Kalandides, 2007: 5, 9). According to Harvey (2012) "city has to embrace the others".

Sheller & Urry (2004: 165) posits that mobilities represent "new urban forms, cultural synergies and challenges to the social relations of the city [...]" and therefore reproduce power relations. Maitland (2010: 177) focuses on the effect of globalization and homogenization not only in the physical existence of transnational spaces but also in their urban imaginaries. The "resonant images" offered by undifferentiated global cities serve to "simulate this urban playground that destroys the urban" (Annibal-Iribarne, 2003: 183). The increasing flow of information has facilitated copying from each other. The successful cases in city marketing generate lessons to learn but cities should not copy from each other. As the cities tend to copy "a successful formula with buildings or events", they are also likely to decrease their competitive advantage by diminishing the uniqueness and diversity (Maitland, 2010: 177). Although there is not a unique formula, similar images of modern architecture are used for global cities (Holcomb, 1994). Jenkins (1999) challenges to this situation by putting the identity of the city forward in the city's product package. Successful urban planning takes years of strategic implementation; thus Jacobs opposes taking a short-cut of copy-paste projects:

"Stop the big projects, as they only will lead to urban monotony. And do not strive for instant success. Sometimes it takes years before abandoned urban areas are brought back to life." (cited in Hospers & van Dalm, 2005: 11)

In the global city model, the homogenization effect as a result of economic activities that cross borders in the form of international trade and investment is underlined (Sassen, 1991: 347-8). Thus, the cities are taking new forms in an environment ruled by the global and transnational structures. While the cities are emerging as global centres for economic financial transactions, their images turn into products shaped by the urban change. In other words, these conditions led cities to adjust their images either as the end result of financial accumulation or to attract investment (Soysal, 2009).

Ashworth (1992: 5) describes the qualities that shape the city within "regional and inter-urban networks", in the web of physical, structural, economical, social and cultural factors and according to their relationships with one another. In this context, the city is the space where production and consumption take place and social agglomerations are formed as existence of a city depends on people and economic activities (Short, 1984). According to Sassen (2007: 3), "global - whether and institution, a process, a discursive practice, or an imaginary - simultaneously transcends the exclusive framing of national states yet partly inhabits national territories and institutions". The discourses of power show itself in the global economic system as a "function of the power of transnational corporations and global communications". The images transmitting the messages and discourses in this global communication system emphasize "hypermobility, global communications, the neutralization of place and distance" (Sassen, 2007: 97).

Flow of signs:

There is an interplay between Sassen's (1991) definition of "global city" and Castells' (1989) notion of "informational city" based on the function of dissemination of information. Place marketing is crucial in attracting global flows of capital as well as the information flow; both are part of "spaces of flows" (Castells, 1989: 170). According to the theory of "spaces of flow", "the more organizations depend upon flows and networks, the less they are influenced by the social contexts associated with the places of their origin" (Castells, 1989: 170). According to this theory, the organizational logics are "placeless" and "independent from the societal logic" (Parnreiter, 2010). Yet, the cross-border connections are not only constituted by particular flows in the physical space. The sociology of space should be studied carefully in order to be able to understand the production of (symbolic) markers representing the transnational space.

Moreover, Appadurai (1990, 1996) claims that globalization is more complex than being only the transnational capital flows between global financial centres. He adds ethnoscapes (the flow of people), mediascapes (the flow of images and symbols), technoscapes (spread of technology), and ideoscapes (global spread of political ideas) to the space of flows (cited in Andersson, 2010: 196). Although Appadurai (1996: 2-9) highlights "electronic mediation and migration to produce a global imaginary", mediascapes are of particular interest in terms of city of signs comprised of images and symbols.

Lash & Lury (2007: 7-14) define the media environment as a "forest of extended intensities, of material signified around which subjects find their way, orient themselves via signposts". The development of mass media and digital revolution affected the communication systems by marking the shift in the permeation of the symbols and messages. The urban spaces become "decontextualized and deteriorated" (López-Varela, 2009: 11), as the borders are removing; the world is shrinking and becoming a global village (McLuhan, 1964).

City Image

Lynch (1960) introduced the city image to the urban realm from the eyes of a city dweller by conceiving the city as a text to be read and the image as a mental map, in his book "The Image of the City". Lynch (1960) proposes three components of city image, which are identity, structure and meaning. Identity and structure addresses physical features of image formation, whereas meaning is related to what we interpret, by looking at these physical structures. The identity and the structure are set and intrinsic to the city, but the meanings may vary from one person to another and they usually do so. Legibility and visibility are the two elements that identify the imageability, which is "quality in a physical object that gives it a high probability of evoking a strong image in any given observer" (Lynch, 1960: 9). These qualities are led by the compositional elements such as colour and spatial organization in the image. Nevertheless, the effect of physical environment as an "independent variable" also impacts on the "social meaning of an area" (Lynch, 1960: 10).

Meaning of place:

The image of the city is produced in a symbol system in which "a host of interests whereby denotative and connotative levels of signification are entwined and new species of urban mythologies, mythographies and place-images emerge" (Lefebvre 1991; Lindner 2007; Shields 1991 cited in Stahl, 2009: 257). Meaning has three levels: firstly, denotative meaning which lies at the lower level and coincides with object recognition, secondly connotative meaning that is middle-level meaning and refers to emotional values associated with the object and thirdly abstract meaning which is a higher level meaning that refers less to the object than to broader values (Rapoport, 1990: 221-3). To be able to infer meaning, one has to have a certain degree of relationship with a place; either directly or through mediation such as image (Carr et al., 1992: 233). Lynch (1960: 11) suggests, "it is possible to strengthen the image either by symbolic devices by retraining of the perceiver or by reshaping one's surroundings". The latter takes the form of urban transformation projects on the political playgrounds. Nevertheless, according to Nasar (1998: 2) the urban change should be a guided one:

> *"The city landscape may have a value as a source of delight to people. Thus, the shaping & reshaping of the city 'should be guided by a visual plan'. To devise such a plan we need to know how the public evaluates the cityscape and what meanings they see in it."*

Sense of place:

Andreoli (1996: 64) describes the senses that form the image of the city "we first think about its look- the look of its buildings, streets and monuments. Thus the image of the city is shaped by its form (physical aspects such as buildings, streets and monuments), as well as the meanings we attribute to it and our memories, our sense of that particular place. The image is strongly related to the sense of place. Massey (2004: 14) argues that the multiplicity of identities, peoples, social relations, and conflicts hosted at a place does not undermine their specificity and unique sense of place. There are meanings in places hiding as the "invisible landscapes" of the city in its image (Gould & White, 1974: 111). The invisible meanings attached to a place may stem from one's own senses.

Mental images:

Mental structures play a central role in the perception of the images of the city as well as the city itself. According to Espelt & Benito (2005: 777), "knowledge, impressions and values based on a series of perceptions" are influential in the formation of mental structures. Lynch (1960: 1-2) implies the variation of perceptions through the surroundings, memories and past experiences. Sometimes they are constructed by the physical experience in the city, sometimes through images and narratives. Whatever is the case, whether a personal experience or not, we have a certain image in our minds. Colomb (2012: 1) says that people have an image of a city in their head through the collection of icons. This may be either result of a cognitive process of association or "social construction of a particular image and meaning" (Lehrer, 2002: 61).

Zukin (1995: 1) sees urban regeneration plans as "a source of images and memories". The collective identity and memory create a sense of belonging through the shared images. Whereas, Hamilton et al. (2001, cited in Maisetti et al, 2012: 3) suggest cultural instruments and public art play a crucial role in urban revitalization leading to "the collective elaboration of new city images". Therefore, the new image (that is intended to be created) is not totally brand new, but it is built as a new layer on top of the existing image. In this sense, a city is more than a representational entity, which is "a space not only perceived, but also lived, experienced and practiced" (Hubbard, 2006: 221).

"Older people still experience the need to translate images into observed reality. When they travel they want to see the Eiffel Tower or the Grand Canyon exactly as they saw them first on posters. An American tourist . . . does more than see the Eiffel Tower. He photographs it exactly as he knows it from posters. Better still, he has someone photograph him in front of it. Back home, that photograph reaffirms his identity with that scene" (Carpenter 1972: 6).

Looking, seeing, gazing...

What is more important than making the image, is the eye looking at it. Visuality is favored by some scholars such as Berger (1972: 7): "Seeing comes before words... the child looks and recognizes before it can speak" as he starts with these words to his book "Ways of Seeing". Jenks (1995: 3) draws the attention to the importance of vision and visuality in Western culture:

"Looking, seeing and knowing have become perilously intertwined... the modern world is very much a 'seen' phenomenon. We daily experience and perpetuate the conflation of the 'seen' with the 'known' in conversation through the common place linguistic appendage of 'do you see?' or 'see what I mean?' to utterances that seem to require confirmation or when seeking opinion by inquiring after people's views."

Kress and van Leeuwen (2006: 163) emphasize the visual representations over the linguistic ones by proposing that seeing is a condition of understanding. Urry and Larsen (2011) makes a distinction between "seeing" and "gazing" by referring to seeing as "what the human eye does" and gazing as "discursive determinations of socially constructed seeing and scopic regimes". The term "scopic regime" is coined by Metz (1981) broadening

Lacan's (1977) "scopic field". The split between the *eye* and the *gaze* is expressed by Zizek (1991: 89): "I can never see the picture from the point that it is gazing at me." According to this, Foster (1988: ix) describes the vision as "how we see" and "how we see this seeing and the unseeing therein". Benjamin (1979: 89) notes *"the unclouded, innocent eye has become a lie, perhaps the whole naive mode of expression sheer incompetence. Today the most real, the mercantile gaze into the heart of things is the advertisement."* He also discusses the problematic of the view around the panorama as an organizing technology of the eye and gives the example of the airplane passenger:

> *"The airplane passenger sees only how the road pushes through the landscape, how it unfolds according to the same laws as the terrain surrounding it. Only he who walks the road on foot learns the power it commands, and of how, from the very scenery that for the flier is only the unfurled plain, it calls forth distances, belvederes, clearings, prospects..." (Benjamin, 1979: 50).*

De Certeau (1984: 91-92) proposes to look at the cities from afar and above: "seeing the whole, of looking down on, totalizing the most immoderate of human texts". He offers the vantage from the top of the World Trade Centre in New York by presenting a panoramic text to the viewer/reader. What interests de Certeau is not the visually constructed "geometrical" or "geographical" space but rather the "ways of operating", the everyday practices, the mobilities that transform the "migrational" or "metaphorical" city into a text of planned and readable city (Schneider, 2008: 25). Any visual representation should be considered with its purpose to reflect the cultural values, not just being graphical demonstrations (Davis, 2002: 10).

The term panoptic gaze, borrowed from Bentham's Panopticon model, does not exactly signify surveillance as Foucault suggested, but stands for a certain degree of power exercised in and communicated to the society through images and representations. Panopticon, cited by Foucault (1974 [1966]) has become "an emblem of the 'politics' of seeing". The gaze is the behaviour created by mechanisms that belong to the social realm of visibility. The images lead to conformity in the society through their messages. Therefore, the panoptic gaze, in relation to the city, could be conceived in the example of looking at the map of the city. We look at a map of a city and assume a view from on high (de Certeau, 1984). It may take the form of aerial images or maps that provide a gaze for the totality of the urban space. Hubbard (2006: 97-8) stresses the role of aerial perspectives in city imaging by its effect on the perception and representation of the city "as a totality which can be easily and immediately comprehended (and by implication, ordered)." On the other hand, the panoptic view allows the ones, who would seek to order and govern our cities, to ignore "the rubbish that piles up in the city's back alleys, hear the constant noise of traffic and people or smell the fumes that choke the streets below" that disturbs the image of a clean and orderly city - "crime, deprivation, death, loss, anger and pain all cease to have an existence in a city that is rendered as a visual ensemble rather than a living, breathing entity" (Hubbard, 2006: 97-8).

Most of the images of the city on the catalogues are panoramic images. Nevertheless, a more personal and emotional connection can be made through cultural signifiers and referrals to books, films and paintings by suggesting flashbacks in mind and reinforcing emotional bond with the city (Stevenson & Inskip, 2010). The emotional connection is related to the perceptual side of the imaging, in other words reception of images. According to Smith (2005: 401-2) an alternative to the perceptual approach is the conceptual approach, which is about the "image formation as a process of communication".

Communicating the image:

Font (1997: 125) identified a public image creation model, "involving the transmission of a destination's identity to the public, with some elements being lost in the noise or reshaped according to personal and external factors". The meanings communicated by the images always go through a 'two-way process' between the observer and the place or the object that is observed (Lynch, 1960: 6). Public image (or overall image) is constituted by "overlapping individual images" (Lynch, 1960: 46). This process takes place at different urban levels; "from street level to levels of a neighbourhood, a city or a metropolitan region"; that form the layers of the image (Lynch, 1960: 85).

Smith (2005: 40) believes that images should be simplified representations reducing the urban complexity yet able to epitomize the whole city. He proposes synecdoche mechanism "where a part of something is used to stand for the whole or indeed where the whole is used to stand for a part" and cites examples of landmarks such as Eiffel Tower or city silhouettes such as NY skyline. On the other hand, MacCannell (1999: 131) counter-argues with the synecdochical urban features as "tourists may perceive them only as symbols of a destination and therefore unworthy of actual visitation."

Another mechanism described by Smith (2005: 405) is "connotation". Connotations are "wider meanings that are dependent on certain cultural associations" (Stevenson 1995: 41). The connotation employs both abstract and arbitrary meanings and takes cultural influences into consideration. However, it is difficult to draw a line between the synecdoche and the connotation in the case of iconic structures that can connote the whole city (Smith, 2005: 406).

The city image might have negative connotations due to unpleasant personal experiences, which do not necessarily stem from the materiality of the urban conditions. The real situation in the city could be disastrous as well, such as "decaying in industrial cities, peripheral locations, little contribution to national economy, unemployment, ongoing crime and incidents such as racial and ethnic clashes, terrorist attacks, assaults on tourists, epidemics or fatal diseases, and natural disasters" (Avraham, 2004: 472). The negativity leads to prejudgments and stereotypes about the place more easily than the positive ones. The low self-image of cities creates a lack of pride for the residents (Avraham, 2004: 476).

Positive images, on the other hand, tend to be clear and favorable images. Clear images provide signs that make the "structural legibility of the city" more coherent (Lynch, 1960). Favorable images stem from the relationship of the individual with its environment or the feeling that the image communicates, which may include clear images. Attracting flows of people and tourism revenues is a crucial factor for developing a favorable destination image (Gartner, 1993). Molotch (1996: 229) posits, "favorable images create entry barriers for products from competing places". The need for differentiation caused by the competition, forces destinations to re-invent their images and position themselves (Şahin & Baloğlu, 2011: 69).

As if the city does not have an image, it would be difficult to communicate the city and its assets to the outside world. That is why the built environment and the city image have become a critical tool for city marketers and those who take role in city branding processes. Crawshaw & Urry (1997: 189) argue that the images used for marketing purposes tend to be positive in an attempt to show pleasing aspects and/or "amplifying the beauty", while eliminating the undesirable aspects. In most of the cases touristic images are modified to "mystify the mundane" and "amplify the exotic" (Weightman, 1987: 229). This necessitates paying a particular attention to the social representations as the shared meanings of the concepts and images. Images are powerful tools as "seeing is believing". That is why media uses images for communication, which also applies to tourism and marketing practices in attracting people to certain places. MacCannell (2001: 27) stresses the role of actors operating in the tourism industry and the means of communication such as brochures, guidebooks, and travel writing that shape the tourist gaze. As there is no unique experience of a city, there is no single tourist gaze, which is constructed through signs (Urry, 1995: 21) in the process of creating "aestheticized spaces of entertainment" (Zukin, 1995: 3-11) and making cities attractive (Selby, 2004: 48).

Lash & Urry (1994: 272) claim "what is consumed in tourism are visual signs and, sometimes, simulacra". Simulacra addresses the imaginary created through the signs (Baudrillard, 1994 [1981]). Accordingly, simulacrum involves negation of the reality as the reality itself has begun merely to imitate the model, which now precedes and determines the real world. Baudrillard (1994 [1981]) argues that the post-modern era eroded the "basic reality" behind the signs by breaking the link between the signifier and the signified. The mass media, with advertising and propaganda as its most effective tools, has changed the understanding of the reality through illusions, defined as "hyper-reality" in Baudrillard's (1994 [1981]) terms. The signs characterizing this phenomenon, in other words orders of simulacra, take three forms: counterfeit (imitation), mass production (illusion), and simulation (fake). Boorstin (1992) links the illusion created by the mass media to the staged mega-events by calling them as "pseudo-events". Media plays a key role in shaping the form and content of the messages while presenting the events to the public. Several studies, especially qualitative ones such as Boorstin's (1961), have demonstrated the effect of media in framing messages therefore making mega-events into "media events". An event is a social construction in which the materiality of sign production cannot be ignored (Galtung & Ruge, 1981).

City of Spectacle

Debord (1994 [1967]) coined the term "spectacle" in the framework of consumption culture and capitalist urbanization. In this framework, "Society of the Spectacle" (Debord, 1994 [1967]) stands for the image-saturated society where advertising, entertainment, television and mass media increasingly define and shape the urban life. We live in a society surrounded by images in which spectacle is defined as "a social relation among people, mediated by images" (Debord, 1994 [1967]: 153). According to this theory, the spectacles make the images consumable objects; as a matter of fact not only images but also the social realities and lived experiences in the spectacles (Jones & Wilks-Heeg, 2004). The signs are inescapable as they are all over the place. Debord (1994 [1967]: 4) describes such social process as "a process of objectification or thingification of social relations and products that extends to the production and consumption of images". Therefore, spectacle can be recognized a synonym to social control and form of power. For Debord (1994 [1967]), the contemporary city is the locus of conflicts and struggles over the spectacle.

City as a theatre:

The spectacle has entered our daily lives following the merger of the culture with the market, in which the consumer culture celebrated the commodity and its spectacle. Culture and spectacle are two pivotal points in city marketing as art and culture play an important role as a creative engine in the new global economy. Mega-events have been an area of practice for cities to exhibit themselves and attract people through the mediated images. This process is described by marketing a city as a staged experience. Cultural strategies are described in connection to the mega-events in the context of consumption culture, therefore "staged experience" refers to "experiences to be consumed, collected, and displayed" (Gotham, 2005: 226-7). Harvey (1989a: 92-3) comments on the situation: *"cities and places now, it seems, take much more care to create a positive and high quality image of a place ... [that is] blessed with certain qualities, the organization of spectacle and theatricality."*

The theatricality of urban spaces highlights the equivalence between the society of spectacle and the society of consumption. The importance of culture and entertainment industries is increasingly parallel to the creative and image-based industries. This reflects on the marketing strategies by blending cultural/entertainment branding with place or destination branding. The spaces without places come to existence presenting a stage of décor. The spectacle presents the city as a theatre stage. The spectators are not only observers but they are part of the spectacle; "they are on the stage with the other participants" (Lynch, 1960: 1-2). As mentioned earlier, the city is a "theatre of social action" (Mumford, 2007), in which a series of events are staged, a multiplicity of roles is performed by citizens and governors, and the whole spectacle is watched by the visitors (as well as the inhabitants). According to Gotham (2005: 227) spectacle is a "theatrical presentation and controlled visual production". Zukin (1995) considers cultural capitals as spaces for art production and consumption at the same time. Short (2012: 88) exemplifies this framework through the case of Olympics:

> *"The games represent a significant regime of international regulation, embody a shared cultural experience and provide an important platform for economy of globalization as transnational corporations advertise in and through the Olympics and lastly they theatricalize the city, making it a media spectacle onto itself".*

Mega-events:

The spectacle is used to refer to the mega-events and their impact on changing cultural and leisure patterns in this book. There are various terms in the literature, evolved in time to address special events and often used interchangeably. Mega-events (i.e. Olympic Games and World Cup), hallmark events (those closely linked with a destination), festivals and other more modest events are all variations of special events, which emerged as "early and encompassing term used in the literature" (Quinn, 2009: 8). Therefore special events range in their themes from sports (Olympics, F1) to trade and business (Expos and Fairs) as well as cultural events (Biennials, ECoC).

Hallmark events were distinguished as an instrument for civic boosterism and image making by establishing a close link with a destination (Quinn, 2009: 8). Ritchie (1984: 2) defines a hallmark event as a "major one-time or recurring events of limited duration", by putting the emphasis on "uniqueness, status, or timely significance to create interest and attract attention". Hall (1989), on the other hand, draws relations between the hallmark events and the large-scale impacts created by them in terms of economic effects, marketing, physical or social impacts, as well as the level of international attention.

Ritchie (1984: 2) defines mega-events as a synonym to hall-mark events. On the other hand, some other scholars approach to the mega-events and the impacts created by mega-events in different contexts. Roche (2000) refers to a larger framework of public events and defines mega-events in this framework by describing three forms of mega-events: The Olympic Games, the World Fairs (Expos) and the World Football Cup. As it can be understood from this categorization, Roche (2000: 1) describes mega-events as; "large-scale cultural (including commercial and sporting) events, which have a dramatic character, mass popular appeal and international significance" while putting the emphasis on the national aspect in distinguishing hallmark events from special events and mega-events. Surborg et al. (2008: 348) assert that the hallmark events and mega-events "have created a dynamic and enduring *spectaculum urbanus* – a constellation of happenings that are impressive to see, designed on a large scale to attract attention, and fundamentally, inescapably urban". This role is appreciated from the tourism point of view "as an effective enhancer of destination image" (Hall, 1992).

Law (1993: 167) gives a definition of mega-events in urban context, which is "large events of world importance and high profile which have a major impact on the image of the host city". Since the research is investigating the impact of mega-events on the city image, this definition is applicable to the research. Although the terminology used to describe large-scale events may vary, and even can be used interchangeably, I use the term "mega-event" to refer to the European Capital of Culture (ECoC).

Global marketplace:

The development of the arts or cultural economy transformed "urban cultures have become valuable economic commodities for sale in global marketplace" (Stevenson, 2003: 97). The cultural products such as music, art, architecture, and food are global sold on the "cultural supermarket" (Mathews, 2000: 19). That is why, it has become a panacea for improving the image of cities, "which pivots on consumption, entertainment and spectacle (Stevenson, 2003: 141) to the increasingly adopted cultural planning approach, aimed at nurturing and promoting local cultural activity in the city" based on the idea of making the host city into a "festival marketplace" (Garcia, 2005: 841-2).

The contemporary urban cultural consumption is characterized by the spectacle what Harvey (1989b) refers to as "bread and circus". The history of urban cultural festivals dates back to Roman Empire; "bread and circus" in the form of entertainment directed towards gaining political power (Eisinger, 2000: 317). The "festivalization of the city" (Harvey, 1991) refers to the thematic development of city images and identities mainly through culture, politics, sports, architecture and design, so and so forth (Evans, 2011: 5-6). The entrepreneurial turn in cities is reflected in the so-called phenomena of "festivalization of urban governance" (Häußermann and Siebel, 1993). Jamieson (2004: 64) claims festivals as means of access to "cultural production and consumption". Although the idea of collectivism[2] as the main motivation behind the festivals is rooted in the past, the recent studies recognized the importance of festivals and events parallel to their importance in tourism. Thus, festivals are also turistified and commodified. If we extend this theory to transnationalisation and globalization of culture, we can say that festivals celebrate the difference on stage but exclude actual social differences in the city. Yardımcı's (2004) analysis of Istanbul festivals supports this view by contrasting everyday life versus festival time and/or reality versus representation. Bianchini (1999: 30) explains this transformation in cultural policies in three phases: "as the age of reconstruction (1940s-1960s), the age of participation (1970s and early 1980s) and finally the age of city marketing (from the mid 1980s to present)". Festivals, in the sense of transformation into the marketplace, comply with the third approach of city marketing (Sassatelli, 2011: 26).

World Fairs, as a part of wider social world, served as "windows on the world", by presenting discourses as sites of representations of the imperial and colonial world. They have served as justification for colonialism through the messages coded in "material progress, technological triumphalism,

---

[2] "collective effervescence" (Durkheim, 1965)

national cohesion, white supremacy and noble savagery" (Short: 2012: 93). Mega-events are the "instruments of hegemonic power" (Ley and Olds, 1988) in the form of "materialism, belief, reliance on technical progress to solve social ills, mass consumption of imperialism and "rightful" hegemony of capitalism" (Short: 2012: 93). Harvey (1989b) and Debord (1994 [1967]) address the hegemonic power in terms of social control and unification for the class-divided society in the context of spectacles. According to Harvey (1989a), they can also be used as a tool for urban regeneration, as they give the host city the opportunity to produce a new and exciting image. Urban spectacles are started to be mass-produced for the sake of profit making and bureaucratic control motives, which force individuals to consume images as passive spectators (Gotham, 2005: 227).

The case of Great Exhibition (1851) in London can be given as one of the earliest examples of special events and Marxist theories of commodity fetishism. In this context, the urban spectacles that gained acceleration in the 19th century reflected on the urban landscapes. A temporary massive structure made from iron and glass is built by Joseph Paxton for the Great Exhibition of London, which is also called "Crystal Palace Exhibition" by naming this temporary event together with its temporary structure. In this sense, the Crystal Palace can be perceived as the "precursor of the modern department store or shopping mall" (Thackeray & Findling, 2002: 104). Benjamin's "Arcades Project", tells the story of shopping arcades of Paris, which can be extended into a new and global imagery for consumption as in the case of Crystal Palace (Pickles, 2003). The World exhibitions are remarkable in the conceptual framework of mega-events, as they reflect on the character of display.

Ephemeral spectacles:

This "transitory but participatory" nature of the spectacle leads to an ephemeral display as Harvey (1989a: 91) describes through "architecture of spectacle". The idea of commodification is applied to culture industries and cities through the concept of "festival marketplaces", which is closely correlated to concept of "architecture of the spectacle". The semiotic reading of spaces of spectacle such as malls, festival marketplaces and leisure parks connotes the "illusory places of pleasure, leisure, hyper-reality and simulated elsewhereness" (Hubbard, 2006: 72). Thus, the temporal dimension should be added to the spatial definition of the mega-events. The "on-purpose built infrastructures" required by mega-events to host the large crowds serve for a short period time and their function may be discontinuous (unless hosted periodically in the same location or transformed). Therefore, by bringing both spatial and temporal dimensions into focus, mega-events can be defined as

"Major one-time or recurring events of limited duration, developed primarily to enhance the awareness, appeal and profitability of a tourism destination" (Getz, 2005: 16).

White elephant phenomenon is used to describe the built mega-projects that were not viable over time (Warrack, 1993: 1). Such projects result in misuse of public resources, negative social surplus. Olympic venues can be given as an example to the showcase projects of the local governments that wish to demonstrate projects having visibility instead of utility. These places often turn into ghost towns after the Olympics leave the city. The world historical events are increasingly condemned to disappear (Baudrillard, 1994 [1981]), as Debord ((1994 [1967]: 20) expresses "when the spectacle stops talking about something for three days, it is as if it did not exist". Media fosters a society "obsessed by the desire to forget" (Kundera, 1996, cited in Clarke, 2008: 138). Mega-events such as Olympics are directed towards achieving this through "saturation of media coverage" for a certain period of time (Stevenson, 2003: 98-9).

In this framework, when mega-events are considered in terms of urban experiences rather than urban representations, their temporality is expressed as "ephemeral vistas" (Greenhalgh 1988). Speaking from the urban point of view, the temporary structures created for mega-events are criticized for being ephemeral vistas, whereas they can become architectural landmarks symbolizing the city. Mega-events facilitate the homogenization through the flow of images and application of success stories to any host city in their bidding and marketing strategies.

City boosterism:

Hosting mega-events may lead to both positive and negative results. It is a costly thing to do, which might result in sunk-costs if the opportunities are missed. Majority of the reasons lying behind hosting mega-events are generally the economic reasons, which are closely linked to globalization. Tomlinson and Young (2006: 1) describe the relationship between the spectacles and the globalization on the basis of potential of the spectacles "to realize shared, global modes of identity and interdependence, making real the sense of a global civil society". A successful hosting of a mega-event offers global exposure, prestige and legitimacy to the host city and the entire country, which is especially desired by emerging economies eager to prove that they have become major players on the global stage (Black & van der Westhuizen, 2004).

Therefore, although the culture seems like the focal point, the economic interests cannot be denied. The mega-events require large public and private investments and the economic interests in these investments are often global with respect to creation of new leisure and consumption habits (Surborg et al., 2008: 342). The scale of the projects often exceeds the urban areas and became national projects of the governments. According to Brenner (1998: 3), the transnational elite promotes the cities to the world economy as the "nodes for transnational capital investment" through mega-events. On one hand, transnational elites seek to build "tourist sites or sights" (tourist gaze/experiences) over mega-events and mega projects and on the other hand, spectacles become opposing tools to dominant meanings and power relations (Gotham, 2005: 241). Mega-events are recognized as important tools for place marketing for creating iconicity and images of places, thus play a role in the global economic system controlled by the TCC (Surborg et al., 2008). The link between the mega-events, global economic system and the TCC is also closely connected to Molotch's (1976) concept of urban growth machine. The terms such as urban growth machine, city boosterism and urban entrepreneurialism are framed in association to globalizing economies and the process whereby city elites promote the economic competitiveness of the city through attracting investment and spurring economic growth. The political interests directed towards cities employ mega-events to support urban growth. Harvey (1989a: 16) states: *"Concentration on spectacle and image rather than on the substance of economic and social problems can also prove deleterious in the long-run, even though political benefits can all too easily be had."*

According to Molotch (1976) the actors who have economic interests in the places with growing value in the city make up the local growth machine by organization, lobbying, manipulating and structuring through their social actions including opportunistic dealing. From this perspective mega-events are related to this theory in terms of increasing land values and the economic investments to be made. This can be also understood when we think of mega-events as the catalysts for urban restructuring and regeneration (Surborg et al., 2008: 342,347). European Capital of Culture Programme portrays this process transforming from social cohesion among the member states into cultural development and urban regeneration (Maisetti et al. 2012).

It is true that host cities attract millions of visitors through mega-events. The nations are in competition because they are interested in not only the economic results but also the symbolic meaning of mega-events. This may take the form of creating the image of a world-city, spectacular structures and architectural achievements as well as showcasing their heritage as in the case of ECoC. Mega-events are believed to provide an opportunity to reinforce the city image or re-image it as part of re-branding exercise. They strengthen the city brand and hence they are likely to increase the brand value (Sirkeci, 2013b). They, not only create the awareness and increase the interest towards the city hosting the event, but also help to achieve world-city status thus making the global connection. There are global centres that already have a global image, recognition and infrastructure, yet these cities want to keep their superiority in the global economic system, and they want to emphasize their physical and organizational capacity to organize such a big event (Shoval, 2002). For those cities that are already known, it offers opportunities to re-invent their images and re-position themselves. Communication is the number one step. The desired image should be communicated truly, while it has to be reliable at the same time, which means the communication should be consistent to reflect on the city's real features and qualities. In this respect, the spectacles are the communication channels conveying the messages of a city to be attractive, dynamic, cosmopolitan etc. for a desirable and favorable image.

The research of Ritchie and Smith (1991) has shown that the image and awareness level of the hosting destination can be substantially improved during and immediately after a mega event. Although this knowledge indicates an image change, it does not denote how specific affective and cognitive characteristics (Baloğlu & McCleary, 1999) of destination images change before and after the completion of the event. The impact of mega-events on the urban change is analyzed by Hiller (2000: 440), through his model in which dependent and independent variables are disaggregated. The analytical assessment of Hiller (2000: 444) draws bold lines between the mega-event as the cause and the urban processes as the effects in order to emphasize that "the mega-event is placed in its full urban context as an urban event rather than something that is parachuted in and then disappears" (Hiller, 1999: 192). This relationship is demonstrated through a longitudinal analysis for both pre-event and post-event phases of the mega-event.

The vast literature on the impact of mega-events concentrates on the economic impacts. Nevertheless, various researches put forward the questions about destination image enhancement, national identity and pride enhancement, and longer-term regeneration outcomes in the form of sporting and commercial infrastructure as well as community building and social legacies. The crucial point from the image-making perspective is to provide a better understanding of how mega events serve as a tool in city marketing in order to improve the image of host cities. The link between the spectacles and the city is further discussed in the next chapter.

Chapter 2: Marketing the city & the city image

The theoretical model (Fig. 1) I developed draws upon the wide array of topics that are brought together in their relationship to city imaging process in marketing. The city image is at the centre. From the centre and above it provides a totality of the whole structure of concepts. Concepts covered in this framework are classified under three main categories (city-spectacle-image) that construct the backbone of the research (Fig. 2).

Representation is explained through defining the concepts related to city image following the conceptual framework developing from broader to narrower in the sequence of city marketing, city branding and city imaging (see Fig. 3). The image of the city and how it is created in city marketing and branding practices is at the core of the conceptual framework.

As I defined city as a lived and imagined space in previous chapter, here I focus on city image from a marketing perspective before going into the how and why of the spectacle and the impact of mega-events on city branding in the case of Istanbul ECOC 2010.

Figure 1. Theoretical Model of the Study

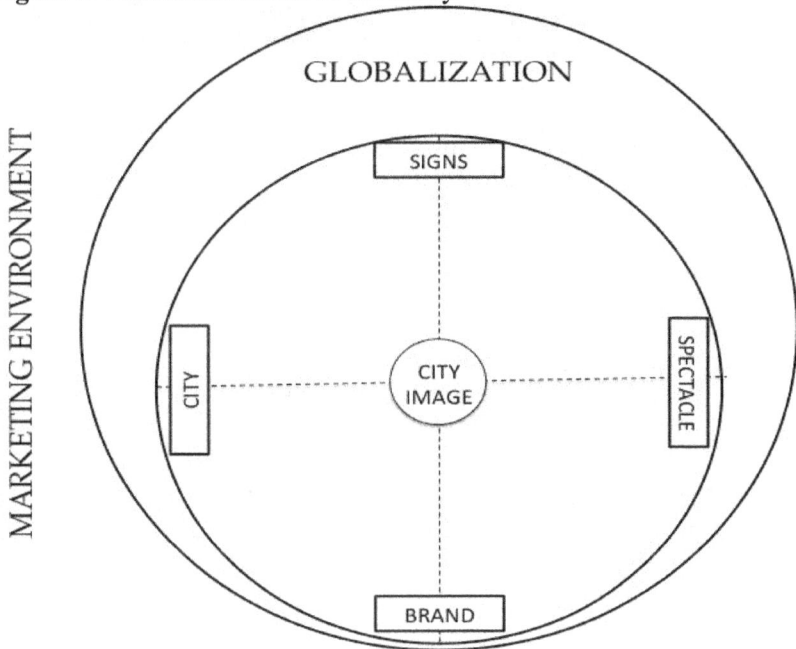

Figure 2. Concepts covered in the theoretical framework

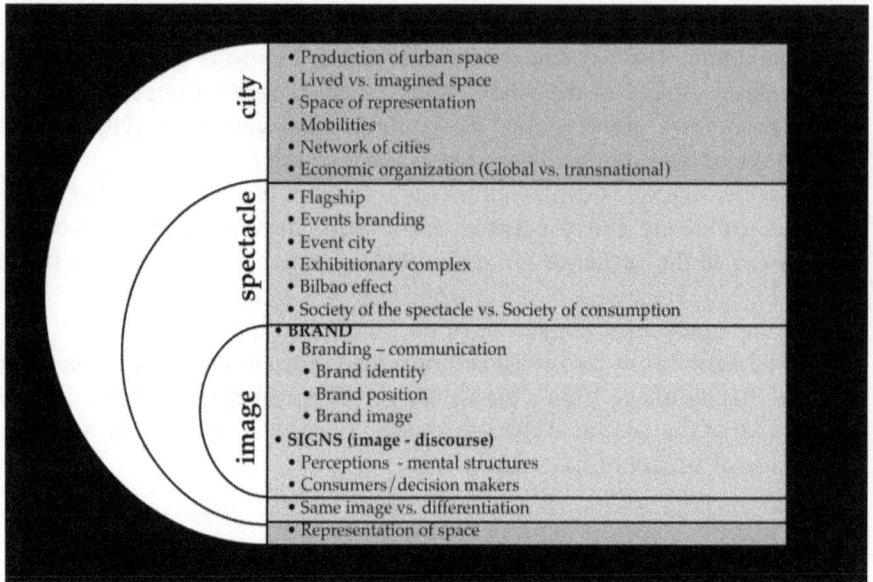

city
- Production of urban space
- Lived vs. imagined space
- Space of representation
- Mobilities
- Network of cities
- Economic organization (Global vs. transnational)

spectacle
- Flagship
- Events branding
- Event city
- Exhibitionary complex
- Bilbao effect
- Society of the spectacle vs. Society of consumption

image
- BRAND
  - Branding – communication
    - Brand identity
    - Brand position
    - Brand image
- SIGNS (image - discourse)
  - Perceptions - mental structures
  - Consumers/decision makers
- Same image vs. differentiation
- Representation of space

Figure 3. Conceptual Framework

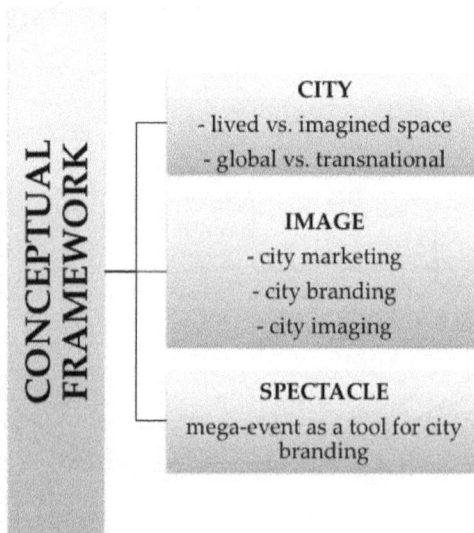

CONCEPTUAL FRAMEWORK

CITY
- lived vs. imagined space
- global vs. transnational

IMAGE
- city marketing
- city branding
- city imaging

SPECTACLE
mega-event as a tool for city branding

City Marketing

According to Kavaratzis & Ashworth (2005: 513) city marketing or place marketing is not so different from product marketing. It is possible to apply the concepts and principles of marketing to places. However, a place, an urban setting is much more complicated than a product since cities have their identities, cultures, urban dynamics, so on and so forth. Therefore, Kavaratzis & Ashworth (2005: 510) comment; "places are not products, governments are not producers and users are not consumers." Also what makes city marketing different and more complicated than product marketing, is the cultural context and the interpretation of the meaning.

Place marketing is also referred to as "selling places" (Burgess, 1982; Kearns & Philo, 1993) which are consumed and being sold on the market. Although selling places mostly means fierce promotional activities, Anholt (2010: 11) claims "countries and cities are not for sale". PR companies and marketing strategies developed by city marketers could have done the most of the work for governments, if it was possible to sell a city solely through a marketing campaign. Yet, national images are products of a collective memory that "are not created through communications and they cannot be altered by communications" (Anholt, 2010: 5). Kavaratzis (2004: 69), claim "promotion comes only after one has something to promote", otherwise the images and the messages turn into empty signifiers. These messages are directed towards shaping the image and manipulating the perceptions for the image: instead of saying "please try this product" they say "please change your mind about this country" (Anholt, 2010: 3).

Ashworth and Voogd (1988: 68) define city marketing as "planning actions designed to initiate or stimulate processes that improve the relative market position of cities in regard to particular activities. These activities are described in terms of economic aspects such as attracting commercial investment, or improving the effectiveness of service activities whether in the public or private sectors. While Ashworth and Voogd (1988) explain city marketing in relation to globalization process, Colomb (2012: 26) builds her definition of place marketing on three blocks: public policy, discourse and imagery (visual representations):

> *"Place marketing is the intentional, organized process of construction and dissemination of a discourse on, and images of a given place (usually a city) and of its development which involves the mobilization of set of actors around that particular task (with specific goals and agenda)."*

Thus, Colomb (2012: 26) focuses more on the spatial practices in place marketing and underlines the role of public with respect to place making by offering a close up on the actors, agenda, political narratives and instruments. Colomb (2012: 26) takes place marketing in relation to the use of spatial metaphors and specific architectural symbols mediating and constructing a defined identity for a specific place. Cultural politics interfere with this process through collective identity and memory formation. The framework suggested by Colomb (2012) provides a more comprehensive definition for this research, as it is interested in discourses created by mega-events as a sign of globalization of culture.

Transnational marketing:

Place marketing has been linked to geographical marketing too (Ashworth & Voogd, 1988). "The geographical and administrative span of the operations, strategy and behaviour" is essential in approaching the marketing activity that draws upon multiple territories. Sirkeci (2013a: 14) names this kind of borderless (or across the borders) marketing as transnational marketing. In contrast to the "economics of simplicity" ordering "the same thing, the same way, everywhere" transnational marketing strategy relies on "flexible and responsive country-level operations" in response to "host country governments' growing demands and customers' rejection of homogenized products" (Sirkeci, 2013a: 15).

Although transnational marketing strategies recognize the importance of local demands, place marketing practices often tend to focus on the international audience to market cities on the global scale. The entrepreneurial turn inevitably shaped place marketing with the influence of heavy advertising, mass media and generally it shows itself in risky urban projects with high profits (Falkheimer, 2006: 1-2). The conflict of interests between public and private actors might cause the process to be top-down instead of encouraging public participation. In this case people are perceived as consumers instead of decision makers.

Experiential marketing:

The cities are lived and experienced but the images of cities are consumed. The sense of pleasure has become part of place marketing through the concept of fun city (Spink & Bramham, 1998), in which pleasure is included as a part of consumption habit as cities are perceived as experiences to be consumed (Reid, 2006: 37). The "experience economy" coined by Pine & Gilmore (2011: 91-2) introduces "designing experiences that are compelling, engaging, memorable, and rich" through the act of "THEME-ing" as in the case of staged events. Thus, Pine and Gilmore (1998) came up with the concept of "experience marketing" or as Schmitt (1999) calls "experiential marketing" as the importance of emotional attachment with places is increasing in marketing. It is believed that the unique and interesting experiences make places and events more memorable. It is also highly correlated with the perceptions of place as it employs six senses – smell, vision, taste, hearing, touch and balance (Kirezli, 2011: 177). Today, place-marketing strategies are directed to create an experience of users of the city, therefore creating a feeling. The sense of place makes the differentiation between the cities, thus plays a key role in city marketing and promotion policies. According to Kavaratzis & Ashworth (2005: 507) the sense of place is constructed through three processes. The first one is the urban planning and design, the second is the urban use, and the third is through the urban representations. The critical question is "how" more than "who" or "what". The everyday interactions with the urban environment go through some mental processes of cognition. As a result of this cognitive processes mental maps are created, which "allows individuals to navigate through complex reality, because our surroundings are often more complex than the sense we make of them" (Kavaratzis & Ashworth, 2005: 507). Therefore, knowledge-based industries, cultural events and leisure are becoming more important in place marketing strategies (Short and Kim, 1998 cited in Surborg et al., 2008: 344).

City Marketing Strategy:

City marketing is highly associated with reimaging strategies (Roche, 1992; Hall, 1994) of places (Stevenson, 2003: 94). The construction, communication and management of the city's image are essential for place marketing as the perceptions matter for the actions. That is why place marketing should be a "conscious and planned practice of signification and representation" in order to shape the perceptions to create desired actions (Firat & Venkatesh 1993: 246). Kotler et al. (1993: 48-9) defined four types of variables as the information sources affecting the perceptions. The first one is personal including family, friends, neighbours etc. The second category includes advertising, salespersons and travel agents as the commercial sources. Mass media is the third type of source, which is defined as the public source. The last one, the experiential source derives from one's own experiences with the place.

In the most of the cases, city marketers and capital groups, who may be lacking the local experience and perceptions of the local people with the everyday life in urban spaces, are responsible for creating the city image. Thus the logos and slogans reflect more of a distant imaginary created than reflecting the local meanings. The global city image, well connected to the world economies, is accessible to millions of viewers around the world (Close et al., 2007: 15). The logo of the Olympic Games is identified as widely as the logos of the mega brands such as Shell or McDonald's (Close et al., 2007: 5).

Slogans, logos, promotional literature (narratives) have been serving as conventional marketing tools for communicating the city image, whereas "staging events, constructing iconic buildings and implementing sophisticated public relations strategies" emerged as practice-based city branding examples (Smith, 2005: 398). The former group of tools is part of the image itself (displayed on the visual representations such as posters and banners), whereas the second group uses city image as a tool to communicate their messages.

Slogans:

Kotler et al. (1993: 151) defined slogan as "a short catch-all that embodies an overall vision of the place". One of the most known is the "Big Apple" for New York, which stands for multiculturalism and the meaning to embrace all the people. Recently there has been a debate to change the slogan as "World's Second Home" giving the city exclusive rights to use it to promote business and tourism.

The cities who became ECoCs of 2010 used these slogans: Pécs – "Borderless City", Essen for the Ruhr – "Transformation through culture, culture through transformation", and Istanbul – "Istanbul, the most inspiring city in the world". Pécs positioned itself as a "gateway to Balkans" in its bidding file. Essen followed the track of Glasgow that has been successful through urban transformation and culture-led regeneration as an industrial city. Istanbul has given weight on the brand value, thus the slogan stands as part of the broader strategy to attract tourists to Istanbul rather than to promote the cultural program itself to potential audiences (Rampton et al., 2011: 76).

Logo:

A destination logo can be defined as "a graphic design used to identify a destination" (Hem & Iversen, 2008: 88). Logos, as one of the most common elements in the marketing communication mix, are considered to be "visual repositories of brand associations" (Pittard et al., 2007: 458).

Slogans and logos are essential for the brand awareness and to distinguish the product package with the strongly associated image constituents in the minds of potential visitors (Morgan et al., 2002). The appeal and packaging of the product has become as important as the product itself in positioning.

Visual Symbols:

The landmarks such as Eiffel (Paris), Big Ben (London), Red Square (Moscow), the Great Wall (China), stand as symbols for their cities (Kotler et al., 1993: 153). The images of these landmarks are often used for promoting the city. Such symbols are used commonly in tourism, for instance in the national tourism promotion campaigns of countries or cities. The messages seek for shaping the international public perception in accordance with the voice of governments and marketers. Advertising aims to create a simple and easily transportable message, but the important thing is distinguishing the product from the other similar ones. Balibrea (2001: 189) defines this message in terms of image, which is "a coherent representation/meaning of the city, one that is easy and pleasant to consume".

City Branding

Branding is essential in the whole marketing strategy (Kotler, 2000), which centres on "people's perceptions" and "mental images" (Kavaratzis & Ashworth, 2005: 507). In the traditional marketing model, brand is defined as a part of the features of the product and/or services and what is communicated about them. American Marketing Association (AMA) defines brand as "a name, term, sign, symbol, design or a combination of these, which is used to identify goods and services of one seller or group of sellers and to differentiate them from those competitors" (Kotler, 2000: 404). Clifton and Maughan (2000: vii) puts the emphasis on the value while defining the brand: "a mixture of tangible and intangible attributes symbolized in a trademark, if properly managed, creates influence and generates value". Branding serves "exposing the brand and creating brand image" (Aaker & Joachimsthaler, 2000). Kapferer (1997: 28) recognizes brand as an external factor, as a sign, "whose function is to disclose the hidden qualities of the product which are inaccessible to contact".

The majority of literature on city branding addresses the topics from the tourism perspective with respect to destination branding. Nonetheless, the work of Kavaratzis (2005: 2-3) includes a variety of areas where city branding can be applied such as place of origin branding, culture and entertainment branding, nation branding, as well as destination branding. Although city imaging and city branding is part of the politics of national governments, city image is more about what is in people's minds therefore it does not have to be associated by political aspects. Hence some of cities have more powerful brand images than the countries they are located in; such as Amsterdam vs. Netherlands (Anholt: 2007: 59).

In this book, city branding is approached from the place marketing perspective directed towards improving the attractiveness of a place by providing distinctiveness and enhancing the city image. City branding aims to create "impressive images and seductive signs" (Kalergis, 2008: 32).

Ashworth (2008) suggests defining what branding is "NOT", instead of what it is, with a special focus on place branding:

> *"It is not a synonym for promotion, [...] Similarly place branding is not just the deliberate shaping and promotion of a place image by a public authority in pursuit of policy objectives. It is also not (as many local branding policies seem to be suggesting) the same as creating a single catchy slogan, logo, house style design and the like, however much these might embody and reflect the aspirations of the place management authorities."*

Ritchie and Ritchie (1998: 103) defined a city brand by addressing the elements and their functions:

> *"A name, symbol, logo, word mark or other graphic that both identifies and differentiates the place; furthermore, it conveys the promise of a memorable travel experience that is uniquely associated with the place; it also serves to consolidate and reinforce pleasurable memories of the place experience."*

Communicating the city brand:

Advertising is usually associated with branding, because advertising communicates the certain qualities of brand to the consumers. Advertising globally requires giving consistent messages and speaking with one voice. The objectives must be balanced when developing a global brand, while local effectiveness of the ads must be maximized (Evans, 2005). Sklair (2006: 26) exemplifies it from the point of images of places that "persuade people to buy (both in the sense of consume and in the sense of give credence to) the spaces and lifestyles they represent." Heavily influenced by the Situationists, Baudrillard (1996: 181) highlighted the importance of spectacle for the consumption of images through advertisements: "We consume the product through the product itself, but we consume its meaning through advertising."

Applebaum (2004: 52) recognizes branding as "one of the most significant symbolization strategies". Dissemination of information through mass media and advertising facilitated the flow of images that brought the transition from exchange value into the sign value through the signs and images. Baudrillard (1981 [1972]) takes a critical approach to the production of meaning in mass media and to the production of event as a sign through the entire system of media and information. The meanings are produced in the form of symbolic exchange, which is transformed into the form of processed, produced, profane meaning through semiotic exchange in advertising (Merrin, 2005: 17). Baudrillard (1981 [1972]: 205) argues that the sign-form, the image, stems from economic-exchange, which is precipitated by modern forms of mass communication and the commodification of culture. The term commodification of culture brings us to an intersection point of capitalism and globalization, if our understanding of the culture here is the consumer culture. In the commodified culture industry, described by Horkheimer and Adorno (1991 [1944]), representation was the mean of mediation (where representation was commodified). In today's "global cultural industry" (Lash & Lury, 2007: 4), everything else is commodified. It is not only representation that matters, communication matters too. In this respect the images of a city are crucial as a communication tool in branding the city.

City branding strategy:

According to Olins (2005: 167) successful city branding depends on few conditions. First, transnational elites (i.e. "representatives of government, industry and popular culture") are influential on the control of capital through investment and funding decisions. Influencing the audience and their perceptions about the image of the city is the second condition, which is communicating the brand image. Third, the opinion leaders are also important for their effect on the communication process. It is essential to communicate the brand image through a logo created by the creative workforce. Lastly, networking is crucial to "influence the influencers" (Falkheimer, 2006: 6). This approach is directed towards visualizing the relationships between the stakeholders and the impact on the communication process. On the other side, understanding the mechanisms of the communication and meaning making process, while paying attention to the cultural codes is essential in order to create successful brands. Although there is not a unique formula to create successful city brands, a number of attributes such as heritage and history, the character of the local people, associations with famous people, capital city status and international city status are applied by the cities and they have become successful. Culture and heritage are the crucial assets for branding as it is not merely about advertising. Branding a place is about "cultural exchange on a global scale and intelligent dialogue" (Anholt: 2005: 140). Therefore, culture is a way of communication and self-expression of a country and its image (Anholt: 2005).

Furthermore, branding is about heterogeneity and identity aspect of the culture can be recognized to have an opposite effect in contrast to globalizing cultures and the homogenizing effect attached to globalization. Baudrillard (1998 [1970]: 88) describes this phenomenon by "industrial production of differences" referring to brands as representational systems, whereas Askegaard (2006) addresses brands as "hegemonic vehicles" of dissemination of ideas and images in a global scale. Bristow (2010: 153) calls it "competitiveness hegemony" referring to the hegemonic discourse behind competing cities and strategies directed to have competitive advantage. One of the greatest effects of branding is believed to be competitive advantage.

Anholt (2007: 7) links all these concepts to the notion of competitive identity. Despite the globalization and its homogenizing effects for cities, identity remains as a distinctive character. Here Sirkeci's (2013a) argument that consumers remain local, national, and culturally embedded, can be extended to claim that identity of cities too remain local and national while also being promoted to a transnational audience. As proposed by Ooi & Strandgard Pedersen (2010: 327) specific to the case of Copenhagen branding strategy, city branding "selectively frames the city, it asserts a unique identity for the place and it provides a set of lenses for people to understand and interpret the city". The emphasis is on the "mobilising and garnering local support, public-private collaborations and engaging with international audiences" in this process (Ooi & Strandgaard Pedersen 2010: 327-8).

Pike (2009: 861) identified three steps in destination branding: "destination brand identity development, destination brand positioning, and destination brand equity measurement and tracking". Brand identity can be defined as "a unique set of associations that the brand strategist aspires to create or maintain" (Aaker, 1996: 68). Therefore, brand identity addresses objectives of the producer whereas brand image is more about the receiver's side, and the "meaning that the consumers associate with the product, based on experiences, impressions and perceptions of the functional, emotional, and symbolic benefits of the brand" (Kaplan et al., 2010: 1291). City image is subjective; therefore, it changes from one person to another. It also differs for the people who are born into the culture of a city compared to an outsider view of that city as the collective symbols and memories affect the perception. Whereas a city might offer a strong sense of belonging for some people, the same city could be associated with disorder and crime (Schweitzer et al., 1999).

De Chernatony (1999: 165) argues that brand identity "is about ethos, aims and values that present a sense of individuality differentiating the brand", and therefore vision of the producers and/or brand strategists and culture are the two elements that are critical to brand building process. Figure 4 illustrates this communication process between the producer and receiver flowing from desired perceptions on the producers' side to actual perceptions on the reviewers' side (Kavaratzis & Ashworth, 2005). Nevertheless, communication is a two-way street. Thus the desired image should match the perceived image.

City branding is a project of multiple stakeholders and influencers including local residents, local authorities, businesses and commercial entities, public bodies, and the media (Maheshwari et al., 2008, 120-1). Virgo and de Chernatony (2006: 379) argue that the complexities of city branding arise from the presence of multiple stakeholders. Therefore, stakeholder management is recognized as an essential aspect in developing a city brand, and measuring city brand equity.

Figure 4. The relationship between brand identity, brand positioning and brand image

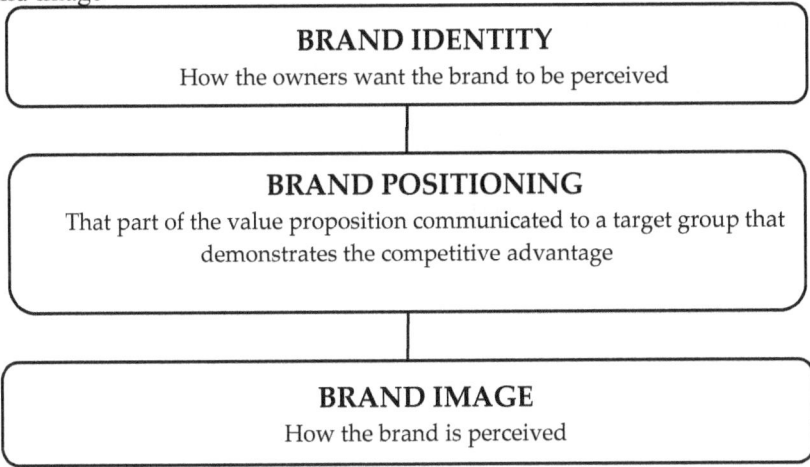

```
┌─────────────────────────────────────────────────────────┐
│                    BRAND IDENTITY                         │
│         How the owners want the brand to be perceived     │
└─────────────────────────────────────────────────────────┘
                            │
┌─────────────────────────────────────────────────────────┐
│                  BRAND POSITIONING                        │
│  That part of the value proposition communicated to a     │
│  target group that demonstrates the competitive advantage │
└─────────────────────────────────────────────────────────┘
                            │
┌─────────────────────────────────────────────────────────┐
│                     BRAND IMAGE                           │
│               How the brand is perceived                  │
└─────────────────────────────────────────────────────────┘
```

Source: Kavaratzis & Ashworth (2005: 508).

The functionality and the added value also have a strong influence on the choice of consumers. The urban infrastructure offered by the city (i.e. Employment, housing, transportation, etc.) is functional but on the other hand people ask for a personal benefit, which stems from their personal associations and experience with the city. This is the added value of a brand, which makes the brand distinctive. It is claimed that the important thing is communicating the core values of the brand, which is the key to generating customer loyalty and brand recognition (Hubbard, 2006: 25).

International branding strategy is closely correlated with brand awareness and brand loyalty as consistent marketing strategy has a potential effect on changing consumer knowledge regarding the brand (Keller, 2003). According to Kohli & Thakor (1997: 208) "creating a strong and distinctive image" positively affects the brand awareness. Brand image communicates these strong, favorable, and unique associations to the consumers through "direct experience, brand information, word of mouth, assumptions of the brand itself -name, logo-, or with the brand's identification with a certain company, country, distribution channel, person, place or event" (Keller, 2003: 70). Visitors can be named as viral agents as their impressions about a place would influence potential visits either by themselves or other people through word of mouth (Anholt, 2010: 89). Visiting and experiencing a place is crucial for personal perceptions. In an ordinary daily conversation, when we are asked about our origin of place ("Where are you from?"), the question is followed by another question: "Have you ever been there?"

How do brands function?

Figure 5. Brand equity
    Brand Awareness
    + Image
    + Perceived quality
    + Evocations
    + Familiarity, linking

    = Brand Assets ➜   Brand added value
                     perceived by customers
                     -   Costs of branding
                     -   Costs of invested capital

                     Brand financial value
                     (BRAND EQUITY)

Source: Kapferer (1997: 37).

Kapferer (1997: 25) explains the value added by brand through the "ability to gain an exclusive, positive and prominent meaning in the minds of a large number of consumers". That is why, the distinction is very important. Brand is more than an identifier; it signifies the place of the product in the mind of the consumer (Kapferer, 1997: 23). Figure 5 (Kapferer, 1997: 37) indicates how brands function through the relationship between brand assets and the brand equity. The asset value of the reputation of a brand is expressed by brand equity.

The city brand should not only be strong but also should be positive. The examples of transformed post-industrial cities such as Glasgow are examples where the city is promoted as being vibrant (Ward, 1998: 192). Additionally, branding should target not only creating an attractive and positive image of a place that is appealing to people, but also achieving consistency between the image and experience to build a long-term value and to achieve repeat visits.

"For a country like Slovenia to enhance its image abroad is a very different matter than for Scotland & China. Slovenia needs to be launched: Consumers around the world first must be taught where it is,

what it makes, what it has to offer and what it stands for. This in itself represents a powerful opportunity: the chance to build a modern country brand untainted by centuries of possibly negative associations" (Anholt, 2000 cited in Sirkeci & Cawley, 2012: 259).

On the other hand, Paddison (1993: 339) argues that the negative image is not replaced; "it is merely pushed to one side, or as the old saying goes; out of sight, out of mind". The impact of the event on improving the image of the city becomes less visible, and the image itself becomes compartmentalised. The image and reputation of a place are closely connected to the place identity. Identity is perceived as the distinctive "positive" associations with a certain place. However, defining the identity of a city is a problematic area. If we discuss it from the branding side, we may come up with cases in which the brand identity is expressed in terms of human traits (Şahin & Baloğlu, 2011: 70-71). This speaks for brand personality. By definition, brand personality is linked to brand identity and brand image although there is an ambiguity in this relationship in terms of city branding. Ekinci & Hosany (2006: 135) applied brand personality concept to destinations and argued "destination personality has a moderating effect between image and behavioural intentions".

The study of Baloğlu and McCleary (1999) differentiates the perceived image by the visitors from the desired image by destination agents. The brand is formulated through examining the brand image and personality of a destination and by matching it to "a desired and fit-to resources image" (Şahin & Baloğlu, 2011: 69-70). Şahin and Baloğlu (2011: 70) state, "brand image is formed by the perceptions of consumers about a brand or product labelled with that brand". Ashworth and Kavaratzis (2009: 525) say "people 'understand' cities in the same way as brands". The city is shaped in people's minds through perceptions and images of the city. Images are crucial in associating the place and the brand as well as the image and reality itself. Images play an important role in the choice of a destination to visit and generally the visitors are in search of that image to be the reality. Anholt (2010: 12) mentions communication (message) is the essential tool to influence public opinion. In this respect, brand image is defined as an external factor, "which is not under direct control of owner or government" (Anholt, 2010: 12). On the other hand, brand equity needs to be managed, measured, protected, leveraged and nurtured over the long term in order to unite people around a common strategic vision, which is the brand purpose. It is also crucial to draw "clear and attractive pattern of development than the rehearsal of past glories" (Anholt, 2010: 12). Thus city branding should be innovative.

Smith (2005: 417) gives the example of Barcelona to illustrate development of a new terminology called personality branding often associated with "The Gaudi gambit". There are similar cases mentioned in the literature representing different ways of branding strategies. Flagship construction is represented by "The Pompidou ploy" in the case of Paris Beaubourg, while "Events branding" is becoming popular through the festivals and mega-events. These strategies are not only directed towards creating awareness, but also developing "associations between the place and attributes regarded as being beneficial to its economic or social development (thus brand utility)" (Ashworth & Kavaratzis, 2010: 513).

Hard branding:

The cultural event itself is the tool for city marketing in the event city. The spectacles strive to do this through the representations. The creative city, on the other hand, is directly related to branding strategies with the aim of upgrading the city image through the transformation of outmoded infrastructures into new usage by the creative labour attracted to the city (Teckert, 2009: 49).

Teckert (2009: 49) explains the phenomena by borrowing the term "exhibitionary complex" from Bennett (1995: 60) and extending its scope into landmark buildings, event city and creative city. The example to the landmark buildings is the Guggenheim Museum in Bilbao by Frank Gehry, which also stands for the commonly used "Bilbao effect" in the literature to describe the influence of urban mega-projects for city marketing. According to Harvey (2013) cities all over the world copy from Bilbao in developing landmark projects and applying them to the mega-events:

> *"The bubble has already burst in Spain and many of the huge projects remain only half finished. Incidentally major events like the Olympic Games, the soccer World Cup and music festivals serve the same purpose. Cities try to secure themselves a prime position on the market - like a rare wine of an exceptionally good vintage."*

Not only cities become commodified places to be consumed and their images become the emblems of consumption culture to attract capital from the urban governance aspect, but also corporations have realized potential of urban spaces and city branding as a part of their whole branding strategy. Evans (2003: 417) explains this by hard branding. The case of Bilbao is such kind, which is as "an attempt to capitalize on commodity fetishism and to extend brand life, geographically and symbolically" (Smith, 2005: 400). Nike Towns can be also given as example, where the shopping experience and commodification materializes into a new symbolic identity (Evans, 2003:

417). Therefore, Nike Towns are "more than just a store" providing "melange of corporate premises, visitor attractions and branding tools" (Smith, 2005: 400). Similarly globalizing cultural sector and industries spread their brands in different locations through franchising.

As such, Gonzalez (1993: 85) links culture-led regeneration in the example of Bilbao to ephemeral spectacles. The politicians focus on urban regeneration projects to improve the run-down areas of the city as well as improving their images. Therefore, it may take the form of urban sanitization or beautification in general. Marketing and advertising, show the positive images of the city in order to make them appealing for the consumers. Maisetti et al. (2012: 3) discuss the effect of urban regeneration and the image of orderly, clean/sanitized city in the context of urban design and marketing. In this context, there are three main trends stated as functional (related to branding), socio-economic (related to creative cities), and lastly aesthetic. Especially the last one highlights "working out metropolitan facades" with the aim of aestheticizing the city (Maisetti et al. 2012: 3).

Ramo (2007) has formulated "urban shopping list" for cities to be repositioned on the market and to be recognized globally. The list includes: Superstar Architect, Ikea, Low-Cost Airline, High-Speed Train, Big Event, European Capital of Culture, Re-Baptism, New Football Stadium, Information Society and Global Brands. Gehry, as the "superstar architect", proved in the case of Bilbao that "ever more cities need ever more icons to relate to" (Ramo, 2007). Big events refer to mega-events with all the infrastructure needs to be created such as new bridges, airport renovations, new train connections, ring roads, stadiums in the case of Olympics, etc. In the end cities become a part of a greater picture. The information society and the flow of knowledge make the cities global brands.

Touristification is mushroomed from commodification by the injection of branding and image-constructing activities into the tourism with a concentration on cultural heritage. It is increasingly becoming targeted at consumption-oriented branding according to the orders of consumer culture and globalization. Attracting global flows (tourism and investment) is vital for urban development (Gold and Ward, 1994). However, globalized forms of cultural flows, in other words "global tourists" (Urry, 1995) are subjected to the effects of cultural homogenization through uniform representations. On one side, the places that are refashioned as global cities are marketed through the mega-architecture projects of brand architects and on the other it gets more difficult to differentiate those cities from each other.

City Imaging & Re-imaging

City imaging:

The city imaging can be approached from different perspectives (Smith, 2005: 399); as a form of communication (Burgess & Wood, 1988); as a means of social control (Debord, 1994 [1967]); as a type of urban governance (Stoker & Mossberger 1994); as a discourse (Philo and Kearns 1993); and as a mode of marketing (Fretter, 1993). Although this research studies the city image in relation to all of these theories, the particular interest is on the mode of marketing and branding as the image is recognized as a part of city brand.

The production of images is defined by the process of producing signs, codes and symbols aimed at shaping perceptions (Teckert, 2009: 50). Gunn (1988) categorizes image formation process into two groups: organic and induced. Marketing and promotion creates images through an induced way. Organic production of the images, on the other hand, stem from popular culture, the media, literature and education instead of being a part of any intentional marketing efforts targeted at particular markets. The symbolic arrangement of images circulates on the global market of cultural industries through means of media such as cinema, television, newspapers, magazines and advertising as well as art and literature (Haarmann, 2005). Therefore, these images, represented in the popular culture, shape "the way in which we know and imagine the city" (Stevenson: 2003: 10).

> *"Many of the dominant ideas about city form that are recognized globally and regarded as ideal or as symbols of urban supremacy have developed resonance not through people's actual experiences of these places but through the imagery encountered in marketing campaigns, film, and other forms of popular culture. It is this relationship between the real and the imaginary city – the city and its representation in cultural texts [...]" (Stevenson, 2003: 112).*

Thus, the symbolic construction of the city image may be realized either in the form of internal processes (perceptions) by the "local actors of the city those identifying their geographical identities with that particular place" or external processes (representation) by/for "people and organizations more or less extraneous to local life and symbols" (Vanolo, 2008: 371). The latter generally affects the choices made by visitors and/or investors (Kavaratzis and Ashworth, 2005).

City re-imaging:

Post-industrialization has restructured urban governance aspired to lure "highly mobile and flexible production, financial and consumption" flows

(Andersson, 2010: 197). Smith (2005: 398) comments on the post-industrial cities with respect to increasing importance of "promotional activities and urban spectacles" in creating images of the city for touristic consumption. Among a number of terms, including civic-boosterism, place marketing, city branding, destination marketing, selling places, he uses "city re-imaging" to define "deliberate (re)presentation and (re)configuration of a city's image to accrue economic, cultural and political capital" (Smith, 2005: 398). Re-imaging encapsulates re-imagining and re-thinking the meanings attached to city image and refers to a repeated process of re-making the city image, or in general terms re-branding the city (Kavaratzis, 2004; Smith, 2005).

The goal of re-imaging the city for tourism is to boost their tourist trade – as in the case of "proliferation of imported "brand name" architects in cities like Shanghai, or Hong Kong and the obsession with visual logos and sound bites (city of culture, city of vitality)" (Abbas: 2003: 143). Smith (2005: 419) stresses the role of city re-imaging in identifying the mechanisms for place-marketing strategies.

Ward (1998) claims that "image production" and "city marketing" is an American invention of the post-modern era, which does not fit to European context properly therefore most of the practices tend to be re-imaging the city through urban regeneration projects. ECoC is one of the most salient examples, which initiated culture-led urban regeneration as the main target of the mega-event. The promotion strategies are criticized for acting like "Trojan horse" for ECoC (Evans, 2003: 426). Evans (2003: 425) argues that the shift from the creation of common market for EU to a "more localized city based initiative" supports the function of culture "as a conduit for the branding of the European Project" (Evans, 2003: 426). Each city seeks branding itself "more European" than others especially in the bidding phase (Palonen, 2010: 102). This is a branding game played on the culture-led regeneration with the most remarkable examples of cities like Glasgow, Barcelona and Bilbao (Garcia, 2004: 312).

Global city imagery:

The globalization and the notion of "global city" are already discussed in the first chapter through framing the city and its image according to the power structures and network of cities. After defining all these nested concepts, it could be useful to discuss the effect of globalization on city imaging under the framework of city branding in order to grasp the meanings and correlations between the concepts and processes.

Globalization is not only about the physical mobilities but also flows of information, which puts the emphasis on communication and branding. Cultural aspects, such as collectivism and cultural symbols, should be considered as the market structure necessitates brand adaptation. Here comes forward the role of culture as well as the vision of the private company or political authority. Adaptation to the international or global markets requires brand repositioning, which is "adaptation of the market position of a domestic brand to one that is relevant to the minds of its foreign customers" (Wong and Merrilees, 2007: 386-7).

The global city imagery is created by combining images of "busy international airports, foreign tourists, inward investment, a cosmopolitan atmosphere, creative industries, cultural economies and an overwhelmingly positive image shared around the world" (Short, 2008: 337). For instance, bidding and hosting the Games is central to communicate this image to the rest of the world. Hosting the Games is "winning the gold medal of global inter city competition for the reimagining as well as remaking" of the representation of the city (Short, 2008: 337). Mega-events offer opportunities for the host cities to "express their personality, enhance their status and advertise their position on a global stage" (Essex and Chalkley, 1998: 188 cited in Reid, 2006: 36). Cities cannot survive without "globally acceptable image as a new testimony of their economical spinoff" (Stupar & Hamamcıoğlu 2006: 27). Accordingly, Rojek and Urry (1997: 31) agree that "those cities with either low visibility or a poor image will not even be considered".

Bianchini (1993: 19) points out the cultural conflicts created by the exclusiveness of the "flagship schemes". The facilities are designed for high culture and wealthy visitors in the form of exclusivity. The conflict arises between the grassroots culture and the high culture where the latter is supported at the expense of the former with the intention of increasing the competitiveness of the city (Miles, 2005: 899). Cities are dependent on consumer icons such as music labels, consumer products, or entertainment studios while creating their global city image, which takes shape at the intersection of cultural industries and arts flagship strategies (Evans 2003, 418). According to Short (2012: 48) cultural industries concentrate in world cities. In the process of re-making the city image, cities project themselves as world or global cities instead of the national.

MacDougall (2003: 257) suggests that "commodities need not serve exclusively as vehicles for the meanings and values invested in them by Western producers, but may be transformed into representations of indigenous or local identities through a process of creolization, in which foreign "goods are assigned novel meanings and uses in diverse cultural settings" (Howes, 1996: 5). The images embodied in these goods will be transformed and emulated by the recipient cultures (Tomlinson, 1991).

Place wars:

Globalization and the increasing inter-dependency between the cities and their economies brought decentralization leading to "transfer of powers and responsibilities to subnational authorities, and increasing competition among cities" (Martins, 2006: 4). Hypermobility and the competition between the cities demolished the "monopoly of command-and-control functions" (Short, 2006: 206). The competition reinforced the international strategies parallel to the entrepreneurial activities and institutional change (Harvey, 1989a). Kotler et al. (1993) describes the competition between the cities as "place wars".

The cities are in competition to have the tallest building in the world or a landmark architecture signed by world-renowned architects. About a year ago, the tallest building in the Western Europe called "The Shard", which is designed by Italian architect Renzo Piano, joined the skyline of London. The Guardian states that The Shard is the investment of Qatar Holdings towering above the British capital:

"If the opening of Western Europe's tallest building – presided over by Hamad, whose country's sovereign wealth fund owns 95% of the development – was a demonstration of Qatar's rapidly growing global visibility and influence." (Beaumont, 2012)

According to the article of Beaumont (2012), this is not the only investment of Hamad who has spent over £13bn in recent years in London on purchasing Chelsea Barracks, Harrods and the Olympic Village through the al-Thanis' investment arm, Qatar Holdings and the Qatar Investment Authority, as the largest shareholder in Barclays Bank. Moreover, Qatar Media Corporation owns al-Jazeera Television. It points out a brand conscious strategy for the "emergence on to the world stage as a considerable diplomatic, cultural and even military player of a tiny state whose huge ambitions to spread influence around the globe […]" (Beaumont, 2012). This example demonstrates the power of transnational elites and corporations in shaping the global cities as well as their images. This kind of urban interventions promoted by transnational capitalist class, have crucial impact on the city image by adding symbolic images in the making of iconic architecture. London could not have been imagined without Big Ben and Tower Bridge. But after the 2000s, London is represented with iconic millennium symbols such as London Eye, Swiss Re Tower and recently added, The Shard.

Image is central to the production of iconicity as the means of representation based upon the assumption that the urban landscape acts as "an ordered assemblage of objects and, thereby, can act as a signifying system" (Gospodini, 2004: 229). Thus, perceptions of the city are affected by images, while the urban space serves as a blank canvas for the image production. Sklair (2006: 43) proposes that "the choice of what buildings and spaces become iconic is never arbitrary".

According to Pearce (2007: 8) "national identity, status and power" are the three main elements of the image of a capital city, which is identified over iconic buildings, cityscapes and monuments. When we think of London as an example, we see that "the most powerful institutions in the nation" such as Big Ben and the Houses of Parliament, Buckingham Palace or the iconic buildings like Swiss Re Tower (Gherkin) has become also internationally recognized. Big Ben and Houses of Parliament give reference to capital's political power, whereas Norman Foster's award winning Gherkin building reflect the global image having no roots with the history and tradition associated with London (Stevenson & Inskip, 2010: 95). According to Maitland (2010: 177), iconic architecture "brand their architects more effectively than they do the place" without paying enough attention to the location and local culture.

Thus, globalization puts the city in a package and markets it as if London, Dubai or anywhere in the world, forgetting about its past, its culture and the most significantly its people. In Istanbul, the transformation after the 1980s remarked the role of city imaging in city branding and place marketing. Istanbul aspires to take its share from the global market by following an economic strategy to attract foreign investment and transnational corporations having their headquarters based in the city. Moreover, mega architecture projects are underway such as Hadid's Kartal project. Nevertheless, pursuing such a change for Istanbul is a big illusion, which is a break off from Istanbul's identity, collective memory and shared meanings.

Accordingly, the image of Istanbul is changing parallel to the emerging orders of finance and capital with the mushrooming new shopping malls, multinational firms with their headquarters in high-rise buildings, five star hotels and the gated communities replacing the old-historical neighbourhoods. The modern contradicts the old, but Istanbul is remembering its past as a glorious capital hosting three empires. History in the modern times is recognized as a nostalgic element of Istanbul brand, yet the most important element of brand identity and added value through the cultural heritage. Therefore, Istanbul is not likely to win this game by demolishing its heritage and adding shopping malls to its central urban area.

Chapter 3: Istanbul: European Capital of Culture 2010

In this chapter, the impact of mega-events is discussed within the framework of three contextual areas: city, image, and spectacle (Fig. 6).

The first part concentrates on the city and urban change through myths, ideology and power and politics. The second part describes the organization of ECoC, as well as the objectives and the strategies by reflecting on the case of Istanbul 2010. Image comes the third, in which the authoritative and historically constituted discourses in the making of Istanbul image are identified.

Figure 6. Contextual Framework

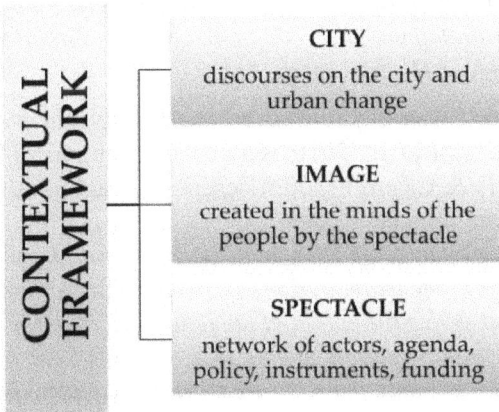

CITY
discourses on the city and urban change

IMAGE
created in the minds of the people by the spectacle

SPECTACLE
network of actors, agenda, policy, instruments, funding

CONTEXTUAL FRAMEWORK

Before jumping into the year of 2010 when ECoC has taken place, a portrait of Istanbul is given by building the layers of history and meaning on top of each other. Geographical and historical facts about Istanbul are outlined that have proven to be dominating the discourses on the urban representations. Accordingly, different stages and political conjunctures are identified in positioning Istanbul as a brand before and after becoming ECoC and the changing meanings associated with the city.

The cultural context is essential in understanding the meaning as the "meanings are context-dependent" (Dey, 2005: 40). Therefore, this chapter constitutes an essential part of research by providing interpretative ground to be integrated into the analytical framework. In this respect, contextual framework acts as a bridge between the theory and methods for a deeper understanding of the meaning and constructing meaningful patterns from the data.

The historical layers of the city are uncovered to narrate Istanbul through myths, ideologies, power and politics. This should not be only recognized as a historical journey back to the past of the city. On the contrary, it takes a combination of factors into account while drawing a wider framework for the understanding of city image formation. Berger (1972: 9) comments that "we never look at one thing; we are always looking at the relation between things and ourselves". That is why this chapter is organized through a cyclical way of thinking instead of a linear way. The image of Istanbul represents continuity through its dialectics and connections between the mythic past and modernizing city.

The City of Istanbul

Istanbul sprawls between the two continents of Europe and Asia that marks the most dominant cliché about the city for being a meeting point between the West and the East. The strategic geographical location of Istanbul attributed historical significance to the city as the capital of three empires.

> *"Istanbul, the capital of the Roman, Byzantine and Ottoman Empires, is the only city in the world which bestrides two continents – a magnificently situated city, as a poet once wrote, 'surrounded by a garland of waters'..." (Freely, 1996: 5).[1]*

The water element, which was highlighted as one of the four elements concept in the bidding project for ECoC 2010, is a strong geographical feature in Istanbul's identity. Sudjic & Casiroli (2009) describes Istanbul as "a city as beautiful as Venice or San Francisco", but

> *"... once you are away from the water, as brutal and ugly as any metropolis undergoing the trauma of warp speed urbanisation. It is a place in which to sit under the shade of ancient pines and palm trees for a leisurely afternoon watching sun on water, looking out over the Bosphorus. But also, in some parts, to tread very carefully. Istanbul has as many layers of history beneath the foundations of its buildings as any city in Europe."*

Istanbul has been a port city throughout the history and the Bosphorus made this city a unique place between the two continents divided by the sea. The Bosphorus adds to the geographical value of the city by making it into a passageway for transnational flows of capital, culture, information and people that occur in the globalizing world. Thus, it can be said that Istanbul owes its importance particularly to its geographic location that creates a natural flow from this passageway. The geographical location of Istanbul plays a key role in terms of enhancing competitive advantage and distinguishing Istanbul (Kurtarır and Cengiz, 2005).

Although its geography is one of the major forces behind the significance of Istanbul brand; history and culture have prominent roles in the construction of brand identity for Istanbul 2010. Batur (1996: xxi) stresses the role of

---

[1] The mentioned poet is the Byzantine historian Procopios: Procopios of Caesarea, Peri Ktismaton, I, V, 2-13. (The Loeb Classical Library, Procopios VII, Cambridge: London, 1971, pp. 57-61)

events and images in creating Istanbul brand as much as its geography. Kuban (2010a: 29) puts the emphasis on the universal status of the city and the role of heritage, which is visible through the monuments ornamenting the city as the gems. Rossi (1984: 92) gives importance to monuments for their meaning and value, which he claims to be "stronger than environment and stronger than memory". In this respect, the importance of monuments can be recognized in terms of mental activities constituting concrete images and collective memory characterizing the city. The city image is based deliberately on the monuments aimed towards "remaining in touch with the past" while "determining the scale and composition of the future city" (İBB Kentsel Dönüşüm Müdürlüğü, 2010: 130).

In this respect, the contemporary city is built on the roots of this rich history. The layers of history, along with discourses, narratives, and features of physical and cultural cityscapes, contribute to build the city image today. According to Uysal (2013: 20) Istanbul's cityscape flourishes on the "architectural synthesis and continuity" shaped by a combination of "Eastern and Western influences". Synthesis and continuity are crucial aspects in rendering the urban change in terms of analysing the impact on the city image. It is not the intention of this research to give a comprehensive chapter on the history of Istanbul, which is neither possible nor fundamental due to the limitations of the research. Therefore, the aim is not pointing out an abstract journey from past to present (like most of the tourism promotion materials do). On the contrary, the aim is making this journey imaginable by elucidating the continuous change and how the city image is affected by this change. In this context, the historical past is conveyed by offering a snapshot to the certain time periods that marked different stages in the urbanization process shaping the identity of the city.

The foundations of today's Istanbul started by the Roman and Byzantine eras. The myth of a city between East and West initiated by the split of East and West Roman Empire extended the discourses attached to the East in the sense of *Orient* after the conquest of Istanbul by the Ottomans. The Republican Era on the other hand, marked the nationalization period in which Ankara became the capital against Istanbul. However, Istanbul continued its rise from being an ex-capital, emerging into a World city. Therefore, the history of the city can be explained through a chronological process of the periods:

- The Roman and Byzantine Period
- The Ottoman Period
- The Republican Period

The history of Istanbul is generally approached and told through the chronology of events; but in this book continuity of events and their impacts on the city image is the major focus. Accordingly, Istanbul is narrated by following the chronological order (while sometimes going back and forth), while, at the same time, the layers of meaning are laid out through myths and discourses. The myths are exposed through the foundation of the city (Roman). The capital status of the city through the imperial ages (Byzantian-Ottoman) is read through the relationship between the power and discourse, hegemony and ideology. The Republican Period cuts this continuity at some extent and produces anti-theses in the creation of contemporary city. There are many intersecting areas in this kind of narration parallel to the continuity of events and a continuous change. The layers are constructed on top of each other, while the new layer does not cover the old one; both exist in the same time. We can see this through the urban constructions. The Ottoman regime neither deconstructed the city, nor reconstructed it, but simply added on the existing ones depending on the topography and functionality (Kuban, 2010a: 25), which formed a mosaic. The layers of meanings are formed parallel to the layers of history. Thus according to this description, Istanbul has many interacting and contradicting layers of meaning.

In this framework, instead of adopting a chronological set-up, Istanbul is read as "imagined" and "lived" space, as noted in the beginning of the conceptual framework. The focus remains on the transformation of the city image surrounded by the historical events and discourses explained through: Myths, Ideology and power, and Politics.

Accordingly, the city of Istanbul is portrayed in a relationship between theoretical knowledge, authority, empirical experience and the spatial practices of knowing city, which is exposed to these three categories or stages defining the urban change.

Myths:

The city, in the sense of today's Istanbul, was seeded by a Greek colony of Megarians in the 7th century BC. However, the first city centre was on the Asian side, in 'Khalkedon' area, in today's Kadıköy. Khalkedon means "Country of the Blind", which was named by another branch of Megarians who came around 660 BC and settled down in the peninsula around Sarayburnu on the European side, across Kadıköy. Therefore, the city of Byzantium[2] was founded by the latter following the advice of the oracle in Delphi Temple to choose the area to establish the city (Eyice: 1980: 90).

The creation of the city is full of symbolic references impacting on the city image. Sennett (1992: 47) explains this relationship and symbolic language with the geometry of Roman astronomy and the application of the grid to the city plan. According to this the sun's movement from East to West is

---

[2] Greek: Βυζάντιον, *Byzántion*

projected as the *Decumanus maximus* while the movement of stars from North to South is projected as *Cardus maximus* as two main axes crossing the city. The intersection point is recognized as the city centre and this point is called *umbelicus* (i.e. umbilicus), which could be thought as the spiritual centre. The Romans dig a hole called *mundus* on the umbilicus and put valuable things dedicated to the Gods, and then cover the hole with a square shaped stone and light a fire. This ritual represents the birth of the city. The umbilicus is marked by the Column of Constantine.

Istanbul was called "Konstantinopolis"[3] (city of Constantine, Constantinople), a name given by its founder, the Byzantine Emperor Constantine. Polis refers to the central cities of the ancient civilizations (Hansen, 2006: 56-9). Greek people used to name the city "polis" in the everyday life referring to Istanbul, or a variation of the word *"stin polis"*, which means "in the city" or "to the city" (Freely, 1996: 3). In time, the name of the city took several forms as Stimbol, Estanbul and İstambol, lastly changed to "İstanbul" (Çelik, 1998: 20).

Ideology and power:

Freely (1996: 4) tells about the transformation of the city from Byzantium into the Christian Constantinople in AD 330. Following the split of the Roman Empire, the official name of the city on the records was "Konstantinoupolis Nea Roma", which indicates the capital status of the city for the Eastern Roman Empire (Kuban, 2010a: 20-2). Some sources indicate that the city is called "Deutera Rome" meaning second Rome, the second capital of Roman Empire (Eyice, 1980: 94). Followed by the announcement of city as the new Rome, it got bigger and bigger in a short time due to its strategic and secure location at the crossroads of trade routes. The city was not only populated in a rapid pace but also its economy improved as a result of trade, so the city became rich. Hagia Sophia was erected during the reign of Justinian as a massive Christian Church. Thus, the transformation of the city was reflected not only to the cultural and economic area but also to the emergence of a centre of Christianity (Krautheimer, 1983: 41). However, Kuban (2010b: 33-34) claims that the new configuration of the city was projected on the Hellenistic city and reflects a combination of pagan and Christian elements side by side.

According to Ousterhout (2010: 124), Constantinople of the 4th century A.D. was a fictional urban formation that is imagined through a common heritage and mythologies (connecting Troy-Rome-Jerusalem) under the auspices of the imperial order. Therefore, Nea Roma was the outcome of

---

[3] Greek: Κωνσταντινούπολις (Krautheimer, 1983: 60)

words, images and urban structures bringing this idea into existence around an ethos, which is not so different from the topos for the global cities today.

Yerasimos (2000: 158) posits the effects of Byzantine architecture on the Ottoman architecture in the context of imperial ideologies and impression of Hagia Sophia. The identity of the city gained a new reconstruction approach through the visual and spatial order of the urbanization in the Ottoman realm through the "construction of Ottoman monuments and selective appropriation of Byzantine sites and monuments" (Kafesçioğlu, 2009: 10). Accordingly,

> *"By portraying, surveying accentuating and at times silencing symbolically significant sites or consequential events, the city's images projected the visions and claims of their makers regarding those particular sites or events and the city at large... A dialogic of representation is particularly pertinent to this subject: products of an era of political and cultural encounters and transformations, these images escape singular interpretations with clear and distinct meanings... The city's commercial and residential fabric was woven from political and cultural process that gave shape to its monuments and images as much as from the workings of daily life. The formation of that fabric and its relationship with the city's monumental structure and image are integral to an understanding of larger urban process..."* (Kafesçioğlu, 2009: 10-11).

The organization of the city, during the Ottoman period, developed around the mosques and public buildings parallel to the discourse of power and the symbolic language behind. Mansel (1996: 33) calls the city of Istanbul, "City of God" linking it to the imperial connotations. It was believed that the sultan or the emperor is the shadow of the God. The mosques represent such relationship. They are assigned by Sultans have more minarets than the little and ordinary mosques. Süleymaniye Mosque and its complex, built by Architect Sinan in the name of Süleyman the Magnificient, joined the imperial symbols of the city expressing its magnificence (Kuban, 2010b: 300). Süleymaniye Mosque does not compete with Hagia Sophia but proves the excellence of its era in terms of architecture. The houses (most of which were made of mud brick or wood) were scattered into the dense urban fabric like a spider net with narrow streets. Such an urban pattern made the imperial structures more outstanding in the urban landscape, while creating a dichotomy in the Istanbul's image. The same type of dichotomy is prevailing Istanbul today with a difference, which is the dichotomy created by the oligarchy of the Ottoman against the oligarchy of the capital in the network of global cities (Kuban, 1998: 13).

Ottoman Empire adopted Islam as the religion of the state but society was formed through a pluralist structure and cosmopolitan in character, which makes the city multi-ethnic, multi-religious and multi-cultural centre (Schmitt, 2011: 131). Non-Muslim members of the community (Jews, Greeks, Armenians, Levantines) gained key roles at the state level under the reign of Ottomans (Necipoğlu, 2010: 262).

The late period of the Ottoman Empire has been the scene of changes and reforms in order to keep up with the advancements in the Western world reflecting on the architecture (Çelik, 1998: 2). 19th century can be cited in terms of changing image of the city following a line from East (impact of Islam) to West (European styles such as baroque) (Çelik, 1998: 26).

At the urban scale the Westernization efforts were directed towards "reviving Istanbul as a modern cosmopolitan similar to its European counterparts" (Aktaş: 2006: 159). While Istanbul's image was portraying a mystic and oriental city in the eyes of Westerners, Beyoğlu and Galata areas emerged as the leisure and entertainment centres in the cultural life of the city with theatres, cinemas, restaurants and cafes similar to the vibrant life of Paris in the 19th century. Istanbul, once being the capital of the Eastern Roman Empire, turned its face to the West again following 'accession, decline and rebirth' (Freely, 1996: 173).

Politics:

With the fall of Ottoman Empire, Istanbul lost its significance as a capital city and Ankara became the new capital of the Republic in 1923. Turkish Republic was born as a modernist, democratic and secular state from the ashes of Ottoman Empire in the aftermath of the World War I (Aktaş, 2006: 160). The first 20 years followed by the foundation of Republic were spent on the revitalization of the country after the war and social transformation in diverse areas from change of alphabet to change in apparel representing the modern state. The foundation of Republic brought strict reforms to erase the Ottoman past.

Istanbul was left unattended throughout the years following the foundation of Republic due to Ankara's new capital status. In the 1950s Istanbul started to get attention from the government. Adnan Menderes, the prime minister of the era, favoured Istanbul more than Ankara and Istanbul became the pupil of the eye again through "beautification" projects (Kaya, 2010: 97-114). The aim of Menderes was making the city into an attraction centre.

Since 1950s the governmental politics for the urbanization of Istanbul has changed tremendously by the emergence of global politics and economics. The interest of the government for attracting tourism and foreign investment to Istanbul turned the city into a marketplace, where the mega-events and mega architectural projects have become the tools for city imaging. Harvey (1989a: 271) criticizes this process of transformation for cities and metropolitan areas for creating "market objects and all-encompassing spectacles". The vocabulary of High-Modernism has entered into the process of transformation of the city in the 1950s as well. Urban demolitions were justified as construction works between 1956 and 1960. Some of the urban renewal projects targeted old neighbourhoods threatening the historical environment, heritage as well as the urban identity. The Chamber of Architects and Higher Board of Preservation of Monuments claimed the heritage at risk (Akpınar, 2003: 154).

The strategic features of Istanbul provide the opportunity for transnational elites to benefit from accumulation and competition through the adaptation to global economic order and strategies for city marketing and image creation (Robins & Aksoy, 1995: 223). However, in its challenge to get its share from the capital accumulation, Istanbul erases its historical accumulation and invites "starchitects" as the magic wand tool to copy-paste their spectacular projects to the selected area of the city. This is the inevitable outcome of homogenization effect of the global order. Thus, the growth in business and industry inescapably affected the urbanization. High-rise buildings of the major national and multinational headquarters started to emerge one by one in the city skyline contrasting with historical characteristics of the urban fabric. Not only corporations and business plazas, but also the architectural emblem of the consumption culture are added to the city such as shopping malls replacing the covered city bazaars, as well as contemporary architecture designs and utopic landmarks, which are away from understanding and communicating the city culture.

The government has a key role in the image making strategy for Istanbul and takes urban regeneration and massive architecture projects at its core borrowing from the Western examples. Some of the new transformation projects for Istanbul are planned to be designer products by world-known architects. This is a way of branding the city mostly illustrated by the example of Frank Gehry's Guggenheim Museum in Bilbao. In this way, the urban spaces become consumable as designer products and the "contemporary metropolis" becomes a "spectacle city" by the proliferation of urban spectacles.

The urban development projects are not directly addressed as the main area of interest for the research but they are highly associated with the city image. The transformed urban spaces such as old industrial sites gain new functions through hosting cultural events such as festivals, biennials, exhibitions and so on. The heritage landmarks, such as Hagia Sophia, are also in such transformation, as they become museums and exhibition spaces. They become the object of exhibition in which the meanings are re-written and re-read over the spaces of transformation. Thus, the image is created and recreated while the past is re-discovered in a different sense in the modern times. Today, most of the urban transformations are targeted at creating spaces of spectacle through the regeneration of the past.

"Galip Dede and Yüksek Kaldırım Streets Are Being Renovated and Beautified"

"We Renovated Our Streets, Now is Time for Our Buildings"

"We are on Duty for a Graceful, High-Quality, Orderly City Life"

The slogans mentioned above are examples of the municipal propaganda for urban transformation that was put on billboards by the Beyoğlu Municipality. Adanalı (2011) comments on the slogans as "going back and forth between a car advertisement and municipal propaganda" and treats Beyoğlu district as "an urban space that needs radical intervention that is hard to contain and discipline". The beautifying project for Beyoğlu is intended to make district a sanitized place with clean and glittering surfaces of the old buildings like a car-wash. Istanbul 2010, on the other hand, claims to be "getting on with the restoration of these buildings and quarters in line with the international standards" (Çolakoğlu, n.d.). Contemporary Istanbul is designated as a "cosmopolitan" and "sanitized" city in order to achieve "international acceptance and recognition" (Robins & Aksoy, 1995: 228).

The present mayor of Istanbul, Kadir Topbaş, perpetuates the vision for Istanbul to become a global city by the support of central government in Ankara. Therefore, the scale of urban transformation is larger than before, while the process of opening to global economies has become more solid as "keeping up with globalization is a central mission of the government, and Istanbul is the privileged arena of operation" (Aksoy, 2010). Istanbul was put forward as a "global city" in the world agenda, as Erdoğan states:

> *"Istanbul is one of the prominent cities in the world and in Turkey in terms of not just its history, tourism and culture but also its economic and commercial profile. I served as mayor in Istanbul for 4.5 years and I had a goal, an ambition in those days to turn Istanbul into a financial capital. Of course, because it was different politics ruling in the central government we couldn't do it then. But now, we are in power in the central government, and also in Istanbul local government... Private sector financial institutions are already here, we are going to move public finance institutions as well as the regulatory bodies and organizations. Istanbul at this point is entering a new restructuring process." (qtd. in Aksoy, 2010).*

As the central and the local government are acting together on a full consensus to realize the project for Istanbul to be a global city, Mayor Topbaş and Istanbul Metropolitan Planning Office started to take the necessary steps for urban restructuring with a goal "to promote the city's image for global viability and competitiveness" (Aksoy, 2010).

When looked at the greater picture, it will not be overestimating Istanbul as a global city of the imperial world. The imperial order created "international markets and global exchange networks, the movement of people the spread of new technologies, the diffusion of cultures and transmission of religion and scientific practices" (Short, 2012: 9) as in today's globalizing world. Being the capital of two 'transnational empires' (Byzantine and Ottoman), marked Istanbul as a culture and trade centre with a cosmopolitan character. The rich culture and history of Istanbul is evident in "the atmosphere or feeling of a place". However, a city should have more than that to be counted as a centre of culture. Today, the cities of culture are associated with the cultural industries they have and their ability to join the "global cultural network". Istanbul is ranked as a mega-city among cities like Tokyo, New York and Mexico City but not ranked on the global city scheme or not ranked as an international centre of culture although has gained the official status of being the European one (McAdams, 2007). McAdams (2007: 162) suggests, "... the future of Istanbul hinges on its ability to integrate and plug-in to the global cultural network not just as a participant, but as an influence." Istanbul as ECoC of 2010 stands for such a challenge to be included in this network and to market itself using the culture as a tool.

The Spectacle of Istanbul 2010

Sassatelli (2009) counts ECoC as one of the programmes contributing the spectacularization of cities. In this sense, ECoC becomes the playground for cities that are fiercely competing against each other to bear the title for the sake of showing off Europe's cultural richness and diversity (Hein, 2010). Diversity is celebrated particularly in the programme of "institutional identity building through culture" suggesting "a new way of imagining the relationship of culture, identity and governance" that has merged into the spectacle of ECoC in the case of a mega-event (Sassatelli, 2008: 230). Therefore, ECoC serves both as a mega-event and "pan-European tool for event-led urban renewal" homogenizing the shared experience of European culture (Palonen, 2010: 89). However, the meaning of this shared experience is created through the assessment criteria by the "European cultural **elite**" (Palonen, 2010: 89).

From European City of Culture to European Capital of Culture

The idea of ECoC dates back to the 1980s in the form of cultural days and cultural months. In 1985, Athens became the first European City of Culture through the initiation of the cultural programme by Melina Mercouri, the

Greek minister of culture. Florence followed Athens and "a whole canon of cities has emerged that are networked into the map of cultural capitals" (Palonen, 2010: 91). Table 3 (European Commission, 2015) indicates the list of cities selected as ECoC from beginning until 2013.

The initial program has developed further and the name is changed from European City of Culture into European Capital of Culture in 1999 (The European Parliament and The Council of the European Union, 1999). 25 years of history of European Capital of Cultures (1985-2010) is explained on the publication entitled "European Capitals of Culture: the road to success" (European Communities, 2009). From its initiation in 1985 to 2004, European Cities of Culture were chosen by the EU Council of Ministers, without the involvement of external experts or any formal assessments, which makes the programme and inter-governmental affair (European Communities, 2009: 5). The programme is launched with an emphasis on the cultural sector in Europe and its contribution to economic growth and social cohesion defined by Lisbon objectives (Council of the European Union, 2007).

Table 3. European Capitals of Culture

1985: Athens	1990: Glasgow	1995: Luxembourg
1986: Florence	1991: Dublin	1996: Copenhagen
1987: Amsterdam	1992: Madrid	1997: Thessaloniki
1988: Berlin	1993: Antwerp	1998: Stockholm
1989: Paris	1994: Lisbon	1999: Weimar
2000: Avignon, Bergen, Bologna, Brussels, Helsinki, Krakow, Reykjavik, Prague, Santiago de Compostela. (final report)		
2001: Porto and Rotterdam	2009: Linz and Vilnius	
2002: Bruges and Salamanca	2010: Essen for the Ruhr, Pécs and **Istanbul**	
2003: Graz		
2004: Genoa and Lille	2011: Turku and Tallinn	
2005: Cork	2012: Guimarães and Maribor	
2006: Patras	2013: Marseilles and Košice	
2007: Luxembourg and Sibiu	2014: Riga and Umeå	
2008: Liverpool and Stavanger	2015: Mons and Plzeň	

Source: European Commission (2015).

European vs. international framework:

When we look at the narratives of the ECoC and the ideals of Europe, there are similarities. The European city stands for a "normative ideal" – a place of freedom, a place for ideas and coming together – referring to both unity and diversity (Palonen, 2010:101). Further discussion can be if "EU really narrates a common European history or creates an image of the European city, or if it creates a range of differences and different perceptions of Europe and through that a narrative of its own" (Palonen, 2010: 101). Lähdesmäki (2011: 139) cites;

> *"The chosen ECOCs are expected to foster the common cultural history and heritage by linking the city's own cultural heritage to the common European narrative" (The European Parliament and The Council of the European Union, 1999).*

The first aim of the program lies in the culture as a key to "unity in diversity" under the European framework, while it has turned out to be "a versatile development tool of cultural policy capable of achieving multiple objectives" (European Commission, 1994). Culture acts as a "glue" between the member states of the EU, which makes the promotion of "shared European culture" central to EU cultural policies (Richards, 2001). Therefore, it is asserted that ECoC is "essentially a political and not a predominantly cultural programme" (Klaic, 2010: 7).

ECoC is a mega-event that has political and cultural dimensions impacting on this process by imposing criteria such as "European dimension" and "city and citizens". What is meant by European dimension, is defined by The European Parliament and The Council of the European Union (2006) as follows:

> *"As regards 'the European Dimension', the programme shall: (a) foster cooperation between cultural operators, artists and cities from the relevant Member States and other Member States in any cultural sector; (b) highlight the richness of cultural diversity in Europe; (c) bring the common aspects of European cultures to the fore." (Article 4 of Decision 1622/2006/EC)*

In other words, candidate cities must present the role they have played in European culture, their links with Europe, their European identity. Although European dimension is a crucial aspect, a city is not chosen as a European Capital of Culture solely for what it is, but mainly for what it plans to do for a year that has to be exceptional (European Commission, 2011). Thus, proposing a unique cultural programme is more significant than the intrinsic historical value of the city. The title is more than a label, therefore the city is asked to draw on its special features and create new cultural events. This means that the cultural events cannot be only the ones that the city usually stages under the "ECoC" banner, or merely highlight the city's cultural heritage (European Commission, 2014).

According to the final report on "Ex-Post Evaluation of 2007 and 2008 European Capitals of Culture", the criteria of the "European dimension" are open to different interpretations that allowed "implementing a wide range of activities with a European dimension but the nature of that dimension and its effectiveness varied" (ECOTEC, 2009: 124). In most of the cases it was undertaken in the form of a broader international dimension through attracting international talent, "rather than specifically European artists" (ECOTEC, 2009: 116).

The programme's framework is wider in its application and recognition. The internationality and transnationality have been impacting on the city's recognition in terms of international projection, international image or international standing that is also reflected on the governments' politics. On the other hand, transnational networking in the case of "city twinning" or ECoC gave opportunities for cities to "free themselves from state control" (De Castro, 1999). The integration into such framework, which the local authorities also recognized key roles played by the transnational relations, is created through flows of information, capital and people.

The development of cross-border co-operation between cultural operators and institutions became more visible in the EU's Culture programme defined for 2007-2013. According to the Programme Guide Culture 2007-2013 cities that are interested in developing projects or receiving financial support for their permanent activities within the Culture Programme. Three main objectives are defined under the scheme: "to promote cross-border mobility of those working in the cultural sector; to encourage the transnational circulation of cultural and artistic output; and to foster intercultural dialogue" (Wilk-Woś, 2010: 79). According to Garcia (2005: 841-2) ECoC is perceived as a "catalyst for cultural regeneration, generating enormous expectations in cities", although the programme "did not originate from clearly structured guidelines as to what would constitute a European City/Capital of Culture".

Istanbul 2010 as a hybrid affair:

As reported in "The Selection Panel for the European Capital of Culture (ECOC) 2010" (2006: 11); European Parliament and Council of Europe took the decision 1419/1999/EC in 1999 to extend the ECoC Programme non-EU member cities during the period 2005-2019 (Palmer, 2004: 42). This brought Istanbul the chance to be ECoC.

The application dossier for ECoC 2010 was presented to the Council of Europe General Directorate for Education and Culture in Brussels on 13th

December 2005. The focus of the official application for ECoC was apparently the EU candidacy and negotiations for membership of Turkey. In this context, Istanbul 2010 is considered as an opportunity to demonstrate Istanbul's identity as a European city. The title is awarded to Istanbul on 13th November 2006, for the year 2010 together with Essen for the Ruhr region (Germany) and Pécs (Hungary).

On the other hand, according to the Final Report published by European Commission (Rampton et al., 2011: 79), the communication campaign of Istanbul 2010 "did not make a particular statement about European dimension". The slogan of international promotion campaign of Istanbul 2010 underlines the vision of a World city as we read "Istanbul... The most inspiring city of the World". In this highly pretentious statement, there is no reference to Europe, not even to Capital of Culture. This indicates a broader scope of branding vision cutting across the European vision. Bağış (Minister of EU affairs, Chief Negotiator and Istanbul Deputy) claimed that ECoC meant to make Istanbul a "World city" more than a "European capital" (Bağış, 2010: 29). Accordingly, the arguments raised by the marketing communication strategy of Istanbul 2010 event signify a higher and a more ambitious target, which is connecting Istanbul to the global city networks.

As the selection criteria put forward "city and citizens" together with "European dimension", Istanbul's bidding process was initiated through a bottom up approach where "city and citizens" were highlighted as the key area. The initiative group was comprised of 13 non-governmental organizations and the support of governmental bodies including municipality, the governor's office, the Ministry of Foreign Affairs and the Ministry of Culture (Çolakoğlu, n.d.). The work has started in 2000 and the initiative group was enlarged with the participation of city administrators, artists, employees at the cultural sector, academics, and representatives of some other NGOs. Istanbul 2010 ECOC Agency was founded for coordinating the joint efforts of public bodies and institutions and for the purpose of planning and managing the activities for preparing Istanbul as European Capital of Culture by 2010 according to the law no 5706 passed on 2nd November 2007 (Bilsel & Arıcan, 2010: 216).

Following the start-up of Initiative Group, Advisory Board is formed as well, which later has selected an Executive Committee (Beyazıt & Tosun, 2006: 6). Nevertheless, the executive committee has changed after the resign of the first group. The latter organization structure was formed under the umbrella of Coordination Committee chaired by Minister Hayati Yazıcı that is divided into Advisory Board and Executive Committee. If looked at the structure of the governance of the latter organizational structure, it is seen that it heavily relies on the presence and control of governmental bodies in a top-down manner (Öner, 2010). Therefore, the initial bottom-up model was not carried successfully and ECoC became the project of the government with speculations, resignations and rumors. In the interview, Korhan Gümüş (Director of Urban Practices at Istanbul 2010 Agency) notes that the change in organizational structure has influenced the decision making process negatively by creating a further fragmentation and polarization (Gümüş, 2010). The shift in the organizational structure changed the "participative objective" from "participation to transform" into "participation to legitimize" (Öner, 2010). The issues related to transparency and equitable distribution of funds contributed to debate about the shady organization of the event while reconciliation is sought for the contention and conflicting demands through "institutionalizing PPPs and inventing instruments of participatory policy making in arts and culture" (Öner, 2010: 267).

The participation of the public is very crucial. When the people feel a sense of inclusion in the process their perceptions would be affected accordingly in a positive manner. In Istanbul 2010, the public and civic organizations were repressed from the decision making-process but they were not hindered to submit projects. Therefore, the public was still encouraged to be part of the event through the cultural events but through a less transparent and democratic process in a top-down manner.

Thus, one of the main critical arguments raised against the organization of Istanbul 2010 lies in the fact that it has become a project of the government. Not only Istanbul itself was ruled by the central government in Ankara but also the cultural programme was subjected to centralization in governing structure. The government has taken a key role in the organization of the event by providing a major budget for the projects. Erciyes (2010) comments on the situation in a sarcastic way that the art and culture life of Istanbul was kept exclusive to the economic crisis thanks to the budget provided by 2010. The new mission proposed by the government was to put forward Istanbul as an attractive touristic destination through the rich cultural history and heritage. Accordingly, an important part of the budget is spent on the restoration projects and international promotion campaigns instead of investing on the cultural projects and to facilitate culture-led regeneration. The urban regeneration projects gained the top importance by attracting 60% of the total budget whereas the rest of the budget was distributed among culture, art, and tourism projects (Öner, 2010: 272) as the success of the event is usually measured in terms of "hotel nights, press millimetres, and urban renewal" (Palonen, 2010).

The financial interests also influence the state's role in preserving cultural heritage, which has turned into means of a cultural renaissance through the renewal of historic areas. The controversial legal and regulatory changes empowered by the state are exemplified in Law No. 5366 for the renewal of historic areas[4]. The urban renewal is targeted at enhancing tourism by improving the urban infrastructure and promoting cultural assets, which is accomplished through well-financed programmes. ECoC can be also recognized as a financing opportunity in this sense, as Aksoy (2009) comments on the investment realized by Istanbul 2010 programme being "equivalent to the Ministry of Culture and Tourism's annual budget towards the restoration and regeneration of the city's rich cultural heritage". Although it was stated that two-thirds of the budget was spent on the urban regeneration and restoration projects, the event did not manage to leave a cultural landmark or a "monumental legacy" such as a concert hall or opera house (Boland, 2011). Instead of adding new cultural landmarks to the city, the existence of the Byzantine and Ottoman heritage was approved by stressing the accumulation through the history of the city. The regeneration projects took the form of cleaning the facades of buildings for a better look or change the face of the city to a modern and global one with financial centres, plazas, five star hotels and shopping malls. The budget from the Commission enabled the large restoration projects to be finished in due time. The historical peninsula has been the primary implementation area for restoration and renovation projects. Thus it was claimed that the historical monuments and sites in the tourism centre of the city are benefited from the event (Erciyes, 2010). Prime Minister (currently President) Erdoğan puts the emphasis on the tourism dimension with the aim of attracting 10 million tourists to Istanbul in 2010 (Aksoy, 2010). However, ECoC is not only a touristic event and the cultural aspects should have been explained more to the audience to convince them why they should visit Istanbul during the year 2010.

Thus, there are various complications associated with Istanbul 2010. According to Palonen (2010), the main concern was presenting the touristic image of Istanbul abroad, rather than the impact on localities. Another issue is the lack of originality of the cultural programme, which includes a number of festivals and series of events. Most of these cultural events are already part of Istanbul's culture life and more importantly Istanbul's image, because they were started before Istanbul 2010 ECoC and they are organized for years on a continuous basis. In the end, ECoC did not really support the active involvement of the citizens as it was initially projected, which led to negativity among the residents.

---

[4] Law no. 5366: Preservation by Renovation and Utilization by Revitalizing of Deteriorated Immovable Historical and Cultural Properties'. Available from: http://inuraistanbul2009.files.wordpress.com/2009/06/law-5366-1.pdf [Accessed 17/09/2012]

ECoC serves as a tool not only for civic pride or participation but also as a branding-instrument in the national, European and international arena to attract tourism and investment. Intercultural communication is largely based on image transfer through mass media and mass tourism. While assuring to meet the criteria, cities design their own programs locally in order to showcase their cultural assets and cultural life or just the opposite in which the international program applies in an attempt to catch up with other cities in the cultural global network. That is why there is not a unique formula for cities to form their cultural programs; few cities concentrate on the cultural fabric and historical heritage of the city, whereas others go for add-on projects on top of what the city already offers as a cultural product. In most of the cases, cities go for a mix-match of these strategies, not coming up with really interesting and original projects. The originality is only stressed in the cultural identity of the city itself. There is the national pride hidden in winning the competition but the creative process is more related to the initial phase of the project and launching the idea. The Guardian journalist Crace (2002) noted "once the thrill of becoming a centre for cultural excellence evaporates, the residue might be little more than a glut of coffee shops". Thus the cultural programme is not always truly original and creative.

Richards & Wilson (2006: 1210) express the familiarity of the audience and brand awareness of the ECoC while warning about the loss of competitive advantage through the serial reproduction the event without creative thinking. The need "to support local culture" and "sustained local creative production processes in the city" is crucial for the competitiveness in the long term (Sutherland et al., 2006: 7). Nevertheless, the study of Palmer (2004) indicates that the long-term development and competitive advantage are not achieved by many ECoCs. The study puts the emphasis on "citizen participation and partnership building across urban cultural and economic sectors".

Accordingly, the changes in the organizational structure reflected on the inefficiencies in the planning. On the one hand, organizational changes through the major involvement of bureaucrats and technocrats rather than civic activists, have transformed the nature of the programme from a creative event into a promotive event. On the other hand, the marketing side of the organization was also criticized for lacking strategy and "decoupling" from the cultural programme and its constituent projects, particularly in its international activities" (Rampton et al., 2011: 76-7).

Thus, the spectacle of Istanbul 2010 presents a hybrid affair, in which the spaces of the city become the theatre stage, the politicians become the actors and the images become a tool for promoting and selling it. Inevitably this affair becomes a stage for conflicting interests among the different social, cultural and political actors. In the case of Istanbul 2010, the resignation of the executive committee marked such a process of conflict.

Besson & Sutherland (2007) claims "the opportunities may be overlooked and indeed wasted, with a huge expense incurred on the part of the city with little or no long-term benefits for its residents". The question is that; if the projects within the frame of ECoC are the outcomes of a strategic planning process for sustainability or if they are short-term projects to create an alluring theatricality.

Yazıcı (2010: 22) expresses the long-term interests "beyond individuals and institutions" by putting the emphasis on the collective venture through inclusion of the local people. This shows us the importance of mega-events, which are very well recognized in city branding strategies, with a focus on its long-term effects. The goals and policies are directed towards the sustainability and improvement but on the other hand in some cases it is hard to see any visible outcome that have a long-lasting effect and that is why it is believed in the temporary effects more than the sustainable effects.

ECoC programme is highly interested in the physical results and recently in the urban change, in other words in making the cities as well as their images. Previous ECoCs "have created cultural industries (e.g. Glasgow 1990), heritage sites (e.g. Weimar 1999 and Ruhr 2010), modern buildings (e.g. Graz 2003) and renovated whole urban cores (e.g. Sibiu 2007) which follow a more general trend in urban cultural policy, seeking economic and social regeneration" (Bianchini 1993; Sassatelli 2006: 35). Although the programme was described with having "pure cultural aims" (Richards and Wilson, 2004: 1936) in the initial framework, it became a catalyst for the urban regeneration, which is mostly associated as a source of "international publicity and prestige" (Smith, 2007: 5). It is expected from this urban spectacle to contribute to the international profile of the city and therefore attract visitors while aiming to "enhance the city image" (Palmer, 2004: 17).

The Image of Istanbul

Istanbul has been attributed certain level of representativeness and gained different meanings for different events in its history. Its foundation as a pagan city and the decoration of the city with Hellenistic monuments, then its transformation into the capital of Christian world and transfer of relics, and then the construction of Hagia Sophia followed by the introduction of Islam to the history of the city while gaining the capital city status of the Ottoman Empire and Muslim world are the signs of symbolic quality of the city. The foundation of the city and the names given to the city stress the relationship between the power and the urban space. In this context, the discourses in connection with the image of Istanbul are reaffirming the meanings of power hidden in the imperial symbols (capital city status, the imperial built structures of the Byzantine and Ottoman times) or Istanbul as a world city at its present.

The spectacularized image of a city takes shape at the intersection of material and discursive production. There have been several attempts by a number of scholars to categorize Istanbul's image according to certain discourse streamlines. According to these categories Istanbul is beautiful but aestheticized and sanitized, it is oriental but modernizing, it is a world city but globalizing. The discourse streamlines will be outlined under three headlines; firstly Istanbul as a "metropolis", and then Istanbul as a "world city" and its aspiration to be branded as a "global city", while lastly the discourses for Istanbul created by Istanbul 2010 event will be explained with respect to the marketing and branding strategy under the slogan of "Istanbul as the most inspiring city in the world". The variety of other discourses for Istanbul is compiled under these discourse categories.

Istanbul: Metropolis

The foundations of metropolis, both etymologically and materially, lies in the antiquity. The translation of the term from Greek origin suggest *"metera"* or *"meter"* means "mother" and *"polis"* denotes the city, combining into "Mother-City" (Farias & Stemmler, 2006: 4). Farias & Stemmler (2006: 5) define Greek metropolises as the "sponsor of a network of colonies", with respect to the "political relations that they maintained with their surrounding colonized area". After the colonial metropolises, post-colonial metropolises re-emerged during 18th-19th century referring to the "relationship between imperial centre and the periphery (Farias & Stemmler, 2006: 6). Metropolis in the modernity was associated with the rapid urbanization process. The contemporary adaptation of the metaphoric meanings of metropolis is of interest; such as festivalization of urban politics (Häußermann & Siebel, 1993), marketing of city images (Ward, 1998) and commodification of culture of cities (Zukin, 1995).

Kuban (2010b: 389) points out the period between 1950-1960 in defining Istanbul and its urban growth as a metropolis. The 1950s symbolizes the end of singular party regime and the transmission to pluralism. This era is marked by significant changes in urbanization. Its influence was felt mostly in Istanbul as the city started to spectacularize through the Americanization and commodity culture. Menderes and his Democrat Party have foreseen a radical urban change similar to Paris of Haussmann with crucial effects on the city image. The image making process for Istanbul in the 1950s was determined by two conditions: firstly, modern and high buildings, and secondly transportation by means of the increase in the number of roads, highways and motor vehicles. Kuban (2010b: 391) posits the parallelism between the modernization of Istanbul and its image rising as a metropolis. Accordingly, the politics of Menderes Government, which were directed towards urban change, should be considered with their impacts on the discourses and the image.

The discourses such as "pupil of the eye" and "jewel of Turkey" (Akpınar, 2010: 174) connote Istanbul parallel to the beautification projects. Kaya (2010: 99) calls Istanbul as the "showcase city" in his claim of the beautification projects directed towards attracting the attention of the world audience and attracting investments. The industrialization started in the 1950s further developed the city into one of the major finance centres in Turkey. The geographical location played key role in the process of industrialization in terms of accessibility to the goods and services. Consequently, migration started to the urban areas, mainly to Istanbul. The gateway to the city was Haydarpaşa located in the Asian side replacing Sirkeci Train Station and the myth of Orient Express. However, this time the newcomers to the city were not wealthy Western visitors, but instead they were the migrants coming from rural areas to Istanbul in search of jobs, hoping to make their lives in a big city. Istanbul's attraction for the flows of people in this era was signified through common themes appeared in the popular culture such as "Istanbul's streets are paved with gold". Istanbul was connoted as the "city of hope" symbolizing the dreams and desires of newcomers to the city. As a result of industrialization and migration, the population of the city reached almost 1 million in the 1950s and doubled by the 1970s, while reaching 5 million in the 1980s (Kuban, 2010b: 524). Contemporary Istanbul has developed to be a "megalopolis", a giant city with more than around 13 million people (Cox, 2012).

However, Istanbul was not prepared to cope with the enormous migration wave and unplanned growth. This era has been the scene for urban transformation and irregular urbanization while the city of hope has become "city of despair" at the discursive level.

Istanbul: World City

According to Kuban (1998: 15), the world-city status of Istanbul is built on the roots of its Greek and Roman heritage. The Ottoman period sustained this status by crowning the city as the capital and maintaining the cosmopolitan structure as well as the monuments. The world-city concept is made visible through these historical monuments communicating the multi-ethnic, multi-lingual and multi-religious structure. The imperial status of the city lasted until the fall of Ottoman Empire but Istanbul enjoyed her world city status through its historical significance mainly due to its ancient past of a universal value (Kuban, 1998: 15).

In opposition to Kuban's approach appraising the historical value of the city, Istanbul Metropolitan Municipality takes the concept of world city central to its marketing strategy for Istanbul especially through "ambitious urban transformation campaigns" (Karaman, 2008). Istanbul Metropolitan Municipality has been projecting Istanbul as a global city since 1980s initiated ambitiously by Bedrettin Dalan (1984-1989) whose vision of Istanbul as a global city by taking the form of catastrophic urban demolitions destroying the identity of the city for the sake of creating a modern metropolis. The destructions were legitimized in the form of urban transformation from "a tired city" of a glorious past resided in the pages of the history into "a metropolis full of promise for the 21st century" (Keyder & Öncü, 1994: 409).

The post-1980s are characterized by the two polarized groups: generation of secular, middle class and professional workers, what Esen (2011) calls "North-Istanbul elites" and rising commercial elites of Islamic-oriented traditional circles politically represented by AKP (Justice and Development Party) – "innovative group". These two groups shared the same vision of "gentrified Istanbul", which is written under the codes of "Clean City" or "Safe City" (Aksoy, 2009). Keyder (1999: 18) comments that 1980s and early 1990s are marked by the political ambiguity and insatiability as well as the "inability of the country to provide the environment for business confidence".

While the city is transformed, Istanbul urgently needs a metaphor to be replaced according to orders of the global city (Güvenç & Ünlü-Yücesoy, 2009). The main aspects defined by Currid (2006) highlight financial and business services and centres of command and control through establishing international headquarters as well as the creative industries referring to the ability to generate art and cultural output. Istanbul is emerging as a hip place for the global consumers and a business centre for the transnational corporate elite with "high-rise office buildings, luxury residential compounds and towers, dozens of shopping centres". This is highly influenced by the massive architectural projects reducing the entire cities and urban areas to market objects (Harvey, 1989a: 271). Brenner (1998: 4) links the world-city theory with the transnational corporations (TNCs) especially concentrating on the world financial centres. Istanbul is emerging as a world-city with an effort of integrating with the world economies through the rise in the number of TNCs and world economic order (Keyder, 1993). Globalization influenced the economic order and tourism has played an important role in the strategies to integrate with the world economy by providing flow of capital. The touristified image of the city has become a marketing tool to attract visitors to Istanbul, to a World city. It has become more salient through Istanbul ECoC 2010 in which it was included as a part of the vision to promote the city image to the world scene. Not only Istanbul 2010, but also a number of mega-events including NATO summit, World Congress of Architects, Formula 1 contributed positioning Istanbul as a World city.

A more globalized aim is lying in the wider picture for branding Istanbul. The conditions for modernizing and globalizing cities determined Istanbul's marketing potential in recreating its image shaped by investment, culture and leisure. Starting from the late 1990s and accelerating in the 2000s under the rule of AKP (Justice and Development Party) the image-making strategies are dominated by "neo-liberal discourses" directed towards showcasing the city at the global stage (Keyder, 2009). The mayor of Istanbul Metropolitan Municipality, Topbaş, states the strategy for city imaging as creating a "fully globalized open city with a different attitude towards the world" (Aksoy, 2010). Although it is vague what Topbaş means "with a different attitude", it is legible in these lines that Istanbul's goal is to be a global city by opening itself to the world economy and finance.

Istanbul, being at the crossroads, is inescapably at the intersection of diverse mobilities. It has been the competitive advantage of Istanbul throughout the history. Sassen (2009) comments on this situation to be advantageous but Istanbul still requires "handling and enhancing network functions" in order to be compatible to fit into global city chart. She proposes three trends among the requirements. The first one is linked to capital flows in which the importance of enhancing economic relations with Asian countries while recognizing EU as the main trade partner of Turkey. This again portrays a city between the East and West. Secondly she mentions the in and out-flows of people. Here, "the diversity of people migrating to and through Istanbul" leads us to the idea of a meeting point between Asia and Europe again. The third trend puts the emphasis on human capital and talent (Sassen, 2009).

The urban transformation of Istanbul could not keep the pace and satisfy the expectations to meet the global city model. Therefore, the efforts in city marketing are directed towards creating the global city image. However, presenting Istanbul through the bridge metaphor between the East and the West had created a projected image and fetishized Istanbul as a consumption object, as a "fantasy city" resting against the historical myths "between the global and the local" as Keyder (1999) claims. The fantasy city hides the negative images and reconstructs the images of the city according to the "Cities of Desire" (Calvino, 1997 [1972]) fetishizing and beautifying cities in the eyes of the people. On the other side 'cities of desire' are withdrawing from the reality and their images are becoming unreal in the world of spectacles. Perhaps the projected images would create "invisible cities" (Calvino, 1997 [1972]) in the future. The homogenizing effect of globalization already gives signals of this projection.

Istanbul: "The most inspiring city in the world"

The promotional campaign for Istanbul 2010 positions Istanbul as "the most inspiring city in the world" with its slogan. However, even before than Istanbul, the "inspiring city" concept was used by Edinburgh branding campaign with the slogan "Inspiring Capital":

> *"There is a drama and magical quality to the city for many people and it is a place that stimulates the senses and imagination. It is a city if contrasts, with a special atmosphere as a result. Its natural beauty along with its intellectual tradition has been a springboard for invention and creativity. From the festivals to the telephone and from the Dolly the sheep to Harry Potter – Edinburgh clearly inspires. Therefore it is the inspiration that is at the heart of Edinburgh brand" (Kornberger, 2010: 91).*

The inspirations of both Edinburgh and Istanbul are meant to create an atmosphere and unforgettable, unique experience for the visitors. Yet, the difference between the two examples stem from their approach to branding. The imaginary created for Istanbul is rooted in its past as an Oriental city in a play of fantasy, whereas Edinburgh puts forward its intellectual assets for creativity as the main inspiring factor.

Istanbul 2010 is only a strategic instrument and a part of the city branding strategy. Istanbul is projected as "the most inspiring city in the world" by stressing the "inspirational exchanges between cultures" (Çolakoğlu, n.d.). In an interview, Yazıcı (Minister of State and Chairman of the Istanbul 2010 ECoC Agency Coordination Board) (2010) expressed that 2010 would be the year to "start the change" in Istanbul. The historical status of Istanbul as a capital city stressed by Yazıcı (2010: 24) as the "capital of all times":

> *"Istanbul is not a European Capital of Culture solely for the year 2010, but rather the capital of all times, a true European capital. It is about time we built Istanbul as a brand and promote that brand."*

ECoC programme presents the image of a European city vibrating with arts and culture that has a clean and orderly look, which is also a highly touristic image. The most liked oriental representations of Istanbul, however, seem to contradict with this picture as these images stress the mysticism and chaotic structure of the city that raises curiosity, because these features do not belong to many European cities. According to Boland (2011), Istanbul is certainly beyond the Europeanness drawn by ECoC and EU framework, yet reassuringly compatible to be a European city.

> *"After so many decades of trying to become Western, Istanbul glories in the rediscovery of a very modern identity. European or not, it is one of the coolest cities in the world." (Newsweek, 2005 [29 August]; qtd. in McAdams, 2007).*

On the one hand modern face of the city of a European look is presented, while on the other hand the cultural heritage is alleged a part of pan-European identity through the historical discourses. Istanbul has a different place among the other example of ECoCs so far, both in terms of being a non-EU city and organizational aspect of the event. Istanbul stands as a polycentric city with more than 13 million people, which is exceeding by far the scale of other cities that have been or are nominated for ECoC, especially in the last decade. Its historical identity and the transformation does not resemble to those transformed from post-fordist city structures. This makes Istanbul distinctive, and it adds to the value at the same time.

On the one hand, messages are directed towards branding Istanbul as a modern Western metropolis and cosmopolitan World city on the surface, on the other hand the sub-meanings signify the glorious past of Istanbul building on the stereotypes and symbolic representations of national heritage. The most common representations of old Istanbul portray the city through scenic or panoramic way or with its everyday life and the imaginary world of Harem (İnankur, 2010: 328). The iconic elements in such representations were often mosques and their minarets (Boland, 2011; Akpınar, 2003: 152-3). The Orientalist images were intended to portray the city in response to the image in the minds of the Western audience.

The marketing strategy has focused on brand values of Istanbul such as "capital for 3000 years, capital of three empires, city of tolerance, cultural diversity, coexistence of 26 ethnicities, mosaic of different religions…etc." (Erten, 2008: 185). In this respect, the history of Istanbul became to represent a symbolic value both for its residents and visitors through the connotations such as "the cradle of civilizations". Newman (2005) suggests that the rich past of Istanbul has provided a large accumulation of cultural capital, therefore "it is a historically dominant city, which makes it less vulnerable to the changing trends in cultural development."

The history of a city is a strong brand asset. Whereas, with the acceleration of consumption culture and increasing globalization, the new and modern are appraised in opposition to the old. Nevertheless, the city does not exist in the past. The global audience is not only interested in visiting old palaces, churches, and mosques, but they ask for entertainment and shopping as well. The marketers strive to answer these needs and therefore they show every possible image of the city to catch the eye to raise interest.

Chapter 4: Posters of Istanbul 2010

Posters are my units of analysis. Posters talk to the audience, they are in the city – on the walls, airports, at the metro stations, at the bus stops, on the facades of the buildings; on-site and off-site, but never out of sight.

While walking on the street, waiting at the bus stop, waiting at the red light or in the traffic the viewers look at posters and whether they notice it consciously or not, the signs give messages. Posters are on display for everyone, each citizen passing by the road, 24 hours a day, 7 days a week for months, thus they are subjected to a broad public visibility. They are potentially seen by all and likely to influence the perception of the city image. In this respect, posters are instruments to rebrand and re-image the city.

The people involved in the social practice, which means production and reception of the text, are called social agents (or interactive participants). Advertising can be seen as the example of "social practice" and the posters refer to the "social event". The French word for poster is "l'affiche", with connotations to public space. It refers to the "public notice that is posted or put up in a public space as an announcement or advertisement" (Timmers, 1998: 7). The communicative function of the poster is essential as it takes place between an "active force" (producer who has a message to sell) and the "re-active force" (audience who is to be persuaded to buy through the message) (Timmers, 1998: 7). This interaction is materialized in the public space.

Posters are used widely in tourism for giving information about the destination. There are also brochures and flyers used for the same purpose but the core is the image as it presents the "exquisite scenery" (Mori, 2010: 7). According to Roma (1917: 18 qtd. in Mori, 2010) "an advertisement is not meant to be observed up close: it must strike from afar, draw people in closer, or be seen at a great distance". In doing so, posters are means of advertising to attract attention through the use of bright colours and compositional elements.

Apart from being a promotion tool to attract visitors, posters convey social and political messages and meanings, through which one can trace a course of social history, evolution of taste, and ideology. The posters of Istanbul 2010 may seem recent for tracing the past, but it should be noted that these posters are part of a larger marketing strategy for the city branding of Istanbul. The projects whether they are designed by different forms of institutions varying from governmental to non-governmental, or by directly Istanbul 2010 Agency itself, they reflect the vision of the Istanbul 2010 Agency in city imaging. Thus, Istanbul 2010 Agency can be recognized as the main actor responsible for planning, organizing and coordinating this process while

Doğan

creating the main discourses and meanings behind the images. Istanbul 2010 Agency used posters as major tools for communicating messages and meanings, and making the city image.

The city imaging is recognized as part of the signification and representation practices, while also being a part of the communication directed at public within a programme of place marketing. Therefore, a sample of posters are chosen and analysed by evaluating their messages in comparison to the strategic communication objectives of Istanbul 2010 in order to arrive a point of integrity in the meaning making.

Sample of Posters

I have classified the posters into two main categories: the official promotion materials of the event, and posters of the sample of cultural projects. The latter is divided into three subgroups defined by Istanbul 2010 Agency. The official promotion posters by Istanbul 2010 Agency are useful for understanding the centralized discourse in strategic image making process. The posters of the Istanbul 2010 projects are variable in their signifiers and useful in investigating the role of cultural events in enhancing the city image.

Table 4. Classification of posters

Istanbul 2010 Agency official promotion campaign		
a) International promotion campaign	b) Domestic promotion campaign	
Istanbul 2010 projects in the year 2010		
a) Tourism & Promotion	b) Urban transformation	c) Culture & art
promotion & communication	urban projects	visual arts
international relations	cultural heritage & museums	music & opera/ classical Turkish music
	urban culture	film & documentary & animation
		literature
		theatre & performing arts
		traditional arts
		education
		maritime & sports
		parallel events

There were only four official posters of the Istanbul 2010 Agency:
International promotion: 1 poster ("Istanbul Inspirations")
Domestic promotion: 3 posters ("Rediscover": Galata, Haydarpaşa, Hagia Sophia)
The second group of posters are selected by using a *stratified random sampling* (Table 4). There were 549 projects selected from a pool of 2500 applications in the ECoC 2010 (Bozkuş, 2012:9). Posters of every single project are taken as the "units of analysis". I have worked on 28 of 549 posters (approx. 5%). This is a representative sample of the Istanbul 2010 projects. I have picked examples from each thematic strata defined by Istanbul 2010 Agency (Table 5).

Table 5. Number of projects in each category

	No. of projects
a) Tourism & Promotion	
promotion & communication	76
international relations	36
Total	112
b) Urban Transformation	
urban projects	47
cultural heritage & museums	29
urban culture	25
Total	101
c) Culture & Arts	
visual arts	41
music & opera/classical Turkish music	48
film & documentary & animation	36
literature	20
theatre & performing arts	15
traditional arts	19
education	12
maritime and sports	14
parallel events	131
Total	336
N	549
n= 5%*N	28

The "culture and art" was the largest segment of events (24% of the total). Promotion and communication comes as the second largest segment with 14 %. Together with international relations, the total number of projects under the tourism and promotion category is equal to 112, which is almost a fifth of the total number of projects. This is closely followed by the urban transformation projects with the total number of 101. Education is the smallest group with 2% as only 12 projects. At the end of random selection, the sample of projects were the following:

Table 6. List of selected posters

Sub-groups	n	Sample of Istanbul 2010 Projects
a) Tourism & Promotion		
promotion & communication	4	1. Golden Routes in the footsteps of Evliya Çelebi 2. "Beyoğlu is Different with Music" 3. call4istanbul 4. Introduction of the Mawlawi Culture and Sema Ceremony
international relations	2	1.Human Cities 2.Istanbul Express-Exploring Multilingualism across Europe
b) Urban Transformation		
urban projects	3	1. Palimpsest Istanbul 2. Project Works for the Land Walls included in the UNESCO World Heritage Area 3. Armenian Architects of Istanbul in the Era of Westernization
cultural heritage & museums	1	1. Istanbul 1910-2010 - City, Built Environment & Architectural Culture Exhibition
urban culture	1	1. Istanbul Woman – Woman Istanbul
c) Culture & Art		
visual arts	2	1. Diver-city 2. Bump into each other – Asia/Europe
music & opera	2	1. Türküyem 2. Tales of Future - 1 city 1011 Vibrations
film, documentary & animation	2	1. If Istanbul 2. İstanbul'da Bayram Sabahı
literature	1	1. International Istanbul Poetry Festival
theatre & performing arts	1	1. Cihangir Insomnia
traditional arts	1	1. Heritage –A Collection from Traditional Turkish Calligraphy Foundation Museum
education	1	1. Sulukule Children's Art Workshop Project
maritime & sports	1	1. Rally of Turkey
parallel events	6	1. Istanbul en Drome 2. Spectres of Trotsky: the Lost Interiors of an Exile 3. In Between. Austria Contemporary 4. "Arie Antiche" 5. "Istanbul – Paris – Berlin" 6. Forum Fashion Week

The second group of posters were mainly from the catalogue of selected Istanbul 2010 projects published in February 2011 (Istanbul 2010 Avrupa Kültür Başkenti Girişim Grubu, 2011) and another catalogue published in 2010 from the library of Istanbul Research Institute of Suna & Inan Kirac Foundation.

I have scanned the posters from the catalogues for analysis with no manipulation. While analysis was carried out on the original posters, the scanned images were used only for representation in reporting.

Form and content

Benjamin (1999) sees the image as the "enabler of human agency" in motivating the will of the people. In this respect, images do not depict reality, but create reality, thus messages are chosen to have an effect to readers. Accordingly, image is of central concern for visual studies as a medium for the transmission of material reality. Two conditions; form and content affect this transmission (Buck-Morss, 2004: 9). Therefore, form and content have been paid greater attention in the initial step of analysis.

Firstly, the description of data is given with a reference to form. It is done by taking notes of the visual details observed only on the surface of the image, which is identified as the form. Content comes the next, as the second source of information, which necessitates a more careful approach to the posters and anchoring the text and image to interpret the meaning at the connotative level. The content of the image tells us about what the image actually means.   As a result, interpretation ideally emerges from descriptive details. The information gathered through description goes further than merely describing the physical patterns related to the design of the posters. Therefore, form and content together are defined as the conditions in developing visual literacy of posters.

Istanbul 2010 Official Posters for Promotion

The international marketing campaign is launched with the slogan "Istanbul, the most inspiring city in the world". The historical peninsula photograph is posterized as the visual icon of Istanbul representing the city abroad accompanied by "Istanbul inspirations" motto. This visual icon targets the World audience for the international campaign. The domestic and international promotional activities differ in their target audience, messages, slogans and visual representations.

The poster of "Istanbul Inspirations" representing the famous silhouette of Istanbul is produced by bringing about 30 photographs of the historical peninsula in Istanbul by the photographer Rainer Strattman. The domestic campaign used different posters, which puts the emphasis on the cultural heritage and landmarks of Istanbul, such as Hagia Sophia, Galata Tower and Haydarpaşa Train Station, inviting viewers and citizens to re-discover the city and its culture with the slogan "Now is the time to re-discover!"

a) International Campaign: "Istanbul Inspirations"

Figure 7. Poster of Istanbul Ispirations

Source: Image courtesy of Özgül Özkan Yavuz (Istanbul İl Turizm Müdürlüğü, 2012).

1. Form

The poster depicts the Istanbul image through the representation of historical peninsula from the sea. The image is located at the upper half of the poster followed by the slogan and the verbal text. The Istanbul 2010 logo is placed on the bottom left of the poster; the colour is grey & white. Below the logo, Turkish Airlines logo is placed as the sponsor. On the bottom right of the poster it is written "Istanbul Inspirations" in gold colour with the biggest font used in the poster.

Advertisers pay attention to composition and framing, how to place the objects on the posters. As the eye reads the page from left to right, there is a general tendency to place the information about the product on the upper left, the product is in the centre as the emphasis is made to product and logo on the bottom right to give a lasting impression (Kress & van Leeuwen, 2006). However, the composition is subject to change and does not follow such an order. The poster for "Istanbul Inspirations" starts with the image, which covers half of the page and extends through both sides like a cinemascope. This may be interpreted as a sign reinforcing the historical meaning, as the cinemascope is an old movie format used in the 1950s. One of the intentions in adapting a wide screen format could be interpreted as amplifying the effect of the image.

The slogan and verbal text is placed in the centre, while the logos of Istanbul 2010 and sponsors are at the bottom-left corner. The lasting impression is provided by concluding with "Istanbul Inspirations" written in gold colour and bigger font size than the slogan, which is at the bottom-right part. The size of the font and the organization of the text divided into two lines both stresses "Istanbul Inspirations" by drawing the attention and brings balance to the composition which otherwise would be imbalanced as the right side would be left blank in a greater portion. The "golden ratio rule" which applies to photography and visual arts also applies to ads for placing the object on the one-third proportion of the page, where eye tends to focus naturally and creates a balance in the composition (Kress & van Leeuwen, 2006). The image cuts the poster into two halves and the verbal messages are placed in the lower part therefore it cannot be said that the golden ratio rule is applied to the poster. It may be rather concluded that the aim of the poster is to put the emphasis on the image as it is an iconic image representing the city. The verbal messages are small sized in comparison to the portion of the image and they are used as promotional tools rather than anchoring the meaning through the image.

2. Content

The main theme of international campaign is "Istanbul inspirations" in its reflection for the city that has inspired many civilizations throughout the history. The campaign stresses the rich historical and cultural accumulation of the past and connects to the modern city. Therefore, the source of the energy of Istanbul is the past, while Istanbul continues to inspire through the multi-colours, multi-voices and multi-faces, in other words multi-layers of meaning. The anchorage between the image and word will be analysed further, through the examination of what the words say and what the images show and if they give the same messages or if they contradict each other. Firstly, the textual meanings are interpreted and secondly the visual meanings are inferred and lastly they are combined to anchor the meaning between the word and the image.

> **Text:**
> "Istanbul... The most inspiring city in the world."
> "Istanbul 2010 European Capital of Culture will further inspire you with its contemporary art and urban culture. Be part of this unique experience."

The slogan for the international campaign of Istanbul 2010 is naming Istanbul as the most inspiring city in the world. The superlative structure of the slogan sounds very pretentious and raises doubts about the status of the city. The mega-events have become the global arena for the competition between the cities. The cities strive for presenting themselves at the most beautiful, most artistic, most creative or most inspiring as in the case of Istanbul, but this does not necessarily mean that "they are" really, than what "they like to be".

Interpersonal voice is used, which seeks to turn the public into active citizens and to win their support by inviting them to "be part of this unique experience". This interpersonal voice is supported by a promotional voice, through which public participation is emphasized: "Istanbul 2010 European Capital of Culture will further inspire you with its contemporary art and urban culture." The purpose of this promotional voice is to put the emphasis on the contemporary art and urban culture as the two inspiring features of the city. However, the linkage between the word and image seems weak. The image of historical peninsula is a mystified object of the past and throws a historical gaze to the city as a powerful representation of its heritage and as a monumental site. The image is stronger than the text in its visual representation of the iconic and the text does not argue with the image. The references for contemporary art and urban culture can be hardly found in the visual representation.

The international campaign was created by RPM/Radar Advertising & Ajans Ultra in which Paul McMillen was the creative director. "Istanbul Silhouette" was produced by the photographer Rainer Stratmann through a collage of 30 photographs, in order to create an "icon visual that will be automatically remembered when Istanbul is mentioned" (Anatolia News Agency, 2009). The choice of angle is purposive in order to capture the landscape of historical peninsula from a wide angle. The photo starts from sea level – discovering the sea, originating from the sea. This represents a gaze connected with the past when Istanbul was (and still is) a port city and western travellers had their first look at the city from here. According to McMillen (2010: 55), representational photos of London and Manhattan are romantic and gloomy, black & white. Photos of Istanbul by Ara Güler can be thought as such. However, McMillen (2010: 55) claims they wanted to add colour as "darker tones help to go beyond the ordinary, to re-discover". This goes hand-in-hand with the national campaign and its slogan "It is time to rediscover". McMillen (2010: 56) states: "When we live in a city we know her better, but admiration of the city is possible from afar", therefore the image presents a panoramic gaze to Istanbul.

When we talk about the modality of the image we see that it is highly manipulated through retouch & refinement. The photo was finely retouched as the satellite dishes, several derricks and other details were cleared off, unpleasant elements on the fields became trees, but there were no major relocations. Those types of interventions and manipulations are common in advertising for making images positive and destinations attractive. The international campaign aims to show Istanbul as a confident and dignified city in the same league with the world's other leading metropolises.

The image has a gloomy affect through the use of high saturation and dark colours. Although sea is represented by blue, in this picture it is lead colour, creating a dark atmosphere. The colour scheme applied to the picture fosters the historic meaning. Yet such kind of preference of dark colours is unconventional for advertising and the tendency to use bright colours to make representation of the objects more glamorous.

The target audience is the international audience as "Istanbul Inspirations" was the international marketing campaign for Istanbul 2010. Hakkı Mısırlıoğlu, who carries out the creative architecture of the campaign alongside McMillen, mentioned that the city would be promoted in 20 countries around the world through printed media, television, advertisements and the internet. The poster of the silhouette is placed in the main squares and train stations and airports of a number of European cities such as San Marco Square in Venice or Gare du Nord in Paris (Radikal, 2009).

b) Domestic Campaign: "Now is the Time to Rediscover"

Figure 8. Poster of Galata Tower

Source: Image courtesy of Özgül Özkan Yavuz (Istanbul İl Turizm Müdürlüğü, 2012).

Figure 9. Poster of Haydarpaşa Train Station

Source: Image courtesy of Özgül Özkan Yavuz (Istanbul İl Turizm Müdürlüğü, 2012).

Figure 10. Poster of Hagia Sophia

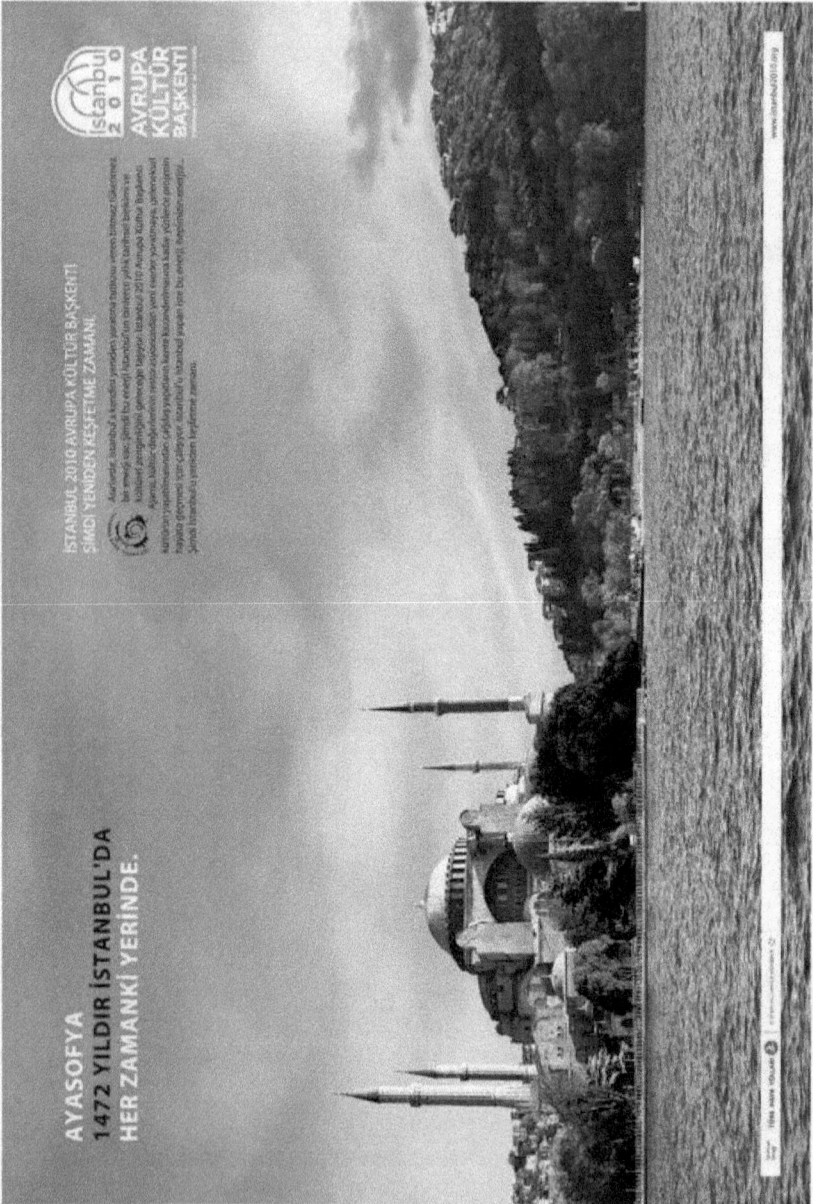

Source: Image courtesy of Özgül Özkan Yavuz (Istanbul İl Turizm Müdürlüğü, 2012).

1. Form

All of the three images used for the national campaigns are arranged in a similar way in their composition. The text is placed on the upper left in three lines, the first and last lines are in white colour and the line in the middle is black colour. The last line does not change but the first two lines changes. The first line refers to the image signified in the poster: Galata Tower, Haydarpaşa Station and Hagia Sophia. In the second line only the numerical figures change in order to denote the age of the monuments to emphasize their historical values.

The text catches the eye of the viewer together with the image at first glance. There is also a large amount of text written in smaller fonts. It is accompanied by a small logo in the shape of Istanbul silhouette like a whirlpool. The text "Istanbul 2010 Enerjisi" (Energy of Istanbul 2010) makes a loop around the swirling silhouette. The headline in bigger font, capital letters and white colour, is the slogan of the national campaign, which applies to all of the three posters. The text also remains the same while the colour changes for visibility purposes. The text is black except the Galata Tower poster, where the whole text is white because the background is a dark colour. Therefore, the slogan and the following text for "Rediscover" series remain with the same content and at the same place in all of the posters. On the right of the slogan there is the logo of Istanbul 2010 in white colour. The logo of Turkish Airlines, as the main sponsor can be found on a white box at the bottom of the poster indicating the web address of Istanbul 2010 (www.istanbul2010.org) on the right. The text is applied on the image, which makes it look like a part of the image. In doing so, form and content merge into each other.

2. Content

> **"Istanbul 2010 Avrupa Kültür Başkenti**
> **Şimdi Yeniden Keşfetme Zamanı"**
>
> "Asırlardır Istanbul'a kendini yeniden yaratma tutkusu veren bitmez tükenmez bir enerji var. Şimdi bu enerji İstanbul'un binlerce yıllık tarihsel birikimi ve kültürel zenginliğini geleceğe taşıyor. Istanbul 2010 Avrupa Kültür Başkenti Ajansı, kültür değerlerinin restorasyonundan yeni eserler yaratmaya, geleneksel kültürün yaşatılmasından çağdaş yapıtların kente kazandırılmasına kadar yüzlerce projenin hayata geçmesi için çalışıyor. Istanbul'u Istanbul yapan işte bu enerji, hepimizin enerjisi... Şimdi Istanbul'u yeniden keşfetme zamanı."

> ### *"Istanbul 2010 European Capital of Culture*
> ### *Now is the time to rediscover"**
>
> *"There is a never-ending energy that gives Istanbul the passion to recreate itself for centuries. Now this energy transcends the historical accumulation and cultural richness of Istanbul for thousands of years to the future. Istanbul 2010 European Capital of Culture Agency is working for the actualisation of hundreds of projects, from restoration of cultural assets to creation of new artefacts, from cherishing the traditional culture to bringing new contemporary artworks to the city. What makes the city Istanbul is this energy, our energy... Now is the time to rediscover Istanbul."**
>
> * *"Translation by the author"*

The slogan "Now is the time to rediscover" aims raising awareness of the city dwellers and asking them to look at their city from a different perspective. The text is informative. The aim is informing the public about rich cultural heritage of Istanbul. On the other hand, the word "energy" is stressed as the transformative power through the connotations to the modern and contemporary. Istanbul is modernizing, globalizing and recreating itself by regenerating the past. Istanbul 2010 Agency comes one step forward as the main actor for facilitating the change: "Istanbul 2010 European Capital of Culture Agency is working for realizing hundreds of projects".

The tone of voice is participative in using "us approach". It says "our" energy and invites the audience to rediscover Istanbul. The audience is recognized as active subjects who are willing to participate and take action. They are not passive consumers. Therefore, it can be said that the energy level and dynamism of the city is kept at two levels – subject and object.

Whereas, the meaning of the message for "rediscover"ing the past is twisty due to the discrepancy between verbal and non-verbal signifiers. To put in another way, what is said in words and what is shown in the image are contradictory. This is a deliberate action in order to surprise and stimulate the audience to rethink. The monuments, which survived from past to present, are iconic symbols of Istanbul. However, they have been subjected to transformation throughout the history. Galata Tower has been restored many times due to damage because of the fires. Hagia Sophia was constructed as a church. When Istanbul was conquered by Ottomans, it was transformed into a mosque and four minarets were added. Today it is a museum. Therefore, the transformation does not only point out the change in physical qualities, but also change in the function. For Haydarpaşa Train Station a different transformation plan is forecasted. It was built and used as the train station as a gate to Istanbul from Anatolia. Its function did not change for almost a century. Nevertheless, a new scenario is projected for the future of

Haydarpaşa to create a complex including yacht club with its marina, a convention centre, a sports centre, a museum, accommodation facilities such as luxury hotels and residences, a commercial and shopping centre, a hospital and rehabilitation centre and recreational areas. The verbal message, on the other hand, proposes a new look on the cultural heritage without communicating the new scenarios. When the people become aware of their cultural heritage, it might be too late that they could have been already gone.

The poster of Istanbul Inspirations was all over the place both in Turkey and abroad since it was the visual icon for Istanbul. On the other hand, these three posters were designed for national campaign. Billboards were the main sites that the posters were exposed just before the event takes on in January 2010 (Dailymotion, 2009).

---

1. GALATA TOWER:

"GALATA KULESI 661 YILDIR ISTANBUL'DA HER ZAMANKI YERINDE."

"Galata Tower has been standing in its usual place for 661 years."*

2. HAYDARPAŞA TRAIN STATION:

"HAYDARPAŞA GARI 101 YILDIR ISTANBUL'DA HER ZAMANKI YERINDE."

"Haydarpaşa Train Station has been standing in its usual place for 101 years."*

3. HAGIA SOPHIA:

"AYASOFYA 1472 YILDIR ISTANBUL'DA HER ZAMANKI YERINDE."

"Hagia Sophia has been standing in its usual place for 1472 years."*

* *"Translation by the author"*

When we take a closer look at each image, we see that they have many common features. As it can be understood from the text, which is in Turkish, the campaign targets the national audience.

The focus is on the buildings (Galata Tower, Haydarpaşa and Hagia Sophia) as the main signifiers in the images and their analysis deserves much more attention, therefore is done separately. Galata Tower, Haydarpaşa Station and Hagia Sophia are featured in the campaign due to their recognisability as landmarks. They are the symbols of Istanbul. Hagia Sophia is a hybrid example, a symbol of two religions. Haydarpaşa was selected as an example of relatively recent history (Mısırlıoğlu, 2010: 58). Galata Tower built by Genoese is an example of multicultural heritage.

Due to the high degree of intervention, the images have low modality but when the goal of the promotional campaign is taken into consideration this does not affect the truthfulness of the image. These images are not true representations on purpose, because they are not designed to make the audience believe what they see, but to surprise them by showing a different image than what they expect to see. The monuments are shown in different places than they are. For instance, Haydarpaşa replaces AKM, Galata Tower replaces Maiden's Tower, Hagia Sophia is relocated on the Bosphorus.

According to the visual codes inferred from the three of the messages, Haydarpaşa image reflects on the urban context with respect to the images of Hagia Sophia and Galata Tower that are not reflecting the urban surroundings and they are literally standing alone. However, in Haydarpaşa image we see an urban public space communicating how the city looks like and how the urban elements communicate with each other.

When we look at these three images separately, the visual codes can be described as follows:

GALATA TOWER

The Galata Tower standing alone in the middle of the sea catches the eye immediately as there is no other object in the foreground of the image and Istanbul skyline is depicted at the background. The viewers may immediately locate Maiden's Tower replaced by Galata Tower in the image. The image detaches Galata Tower from its historical surroundings by locating it in the middle of the sea. The tower stands as a divine figure. It is also a phallic figure according to the "architectural genealogy of tower".

The composition of the image applies to the gold ratio principle, placing Galata Tower at the left on the 1/3 line. The horizon is also located at the lower 1/3 line, not cutting the image through the middle line. Although the emphasis is on the Galata Tower as the main figure, the image is dominated by the sea and the sky. These two elements are associated with the "Four Elements" idea of Istanbul 2010 project at the initial programme. Sky refers to the "air" and sea refers to the "water". The blue colour is dominating the picture through the sea and the sky, which are cut by the Istanbul skyline and a pinkish colour in the horizon like the sunset. However, the tone of blue is dark. Instead of calming effect, it creates a stormy and turbulent effect. The sky is heavy with clouds. It is not a crystal clear sky but is opaque. This is not an attractive image in the sense of advertising. In general terms, advertising images use bright colours to catch the eye. Although it is supposed to be promotional and the main intention is to attract people the atmosphere is gloomy and disturbing.

HAYDARPAŞA STATION

The signifiers "sky" and "water" may be associated with the concept of "4 elements: water, air, earth, fire" which was the main idea in the bidding document of Istanbul 2010. However, the use of water element is bizarre. Haydarpaşa has direct contact with water in reality, whereas it replaces AKM (Ataturk Culture Centre) in Taksim square in the image. The image represents a city square with no reference to water. This is just the opposite of the other two images, which are normally located in the inner city but represented through contact with water. In this sense, the image for Haydarpaşa differs from the other two images.

Haydarpaşa represents being the "gateway" to the city both through the sea and railways. It is a transportation hub as a station and as a port. Therefore, it reflects strong connotations for mobility. The immigrants coming from Anatolia enter the city through Haydarpaşa. In the image, Haydarpaşa is surrounded by the modern city life and modern/contemporary architecture. The Marmara Hotel signifies globalization and tourism introducing uniform architecture and homogenous cities. The depiction of an old building in a modern area stresses the contrasts. It is represented in a busy and crowded urban area, which highlights the urban qualities of Istanbul. Interestingly the architecture of Haydarpaşa fits to be an opera or theatre building in most of the European cities. This is, most probably, due to the architectural style of the building. When we think of the function of AKM (Ataturk Culture Centre), we can infer the meaning of entertainment connected to the concepts of theatricality and spectacle.

In this picture, we see the public space, a square in the city, public transportation, high buildings, The Marmara Hotel (on the right), and the monument. Thus, it is full of references to the metropolitan character of Istanbul. The composition of this picture is chaotic, it is full of other elements, distracting the audience but the focus is clearly on Haydarpaşa. The chaos also reflects upon the dynamism, the crowds and traffic reflects on the energy of the city.

HAGIA SOPHIA

The composition resembles the first image with Galata Tower. The golden ratio applies to the horizon and where Hagia Sophia stands (1/3 line on the left). The focus is on Hagia Sophia as the background is a landscape through the blue and green - earth, sea and sky. The red colour of Hagia Sophia is inviting and intriguing, it says "Come in". The function of Hagia Sophia as a religious place, both as a church and a mosque to which is now added museum function, represents the multiculturalism and openness, which matches with the signified. Yet it stands alone on the shore just like Galata Tower image as if it has no visitors and it is separated from its context as a sanitized object.

1. Istanbul 2010 Posters of Cultural Projects

The second category of posters comprise of the posters from the sample of Istanbul 2010 cultural projects. A total number of 28 posters will be analyzed by applying the same structure of analysis based on form and content.

The posters are classified into three groups:
a)   Tourism & promotion
b)   Urban transformation
c)   Culture & arts

The selected projects under these groups are also classified into subgroups with respect to the strata that they belong to in the programme book of Istanbul 2010 Agency.

a) Tourism & Promotion

Promotion & communication

1.   Form

"In the footsteps of Evliya Çelebi" is one of the themes for Golden Routes projects. Another project is "in the footsteps of Piri Reis". The project is comprised of concerts, dance and conferences in different European (mostly East European) cities from Plovdiv to Oberhausen, including two other cities of ECoC 2010; Pécs and Essen. The list of the cities included in the programme of the event is listed on the lower right side of the poster designed by Fenni Özalp.

When we look at the organization and composition of the elements on the poster, we see the logo of the Golden Routes event on the top left and the logo of Istanbul 2010 on the top right corner. Both of the logos are printed in white. The logo of Golden routes is placed on dark blue/purplish background on a rectangular frame, whereas Istanbul 2010 logo is directly applied on the background of the poster, which is red and has some patterns changing in tone of the same colour. The title of the project is placed under the logos in big fonts and getting bigger from top to bottom line in which "Evliya Çelebi" is written with the biggest font size.

The image is depicted in a frame like a TV screen. The frame line is blue and on the top under "Evliya Çelebi" the date of the project is announced, "20. September–16 October 2010". The image is a sketch representation on yellow-orange-brown tones, which feels like an old image. Under the image the details of the cultural programme are given under three titles: Concerts, Dance and Conferences. The date, place and the name of the event are listed in small fonts and white colour. At the very bottom line of the poster, the logos of official institutions from the collaborating cities are displayed, most of them being the logo of Municipality such as Sofia, Prizren, Belgrade or cultural institutions such as Macedonian Opera and Ballet-Skopje or Enjoy Jazz Festival-Mannheim. The cities of Pécs and Essen are represented with their ECoC 2010 logos. The logos of Turkish Ministry of Foreign Affairs and Turkish Ministry of Culture are also listed, which stand as an evidence of predominance of governmental agencies.

2. Content

When we look at the image it is like we are looking at a TV screen and watching a historical film or documentary. Such representation of a TV screen also connotes the spectacle and spectacularization of culture and history. The main figure is the sketch of Evliya Çelebi (who is a historical figure, a traveller and travel writer) on the horseback. A bus follows the footsteps of Evliya Çelebi. Although Evliya Çelebi is depicted as an ink sketch figure without colours, the bus is painted in blue and red in harmony with the logo of Golden Routes and red used in the background of the poster. The bus carries the logo of Golden Routes and the ECoC year 2010 is represented in numbers next to the logo. The representation of the logo and Istanbul 2010 is in harmony with the logos on the top and fosters the symbolic meaning through stressing brand identity and communicating the brand elements in their most recognized forms.

Evliya Çelebi is a historical figure, who belongs to the past. The way of depiction on the horseback, when there were no motorcars, fosters this meaning through a realistic depiction. On the contrary, the bus represents today. In other words, Evliya Çelebi stands for the history and the bus represents modernity. The bus is depicted in a fast movement, jumping. In its literal terms, motor vehicles are fast means of transportation. In today's world communication and transportation have high speed due to the advancements in technology, which facilitate mobility. The second meaning of the "jump" can be denoted as dynamism. Energy and dynamism were stressed through the motto of the national promotional campaign "Our energy is from Istanbul". Both Evliya Çelebi and the bus are moving from right to left, which is not usual for the eyes as the eye reads from left to right.

• Golden Routes – in the footsteps of Evliya Çelebi

Figure 11. Poster of Golden Routes

Source: Istanbul 2010 Avrupa Kültür Başkenti Girişim Grubu (2011).

When we look at the direction of movement in the films and photographic images the usual way of representation is from left to right if there is not a specific aim or meaning. When we think of the timeline of events the starting point is schematized with the past, older events evolving through present and to the future following a line from left to right. As Evliya Çelebi moves from right to left, it can be interpreted as a journey to the past. Therefore, the bus follows the footsteps of Evliya Çelebi through a historical journey. The cities listed under the bus stand as the stops of this journey. When we further look at the image we see birds in the sky. Although the sky is not painted in blue colour, the eye makes the separation through a horizontal line. There is the silhouette of minarets and pinnacles with a cross and birds are flying over. The birds can be interpreted as migrant birds accompanying this journey. They follow the same direction. The representation of mosques with minarets and the crescent on the top and churches with cross points to a multicultural journey through religious representations. The cities visited represent different religions and cultures.

- "Beyoğlu is Different with Music"

Figure 12. Poster of Beyoğlu is different with music

1. Form

This poster is not scanned but taken a snapshot from the catalogue by the camera. In doing so, the image is distorted due to light and macro settings of the camera, which means it does not reflect the true colours and it is not high quality. Yet this is only representative image and the analysis is done through the image printed on the programme of Istanbul 2010 events.

The title of the project "Beyoğlu is different with music" is written at the headline of the poster in white colour over the red background. It is written in three lines and the initial of Beyoğlu, the "B" letter is transformed into the clef sign therefore the letters are like the notes on the treble clef. "Başkadır" which means "is different" is written bold, thus the emphasis is on difference. The background is fading to white from top to bottom. At the centre there is a yellow circle like a big sun. The tram is the famous and nostalgic Beyoğlu tram traveling on the line between Taksim-Tünel, which is written at the head of the tram (number 2). There are two shadow figures at the back of the tram; one wears a hat and the other at the backside is playing a wind instrument. The notes are flying over the tram. The logos are listed at the bottom of the poster as usual. On the left corner, there is the logo of the Foundation for the Beautification and Protection of Beyoğlu. This stands like a separate logo as the creator of the project. The other logos of the partners and supporters (all are governmental structures composed of Beyoğlu Municipality, Istanbul Metropolitan Municipality and IETT – Istanbul Electricity Tram and Tunnel General Management) and the logo of Istanbul 2010 is listed on the bottom right of the poster.

2. Content

A tram is a means of public transportation, a routine of everyday life in the city. The red tram number 2, traveling from Taksim to Tünel and back is symbolic to Beyoğlu as the most crowded pedestrian street of Istanbul, İstiklal Street cannot be imagined without the tram going up and down. The tram is still functioning today for transport purposes but the meanings attached to the tram is rather nostalgic as it was the main public transport during the 19th century when İstiklal Street was named as Grand Rue de Pera. IETT, which stands for electricity, tram and tunnel, takes its name from the developments occurred around Beyoğlu during the 19th century; first electricity tram and first underground transport system called tunnel between Karaköy and Pera. Therefore, tram is not only important to Istanbulites as a means of public transportation but also symbolically as a means of representation of the urban history and identity of the place. The project suggests another function and meaning to the tram, which is music. The couch at the back of the tram is designed as a stage. The music bands and young professionals or amateurs play on the tram while the tram is moving on its regular track on İstiklal Street. A spectacle is created in the public place, in the streets and on the tram, which has become the part of city life for the city dwellers and users of Beyoğlu. Music has always been an important part of life in Beyoğlu in all times. There is not even a day Beyoğlu is without music. Different types of music are heard from the book and music stores, restaurants and cafes and they mix into each other. Beyoğlu has been the main place for nightlife and live music as well. İstiklal Street has been the main stage for the street performers. Therefore,

Beyoğlu has been always existed with music and the music performed on the tram adds a different colour to İstiklal street as the tram goes by.

- Call4istanbul

Figure 13. Poster of Call4istanbul

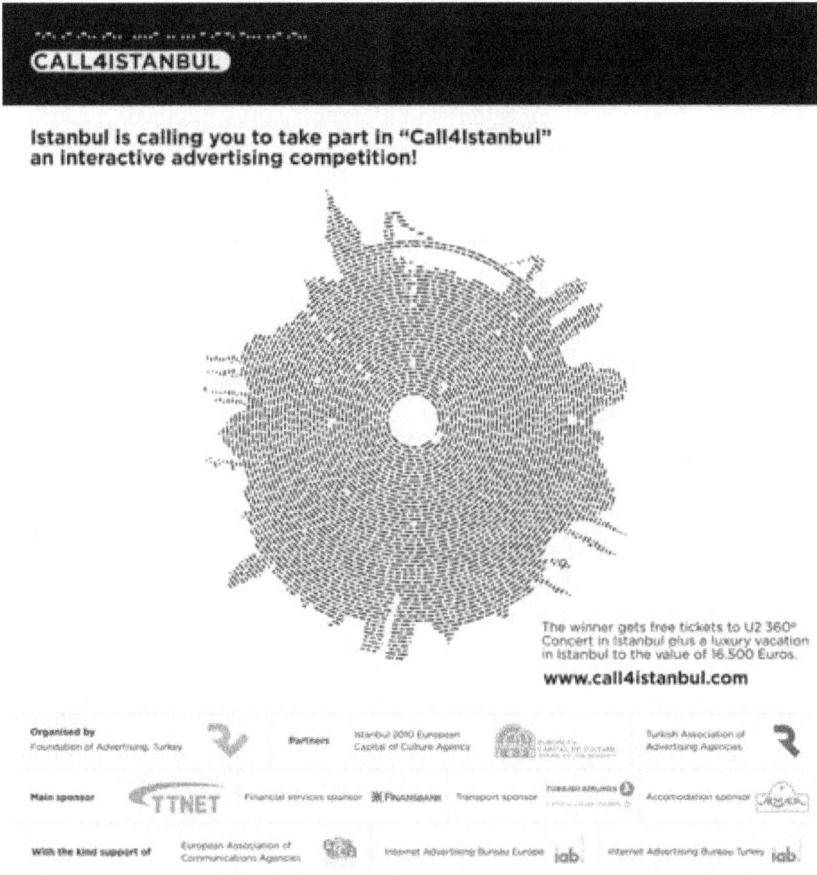

1. Form

Call4Istanbul is an advertising competition targeting young professionals and the call was opened through the internet as well as Facebook and twitter pages. The front page of its website is designed like the poster itself. The organization of the poster reflects the same manner with minor differences such as the absence of the links on the left side. The logos are placed at the bottom of the page. They are classified as organizers, partners, sponsors and supporters. The logo of the event is at the top left corner of the page. It is placed like a headline, white on black. The slogan is positioned below the logo, which is written as "Istanbul is calling you to take part in 'Call4Istanbul' an interactive advertising competition!" In the centre, we see an image on the white page representing the silhouette of Istanbul rounding up the circular image. The words below the image on the right side mention the awards for the winners of the competition, which are free tickets to U2 360° Concert (also included in the programme of Istanbul 2010), vacation worth of 16,500 Euros. The website is given "www.call4istanbul.com" as the applications are made online through the website.

2. Content

Although the importance of the posters has been emphasized by Istanbul 2010 Agency in the published material and also in this thesis, Call4Istanbul can be recognized as a distinctive event that communicates with its target audience and participants online. The main reason is that, it is an interactive advertising competition based on web and digital advertising. It is also communicated through the support of IAB (Internet Advertising Bureau) Europe and Turkey and EACA (The European Association of Communications Agencies) in order to involve European media as the competition is open to participants from and abroad Turkey. The aim of the competition is to prepare a website called "Web City" promoting Istanbul to a group of target audience aged between 18 and 25.

The slogan is inviting and participative, calling the audience to participate to the competition. The slogan emphasizes that the competition is interactive. The title of the project anchors the meaning with the slogan as it is a call for creative people who wish to design a web-based advertising campaign for Istanbul. The title is written as "call4Istanbul". The number "4" replaces the word "for" as their pronunciation is the same. This kind of language is commonly used in communication through mobile and web applications especially among youth. Therefore, the title gives clues about the target audience and about the project based on web advertising. The verbal text communicating the awards for winners is intended to raise interest to the competition and to encourage participation. The information for free tickets for U2 concert, which is another Istanbul 2010 event, accomplishes cross promotion of the two events of Istanbul 2010 in one poster in which the target customers are thought to have same or similar attributes.

The image is like a tree trunk. As known the rings on the tree trunk show the age of the tree. The older the tree is; the more rings it has. Istanbul has a rooted history. The tree trunk figure is also related to culture in the theoretical framework of Simmel (1994). According to this, the cultivation of a pear tree is "latent in its natural structure or energies", but on the other hand a tree trunk made into a ship's mast is the work of culture because "the form of the mast is given by the shipbuilder, which is not inherent in its nature" (Frisby & Featherstone, 2000: 40). The historical monuments, such as Galata Tower, Sultanahmet Mosque, Bosphorus Bridge and some skyscrapers, are depicted together with the modern buildings on the outer part. The image also looks like a fingerprint, in which the representations of the city are coded in the ridges in graphic design.

• Introduction of the Mawlawi Culture and Sema Ceremony

Figure 14. Poster of Sema Ayin-i Şerifi

Source: Istanbul 2010 Avrupa Kültür Başkenti Girişim Grubu (2011).

1. Form

The poster is designed by Özer Duru. The text is in Turkish. At the background there is the figure of a whirling dervish, the image is black and white. Yellow and white colours are used for the text, where the headlines are yellow and the text is white. On the top right corner, we read "Sema Ayin-i Şerifi" which means

Noble Ceremony of Sema, which is written in the biggest size of font, therefore the emphasis is made on Sema ceremony. On the corner above, again right, there is the logo of International Mevlana Foundation that was founded in Istanbul in 1996 for whirling dervishes and mawlawi culture. The text is placed on the right side of the poster and gives information about the type and time of the ceremonies planned as well as the fee for entrance. At the bottom part (right side) the logos of Ministry of Culture and Tourism of Turkey and Istanbul 2010 are placed together. The projects grouped under "tourism & promotion" title carry the logos of both Ministry of Culture and Tourism and Istanbul 2010, which apply to all of the posters. Under the figure of whirling dervish (bottom left corner) the contact address of Mevlevihane of Yenikapı is given where the ceremonies are taking places.

2. Content

The poster is simplistic in its composition and arrangement. There is only one figure, which is powerful and effective in representing "semazen" and the way of ceremony; whirling around. The background is wooden ground. The light falls on the wooden ground from the top like the reflection of the moon on the water. Since we do not see the source of light it is like a divine light that contributes the meaning of a religious ceremony. The image is a bit out of focus reflecting the movement of whirling dervish. The photo is exposed in a longer time deliberately to capture a sequence of movements and continuity rather than capturing a single pose. We are looking at the image from a higher point, which means the photo is taken from the top. The dervish is facing bottom right corner through a diagonal line. The viewer is not face to face with the dervish who seems like he is not paying attention to outer world, he is inert. The practice of whirling has a meditative meaning therefore the act is a journey into oneself and to the God. Sema is a religious ceremony that has deep meanings in the cultural context. Nevertheless, the poster is successful in conveying the messages through a simple and effective design. The connection between the image and text is well established; both are informative about the act that is taking place in the event and the programme of the event(s). Therefore, the anchorage between the image and text is strong. There is not much of connotative meaning; the signifiers and their signifieds are kept at denotative level through giving simple messages.

International Relations

• Human Cities

Figure 15. Poster of Human Cities

Source: Istanbul 2010 Avrupa Kültür Başkenti Girişim Grubu (2011).

1. Form
The poster is a collaborative work of two designers; one from Brussels, Guillaume Bokiau, and the other from Istanbul, Ahmet Sefer. The collaboration is also represented through the flags of European Union and Turkey on the top left corner of the poster. The verbal message "This project is funded by the European Union" secures the symbolic meaning inferred from the EU flag. The title of the project "Human Cities" is positioned at the top left corner, in capital letters and red colour. The title ends with a slash and

after the slash the venues of the event are mentioned, which are Eski Galata Köprüsü (Old Galata Bridge) and Santralistanbul. The verbal text is in Turkish and it spreads over the image in small caps. Thus the letters are overlaid on the image, yet the letters let the eye to see the background through increased transparency, and white colour helps to increase legibility. The verbal text "*kamusal alan tasarlamak*" can be translated as "designing public space", which is written in four lines and the last word "*tasarlamak*" (to design) is hyphenated. Under the text there is the year 2010 in red colour. 2010 denotes ECoC 2010, not only the year of the project. The dates of the project are given as 29/09 and 03/10 on the left side. "Brüksel" (Brussels) and "Istanbul" are mentioned to stress the collaboration and Istanbul Design Week concludes the verbal text, which stands like a full point at the end. The projects web address (www.humancities.eu) is mentioned at the bottom right corner and there is a wheel like figure entering in the frame. This figure seems like a logo but when the webpage is checked, it has been observed that the logo of the project is Human Cities ending with a slash at the left corner. The logos of the supporters are listed at the bottom line, where the logo of Istanbul 2010 is the first one. The background of the poster is an image of the waterfront of Karaköy and Galata Tower is in the focal of the picture. There is a hexagon in the middle of the poster, red and transparent to a certain degree. The hexagon frames the object at the background and draws the attention to Galata Tower, rising on the block of buildings.

2. Content

The image has multi-layers of meaning built on layers of words and image. The image itself at the background is also layered through bottom-up; the sea is the first layer, and then comes the land and then the sky. Therefore, the image is like a collage rather than a mono-block image. The image has low modality due to pink colour. The sea is pink, the sky is pink and it feels like we are in a dream, fantasy world. The act of "designing", which is the main idea of the project, mingles into dreaming and imagination. The gaze of the viewer is affected in two ways. First, it feels as if we are looking at a real landscape through a filter behind the camera turning the image into an illusion. Second, the hexagon is like a viewfinder of the camera. It frames the object and directs the gaze of the viewer to the focal point, to Galata Tower. Another comment can be that, the hexagon not only frames the image but also it might represent the boundaries that frame the public space. The public space is at the focal point of the project as the key concept is "designing public space". The latter interpretation secures the meaning through the anchorage of image and text.

- Istanbul Express - Exploring Multilingualism across Europe

Figure 16. Poster of Istanbul Express

Source: Istanbul 2010 Avrupa Kültür Başkenti Girişim Grubu (2011).

1. Form

The poster is designed by Maartje Alders. The Turkish and European Union flags stand on the top left corner of the poster as "this project is co-founded by the European Union and the Republic of Turkey" written under the flags. The flags and the text are used by all of the posters grouped under "international relations" title, so this is a compulsory element for this group. On the bottom left corner the logos of other supporters are listed, where Istanbul 2010 logo takes the second order this time. The logo at the end belongs to NISI MASA (European Network of Young Cinema) of which web address can be found in capital letters at the bottom right corner. The image is depicted on a white background. Since the project is about the film we see a film ribbon stretching from left to right as it enlarges to the corners through the right and projects a perspective. Inside the film ribbon, the Bosphorus Bridge is depicted extending from left side to the upper right corner of the poster, overreaching the film ribbon. A star is shining under the bridge. As the film ribbon stretched the dark blue tone gets lighter and turns into green. The film ribbon has only two frames the first one is smaller as it is cut. In the first frame we see the bridge pier. The second frame is larger and we see the full frame like a window. The date and title of the project;

"20/09 to 16/10 2010": first line

"Istanbul Express": second and third line

"Exploring Multilingualism Across Europe": fourth line

The verbal text is in English and emphasis on "Istanbul Express" in bold and capital letters also bigger size.

There are four kids depicted, sitting in a cinema hall, looking at the screen. The three boys in the front row are exposed with the full body although we can only see the half of the face of the girl sitting at the back row.

2. Content

The most powerful reference for Istanbul is the Bosphorus Bridge, which can be interpreted as a cultural dialogue bridging between European Union and Turkey through cinema. That is why the bridge overlaps with the film ribbon and stretches together. The same thing can be said for the film ribbon through the other way around. The film ribbon is stretching like a bridge as the cinema connects two different cultures to each other. The film ribbon is like a window frame, which can be interpreted as window onto the world. As cinema is a spectacle itself, the enlarged frame of film ribbon also stands like the screen, which the children are looking at.

When we look at the children, we see that they have different expressions on their faces. One seems surprised, the other is bored, and another child seems interested. Only half of the face of the girl sitting at the back row is displayed, so it is not really possible to comment her expression but she looks at the screen like the other children as we can follow her gaze through her eyes. The clothing style of the children tells us that they are school children, but it is a bit old-fashioned. A nostalgic atmosphere is created through the old clothing style. It is also a black & white image, which reinforces the feeling of nostalgia.

The change of colour from blue to green, show that there is a flow, as the film is playing on the screen, or the spectators are experiencing an inner journey through the imaginary created by the cinema. As the key concept of the project is "multilingualism" the contextual interpretation is the journey across Europe through different cultures connected to each other. Crossing the bridge signifies "exploring multilingualism across Europe". There is a shining star under the bridge, but the meaning is not clear. It can be understood as the guide star showing north direction, but it stands alone and interferes neither with the image nor with the text.

   b) Urban Transformation

Urban projects

•   Palimpsest Istanbul

1. Form
The poster has a white background. On the upper part, the name of the project "Palimpsest İstanbul" is printed in the biggest font size. The name of the artist "Laleper Aytek" is written below in a smaller font. All the words are printed in black letters. The logos are placed at the bottom of the poster. On the bottom right corner, there is the Istanbul 2010 Logo, also in black colour. The logo of Institut Français d'Istanbul is in the middle next to Istanbul 2010 logo and on the bottom left corner there is the contact information of Institut Français d'Istanbul. The photographic image is placed in the centre of the poster. There is no reference to the image in verbal text. The text is just informative about the event.

In the image we see a female mannequin in the foreground. It stands as a sculpture, the shoulders and the nose is damaged. The head is cut therefore the half of the face, the right eye and ear is missing starting from the forehead. It wears a red vest. The background is out of focus but still we can read "T.C. İSTANBUL BÜYÜKŞEHİR BELEDİYE BAŞKANLIĞI" (Istanbul Metropolitan Municipality) "İSTANBUL METROSU" (İstanbul Underground) and "YENİKAPI İSTASYONU" (Yenikapı Station) on the board behind.

Figure 17. Poster of
Palimpsest Istanbul

Palimpsest İstanbul
LALEPER AYTEK

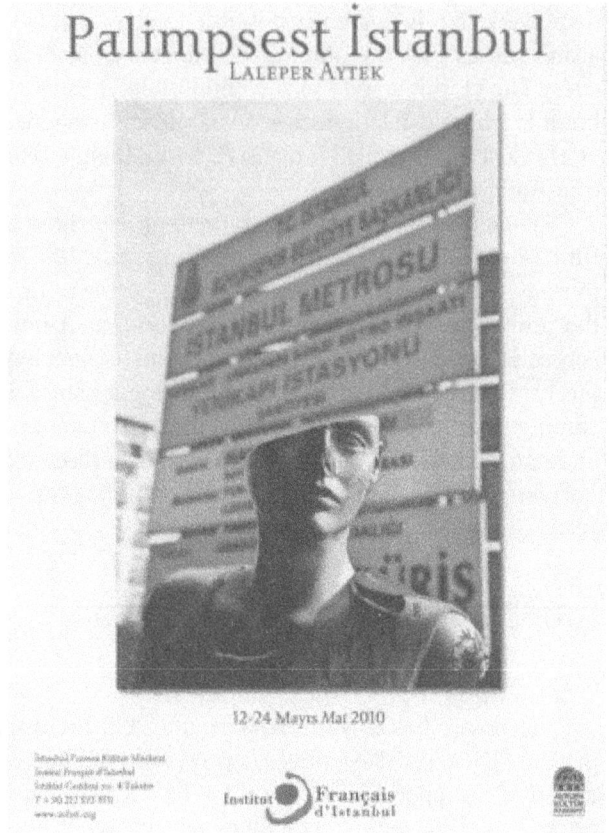

*Source: Istanbul 2010
Avrupa   Kültür
Başkenti   Girişim
Grubu (2011).*

12-24 Mayıs Mai 2010

2.   Content

The image is a depiction of the urban area but the way of representation is not conventional, actually rather unusual. We cannot know if the mannequin was there when the photo was taken or if it is placed there by the artist, therefore the modality of the image is low because it is like a fiction. On the other hand, the image has a high modality if we concentrate on the background, which is usual for everyday life depicting the construction area in the urban space.

The image is taken at the archaeological site of Port of Theodosius in Yenikapı, where the excavation works are undertaken for the underground system construction. Since the archaeological excavation gives us clues about the history of the area we can establish connections between the signifier and signified in a wider context. The image has multi-layers of meaning like the archaeological layers in the excavation area. The excavation uncovers the layers of history and the visual analysis uncovers the layers of meaning. The title of the exhibition, "Palimpsest Istanbul", is also full of references to the layers of the city. Palimpsest means "something having usually diverse layers or aspects apparent beneath the surface" (Merriam-Webster's online dictionary, n.d.) in the urban context. The literal definition of the palimpsest according to OED (Oxford English Dictionary, 2008a) is "a parchment or other surface in which later writing has been superimposed on effaced earlier writing." The modern is constructed on the ancient layers. Therefore, the "new" is superimposed on what has been there earlier.

The site where the image is taken, Port of Theodosius, belongs to Early Byzantine Era. The mannequin figure in the front can be compared to the roman sculptures as if it is one of the unearthed objects during the excavations. Although the mannequin is female, the red vest is similar to the vest that the Roman warriors used to wear. Therefore, the mannequin can be interpreted an iconic representation of the past. The mannequin is represented like a portrait sculpture. Her head is slightly turned to sideward (right to the viewer). Although the viewer is not in direct eye contact with object, the gaze is kept at the eye level. The expression on her face is frosty. The focus is on the mannequin, while the background is blurred and it does not contact with the figure in the front.

When the mannequin figure is interpreted at the denotative level, it refers to the modernity. It represents shopping, fashion and exhibition as the signifieds denoted in the post-modern consumption culture. The mannequin belongs to the window of a shop, where consumption takes place. It is the communication tool to show, to exhibit the goods. The viewer is encouraged to "buy" or "consume". Therefore, the mannequin connotes consumption culture and therefore linked to "spectacle" as a secondary meaning. The images are directed at consumption in the society of spectacle. The modern is a floating signifier; it does not communicate with the past. The lack of communication between the past and present is reflected on the lack of communication between the archaeological site and its surroundings. The face of the mannequin is half in the light and half in the shade.

The image pays an effort to connect the past of the area with the political interventions made today by the government. The image shows how the binary oppositions such as past and present as well as the ideologies on public and public space communicate, in other words "cannot communicate", with each other. The signs of "Istanbul Metropolitan Municipality" and "Istanbul Underground" position government as the subject of power for the urban order. This is the interpretation at the connotative level that is closely related with the context.

• Ghost Buildings

Figure 18. Poster of Ghost Buildings

Source: Image courtesy of Cem Kozar (Pattu Architecture. 2010).

1. Form

The poster is bilingual, in Turkish and English. On the top left corner of the poster there is the logo and the title of the project "Ghost Buildings" and also the web site address "www.hayal-et.org". The logo of Istanbul 2010 is on the top right corner, which is accompanied by "Energy of Istanbul 2010" logo, as the supporter of the project. Below, there is the logo of PATTU Architecture Research Design Company as the creator of the project. The other logos are listed at the bottom of the poster. In the image, in the centre, we see a pile of monumental buildings on top of each other. They look like they are dumped like trash. They are separated from each other by red dots, through which one thinks they are out of paper to be cut, in order to separate them. The stand together but they are separate. We understand that they are old representations of the old buildings from the depiction of human figures dressed in old style, most like Ottoman. The text above, in red colour, poses the question; "These buildings once stood in Istanbul, what if they still existed?" The verbal text is strongly anchored to the image and gives a description about the buildings. From the verbal expression, we confer that these buildings are not standing today; they are the historical representations of the old buildings. The question in the second part of the sentence is proposing a scenario directed at the present time. The question is participative and it invites the audience to re-think the past and present and to imagine possible urban scenarios.

2. Content

"Ghost Buildings", which refers to *"Hayal-Et Yapılar"* Turkish. *"Hayalet"* means "ghost" if it is translated on denotative level. But it has also a secondary meaning if we take it in the form of imperative *"Hayal et"*, which stands for "Imagine". Hence the project is about creating urban imaginaries for the historical buildings they could not have survived today. On the connotative level the title provokes the urban imaginaries for destructions as well as the fictitious urban scenarios for reconstructions. The term urban imaginary refers to "the interpretive grids through which we think about, experience, evaluate and decide to act in the places, spaces and communities in which we live" (Soja, 2000: 324).

The monumental structures represented in the image are depicted with public figures. Then we understand that these buildings were public places and had important functions in the city as a church or religious buildings in general terms, military barracks, palaces and so on. It is possible to infer functions of the buildings from the signs such as cross or structural elements such as dome, towers or from their architectural styles. The public and the details how they are dresses also give clues, for instance some of them are depicted in military uniforms which points out a military buildings or they are depicted in the army organization for formal ceremony in front of the palace. Some figures as dressed in Western style with hats instead of tarbush, which represents the late Ottoman or Republican period therefore a later period. It can be also conferred that the buildings belong to different eras. They are depicted as if in the process of demolishing, falling on top of each other, making a huge pile of stones. On the other hand, they look like paper dolls to be cut of the paper and to be dressed-up. Dressing-up the building would signify the reconstruction. This is the fiction part in which the urban scenarios are produced for today by looking at the past and the urban narratives.

The project can be perceived as a documentation of the history as it provides an archival presentation of the demolished buildings, which are invisible today. The new layers and new buildings, new structures are added on the earlier layers. The city is constantly reconstructed; it is like a living organism. That is why deconstruction is not always associated with negative connotations. It is a condition for the existence of the city recreating itself. However, sometimes, the deconstruction took place can be an unrecoverable mistake. One of the examples included in the project and also one of the hot debates today is Taksim Artillery Barracks, which were demolished for the organization of the area as a park according to Proust plan in the 1950s. In the minds of the young generation, there has been always a park. Today the government presented an urban project to re-organize the whole area and to re-construct the barracks through a project of regenerating the past. This brings the "Rediscover" campaign of Istanbul 2010 Agency into minds, in which the signifiers were the monumental buildings but still standing today, and the signifier was rediscovering the past. Although it looks like these two have something in common their aims and methods are different from each other. "Ghost Buildings" project suggests a critical look to the political power shaping urban environments. Reconstructing the deconstructed monuments that break off from the urban context and meanings is solely the representation of the past, yet unable to communicate with today. That is why although the project takes the deconstruction essential for the existence of the city, erasing the past from the memory of the city is equal to killing the city. Thus the binary oppositions are revealed through the process of deconstruction and reconstruction. Therefore, one of the main distinctions of "Ghost Buildings" from "Rediscover" is the idea of bringing the deconstruction forward. The main objective of "Rediscover" campaign is raising the awareness by inviting the audience to re-look and re-think of the history. "Ghost Buildings" project aims reconstructing an urban memory through a critical approach to the ideology and power behind the deconstructions, in its critique for the narrow minded urban practices taking old buildings as urban trash, and simulating the history as restoration.

• Armenian Architects of Istanbul in the Era of Westernization

Figure 19. Poster of Armenian Architects

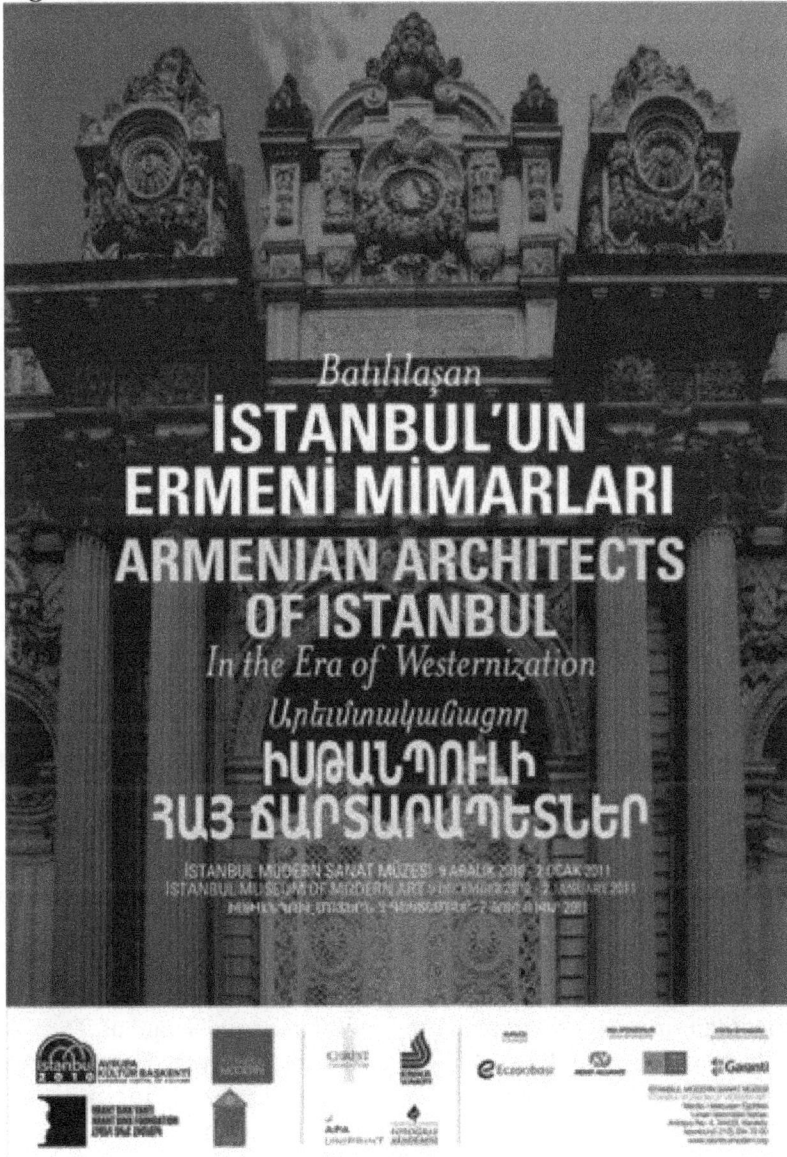

Source: Babalık (2010).

1. Form

The poster is designed by Erkal Yavi. The image shows Dolmabahçe Palace built by Balyan architects of Armenian origin. The picture is cut into two parts through colour separation. The upper side of the image is blue like sky and lower side is brown like earth. It is cut just above the arc of the gate, separating the columns from their heads. The architectural elements show a great variation in style, pointing out the eclectic style of the palace. Greek columns give reference to neoclassical style whereas the pediment reflects a synthesis of baroque and rococo. The royal monogram on the pediment shows that this is the "Gate of Sultan".

The verbal text is written in three languages. On the upper side (blue section) the title of the exhibition, "Armenian Architects of Istanbul in the Era of Westernization" is written in Turkish, and it is repeated in English and in Armenian consecutively (in brown section). The date and place of the exhibition is also given in these three languages in smaller fonts below the titles. The logos of the sponsors are listed at the bottom of the poster on white background separated from the image. The logo of Istanbul 2010 is the first logo on the left followed by the logo of Istanbul Modern where the exhibition took place.

2. Content

The poster invites the viewers to meet the Armenian architects of Istanbul who have put their signatures to the renowned buildings and palaces of Istanbul. In the picture we see the "Gate of Sultan" of Dolmabahçe Palace. The gate figure invites viewers inside. Although the doors are closed, gate represents entering and exiting, into and from, in and out. Passing the threshold means passing to another level, another world. The viewers enter the world of Armenian Architects through this gate. The architects of Dolmabahçe Palace are Garabet Balyan and his son Nigoğos Balyan who are the members of Balyan Family, Ottoman Imperial architects of Armenian origin.

The "Gate of Sultan" has imperial connotations, meanings of power, authority and hierarchy. Eclectic architecture of the Palace reflects on the cosmopolitan structure of Ottoman Empire and its capital Istanbul. The verbal text, which is written in three different languages, is a sign. The text stresses "Westernization". Word and image is highly linked to each other. Dolmabahçe Palace was built in the late Ottoman Period, when the Westernization effects were started to be felt both is the political arena through the reforms called "Tanzimat" as well as in the area of art and architecture through the increasing influence of Western and European styles. Dolmabahçe Palace is a synthesis of Western styles such as Baroque, Rococo and Neoclassical blended with elements of Ottoman and Imperial architecture and arabesque. Therefore, it is a good example reflecting the cosmopolitan structure of Istanbul in the Ottoman era and projects the effects of the synthesis on architecture, which is one of the most important elements in visualizing the city.

The exhibition place, Museum of Modern and Contemporary Arts of Istanbul gives clues about the transformation of Istanbul and it gives the chance to the audience to follow the traces of Ottoman past in Westernization period in a modern and industrial building. Neither is controversial, nor opposing to one another but they exist together through a synthesis in harmony.

Cultural heritage & museums

• Istanbul 1910-2010 - City, Built Environment & Architectural Culture Exhibition

1. Form

The exhibition is organized and designed by Bilgi University, Department of Visual Communication that also the designed the poster of the exhibition. The poster is divided into two parts, where the image of Istanbul is on the top and the verbal text on the lower part on a black ground. The words are printed white and yellow on black for the ease of reading. It is printed in two languages, Turkish and English. The eye first reads "Istanbul 1910-2010" from left to right in big fonts. "Istanbul" is yellow, and "1910-2010" is white, which highlights Istanbul in the text. It is continued below in very small fonts even hard to read: "City, Built Environment and Architectural Culture Exhibition". The information about the exhibition; dates, place and curators are given on the right. Logos are listed at the bottom of the poster as usual. The logos of Istanbul Bilgi University and SantralIstanbul are on the left corner on the bottom as the organizers of the exhibition. The logo of Istanbul 2010 stands alone and it concludes the text at the bottom left corner as the main logo of the event. The photograph is by Cemal Emden, which is noted on the bottom right corner of the image, but it is so small that almost invisible as well.

2. Content

As it can be understood from the title, the exhibition covers a century from 1910 to 2010. It is a documentary project for exhibiting the change of Istanbul through the transformation of the built environment and the architecture in different periods. In the image, 2010's Istanbul is depicted with high-rise buildings, crowds of buildings and traffic, as a city under the cranes. Actually

Istanbul is not recognizable through this image as the image can be anywhere in the world. It is a representation of an industrial place, a post-modern city

Figure 20. Poster of Istanbul 1919-2010

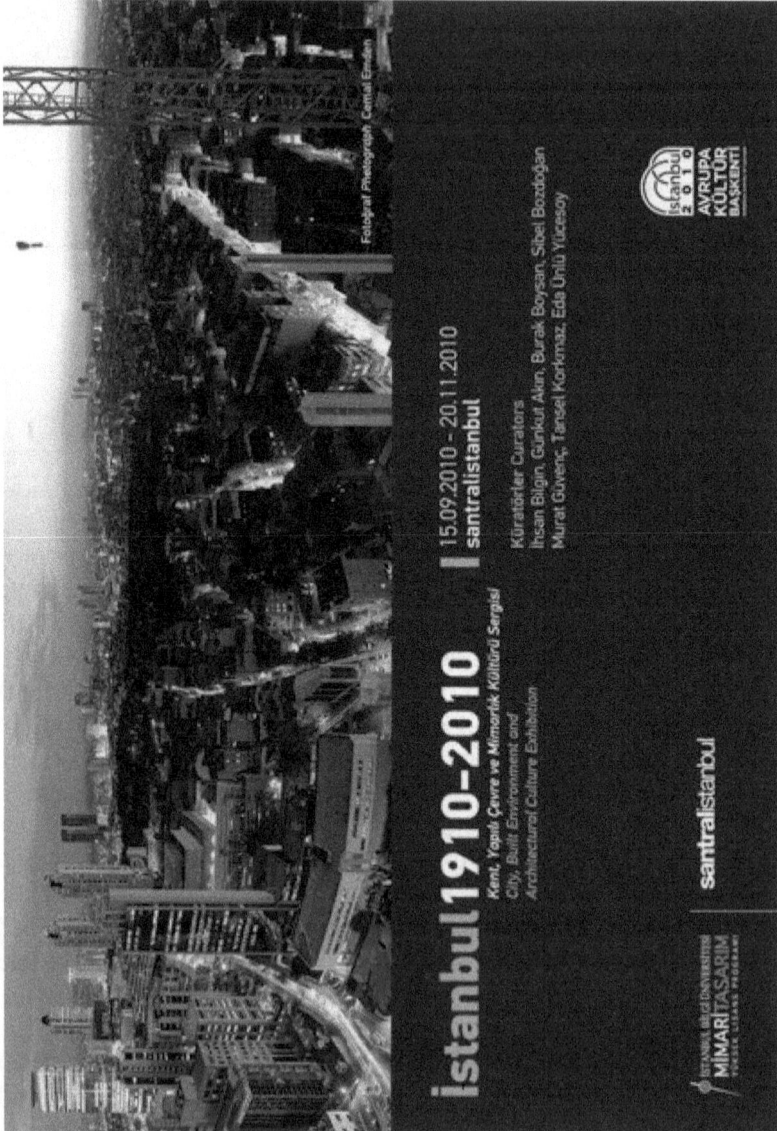

Source: Istanbul 2010 Avrupa Kültür Başkenti Girişim Grubu (2011).

under the attack of globalization through homogenizing cities. It can be Shanghai, London, New York, or Chicago... There is no direct reference to the qualities of Istanbul that are symbolic to the city. The only connection that the viewer may confer that this is the image of Istanbul is through the anchorage between the word and image. The text below says "Istanbul", so the viewer believes it is Istanbul.

Although the vast majority of the representations in the posters focus on cliché images of Istanbul like Galata Tower and the silhouette through historical connotations, this image represents Istanbul as a modern city. It is dynamic; the energy is flowing on the streets, which is depicted with the cars and their lights on the move. The city is overcrowded and the land is not enough, as the buildings are rising on top of each other. The image is chaotic. The eye cannot focus on one point on the image but keeps gazing through it. The image clearly portrays the urban sprawl and disorder of the city. The crane on the right side signifies the never-ending construction in the city. The city has been a construction site for mega-projects of star-architects. The skyscrapers on the left are mushrooming and the height of the crane is a sign of one more high-rise building to be added on.

The image presents a panoramic view to the city from a high angle, which could be the rooftop of one of the skyscrapers, even the tallest one which is being constructed as the crane is very close where the shot is taken. The height connotes power and authority. The gaze is like a CEO's gaze to the city from his office on the top of the tall plaza. The time of the day is sunset, the rush-hour. Although it is time of sunset, it is not a romantic image. It feels like an industrial place and business district. The horizon seems like extending to infinity. The city seems endless.

Urban culture

• Istanbul Woman – Woman Istanbul

1. Form

The poster is designed by Sibel Erbayat. The poster has a black background. The title of the project is centred in the top with white letters. There is an open book in the centre of the image. The letters are flying from the book and they form shapes, shape of a woman with the hat, the silhouette of Istanbul with minarets and Bosphorus Bridge. We cannot really know if the words are flying over or if they are falling onto the book. The latter seems more logical because we read the words from left to right and we continue reading the sentence falling on the page. The sentence ends with a triple dot. Although not all the words can be read, the eye picks "Istanbul" and "*kadın*" (woman) easily as their size is bigger. We read "Istanbul" falling on the page of the book, under the pier of the bridge, on the hat of the woman; we can read "*kadın*" on the pier of the bridge and under the shoe of the woman.

111

Doğan

The logos are on the corners of the poster at the bottom; "Kadın Eserleri Kütüphanesi ve Bilgi Merkezi Vakfı" (Women Works Library and Information Centre Foundation) logo on the left, the address of the organization in the middle and the logo of Istanbul 2010 on the right.

Figure 21. Poster of Istanbul Woman – Woman Istanbul

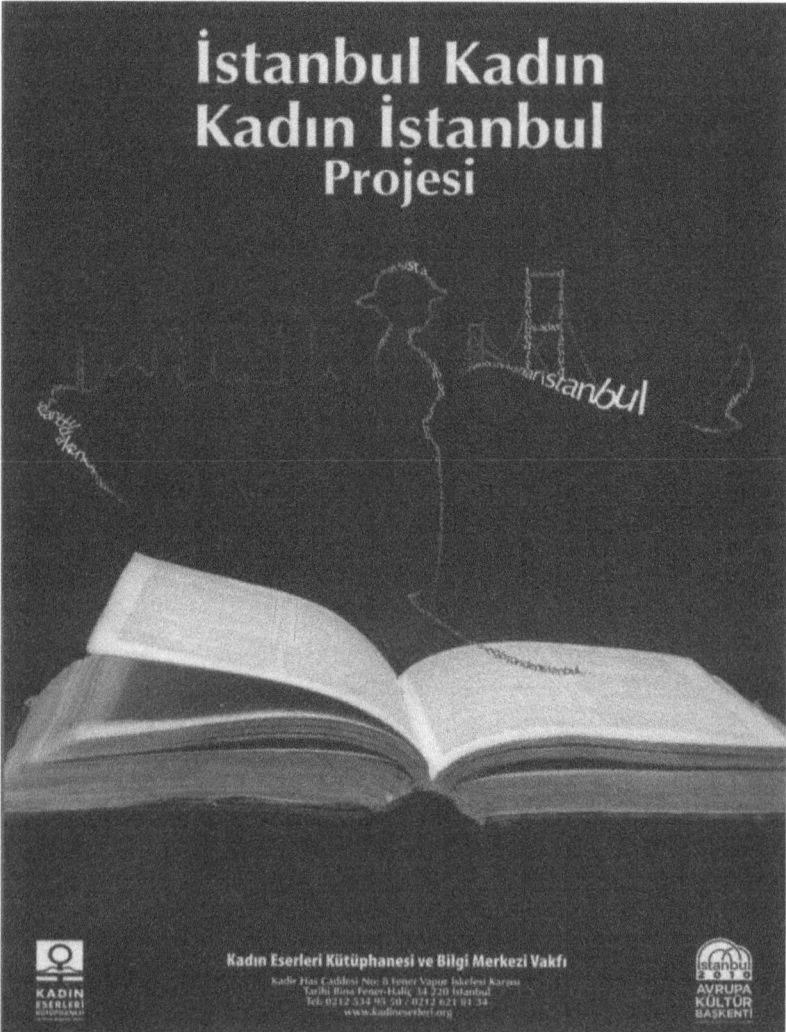

Source: Istanbul 2010 Avrupa Kültür Başkenti Girişim Grubu (2011).

2. **Content**

The project is created by the library on women works and a book has been published as an outcome of the project. That is why we see a book in the centre. Otherwise, it could have been interpreted as a literature project, which is also not so wrong to say because the project was about organizing talks with the theme of woman and women in history. The speakers invited to the talks are among the woman writers; therefore, the book connotes literature, together with its meaning in denotative level as the printed material. As the focus of the project is "Istanbul" and "Woman", repeated in the title of the project, the representation through letters flying over the book signify Istanbul through its symbols and a woman also through a symbolic sign. The woman is depicted with a hat, although hat is a masculine representation. If we think of the public toilettes in the restaurants and hotels the gents is represented with a hat and the ladies is represented with a shoe. The shoe figure with hills is on the right of the image pointed upwards. It is not connected to the image. It is discontinuous and stands as a dependent figure. As a secondary meaning to hat, it can be interpreted as a symbol of modernism and urban women. Hat is imported from the West. The immigrants from Anatolia cover their heads, therefore hat connotes the western woman living in the city. Yet the woman figure in the picture stands like a ghost figure. It is floating in the air like spirit. The Istanbul silhouette is like the smoke of cigarette. In doing so Istanbul is mystified and the woman is depicted in an enigmatic character.

c) Culture and Art

Visual arts

• Di-ver-city

1. Form
It is a black white image with a male figure posing to the camera in the centre. We see the full posture from toe to head as he is standing. His hands are open to the sides, the right palm facing the ground and the left palm is towards the audience. His body is half turned to the left of the viewer. His left food is one step further than the right one in the front, pointed towards audience. But the upper part of his body is leaning backward. He gives a full posture opening to the audience.

The photo is taken at Studio Osep Beyoğlu as the poster is stamped by the cachet of the photography studio, which is seen commonly on the photographs of that period (1970s). The credentials for the image are mentioned in the Poster Catalogue as follows: "Designer: Krzysztof Bielecki, Photograph: Tayfun Serttaş, Studyo Osep". The photograph taken by Studio Osep is included in the documentary project created by Tayfun Serttaş that is why the credentials are given to both of them. We see the logo of Centrum Sztuki Wspolczesnej Zamek Ujazdowski (Centre for Contemporary Art Ujazdowski

Castle) in Warsaw on the top left corner. Divercity Project was realized in the frame of the Warsaw City preparations to the title of European Capital of Culture 2016, therefore CSW is the co-partner of project from Warsaw.

Figure 22. Poster of di-ver-city (*Source: Serttaş, 2010*)

On the right corner there is the date for exhibition. The text is dispersed throughout the poster at right and left sides, giving information about the curators, exhibition design companies, opening hours of the exhibition. The title of the exhibition "di-ver-city" is written in big fonts, but small caps, in light pink colour. The title is centred in the poster overlaid on the male figure. Below the knees of the male figure the text continues with different font type and characters of letters. "Learning from Istanbul" which is the sub-title is also in pink but in capital letters. The names of the artists are listed below. The names of the artists and "Learning from Istanbul" are separated from each other through the line which the floor and the background is separated from each other like the horizon line. At the bottom line of the posters the logos of the organizers, partners and sponsors are listed as usual.

We learn about the story of production from the Activity Report of Istanbul 2010, the second book of the series about the symposia, panels, promotions and exhibitions entitled *"Anla! Anlat!"* (Understand! Tell!). It is noted that "Divercity" addresses İstanbul recreating itself as the city of desires, imaginaries, narratives and fiction (Istanbul 2010 ECoC Agency,

2010a: 76-77). The project draws attention to the polyphony and fragmentation in the city through the personal observations of the artists. The city image is shaped by the imaginaries of artists conjuring the city.

2. Content

There is no direct visual reference to Istanbul in the image although the text mentions "Learning from Istanbul". Therefore, we know that the project is about Istanbul but there is no visual clue of it in the sense that we are used to see that reminds and represents Istanbul at the denotative level. That is why the analyst should look beyond, what is behind the scene rather than what is shown, to be able to interpret the codes in the image visually. In other words, we should be looking at what is "not" in the image rather than what is in the image in order to be able to read between the lines.

The male figure in the centre, establishes a good level of communication with the audience through body language. His gestures are raising interest and attract the audience. His face and his gaze are directed towards the audience, establishing an eye contact. The eye contact can be said to have hypnotizing effect; it is such a direct gaze. He seems like a public figure in show business; an artist or rather an illusionist. We confer that he is an illusionist because of the positions of her hands, the gesture. The way of clothing also resembles to the clothing style of illusionists, formal suit but no jacket, vest instead. No tie but neck cloth instead. He also resembles to the figure of joker on a playing card, not in clothing style but due to the style of written words in front of him. "di-ver-çity" is hyphened into three lines and it is divided into two parts diagonally like the joker figure is divided diagonally from his belly and below the figure is upside down again showing the same image of joker like a reflection on the water. In this image the male figure is posing in full and complete posture, the figure is not cut but just the words are cut. He raises curiosity and expectation among the audience, as the role of the illusionist is to surprise and amaze the audience.

The sign of illusion or show connotes the spectacle, that the urban space has become the theatre decor and the scene of spectacle where the inhabitants have become the spectators. The light pink colour of the word "divercity" is picked for the fantasies, dreams and desires in the world of illusion. If we carry the analysis one step further to become closer to the ideologies and social and political context in the urban realm, we can say that the figure represents a politician figure full of tricks and illusions. The desired reaction, however, is a loud applause for the mega-projects realized by starchitects and brand names such as Zaha Hadid, Frank Gehry, Norman Foster, Renzo Piano and so forth. The poster raises the question of spectacle and urban change taking place in a top-down fashion in Istanbul.

When we focus on the technical and physical features as well as the compositional elements on the surface we see that the black & white image is a true representation. It is an old photograph taken in "Studio Osep" in Beyoğlu, which is one of the oldest photography studio of Istanbul. Although the figure is posing to the photographer, which may be interpreted in fictive way decreasing the truthfulness of the image, the image has a high modality. We can comment on the image as a true representation, a document of the past. The black white images have documentary and archival value as they refer to the times when the colour photo was not invented.

"Di-ver-city" was a project realized through the framework of preparations for Warsaw ECoC 2016 bridging over two ECoCs Istanbul 2010 and Warsaw 2016. That is why the image is full of references to the visual culture in Warsaw in the 1970s. Since the project brings artists and curators from Istanbul and Warsaw, the context of the both cities and countries are important. The question why this image is chosen for representing all the works in Divercity project can be explained by the shred images, and meanings inherent in both of the urban visual cultures. The context in Warsaw should be understood through the period of transformation from Soviet Regime to modernism. The connotations for modernism draw similarities between the transformation processes that most of the countries (especially Eastern European) passed through in that era. If we take the context into consideration and note that the project is between Istanbul and Warsaw, we may conclude that the poster communicates with the international and local audience at a very good level in transferring the codes and in representing the project through this image.

- Bump into each other – Asia/Europe

1. Form

The poster uses the map of Istanbul laid as the background image. The blue represents the sea (Bosphorus and Golden Horn) and white represents the continents of Asia and Europe. The title of the project is written in quotation marks "Bump into each other – Asia / Europe", in bold black letters. The quotation marks are facing different directions. Above the title we read "Assocreation", which gives reference to the designer of the project. The dates are given below the title line. The text is giving very detailed information about the content of the exhibition. The text is in two languages, Turkish and English, divided into two columns, which is positioned on the European continent at the upper part of the poster. Two points are marked on the map, one on the Asian side, Üsküdar IDO (Üsküdar port for seabusses) and EminönüIDO (Eminönüport for seabusses). The text in red is in Turkish

"Bulunduğunuz yer burası..." indicating Eminönü and "... ve burası!" indicating Üsküdar and the text in yellow is in English "You are standing here...", "... and here" consolidate the meaning of the sign. The yellow dot is surrounded by the red circle, the same colours with the text anchoring the elements to each other. The texts are communicating to each other as the second sentence is continued from the first and they are crossing over. The English and Turkish words have changed the places, while the text in English says "You are standing here..." the Turkish text for the same point of reference can be translated as "... and here". So it may be concluded that the sentence in one language continues in another language and they complement each other.

The logos of the sponsors and partners are listed at the bottom of the poster. They are depicted in white colour on the blue of the sea. On the bottom right corner, we see two logos in blue placed on white background on the Asian side. The logos are in blue colour, which is distinguishing them from the rest of the logos. Actually it is only one logo, that is the Istanbul 2010's logo and next to it, there is the logo of national campaign "The Energy of Istanbul 2010" highlighting Istanbul 2010 ECoC Agency as the supporter of the project.

2. Content

The signs of text and image are anchored to each other like the bridges connecting the two continents. Asia and Europe are linked with strong ties. The project aims to foster the sense of connectedness through sensors placed on the sidewalks in the public place. The impulses are transferred digitally to the other city therefore enabling the agents to communicate to each other in different places. The city is like a living organism stimulated by the steps of people and gives a response. The map of Istanbul on the poster is one of those city maps that you can find on the informative boards at certain places throughout the city. However, the map does not give any information about the city. Basically, it is blank. On a blank map, one cannot figure out the meaning of bumping into each other, as there is no reference to the population density, traffic and crowds. The map shows only two points, hear and here, Üsküdar and Eminönü. It can be said that there is a unity in time and space. While you are here, you are also there and vice versa. The expression "Bump into each other" connotes coincidences and encounters. The project communicates the encounters taking place in different cities as if it happens at the same place.

Figure 23. Poster of Bump into each other

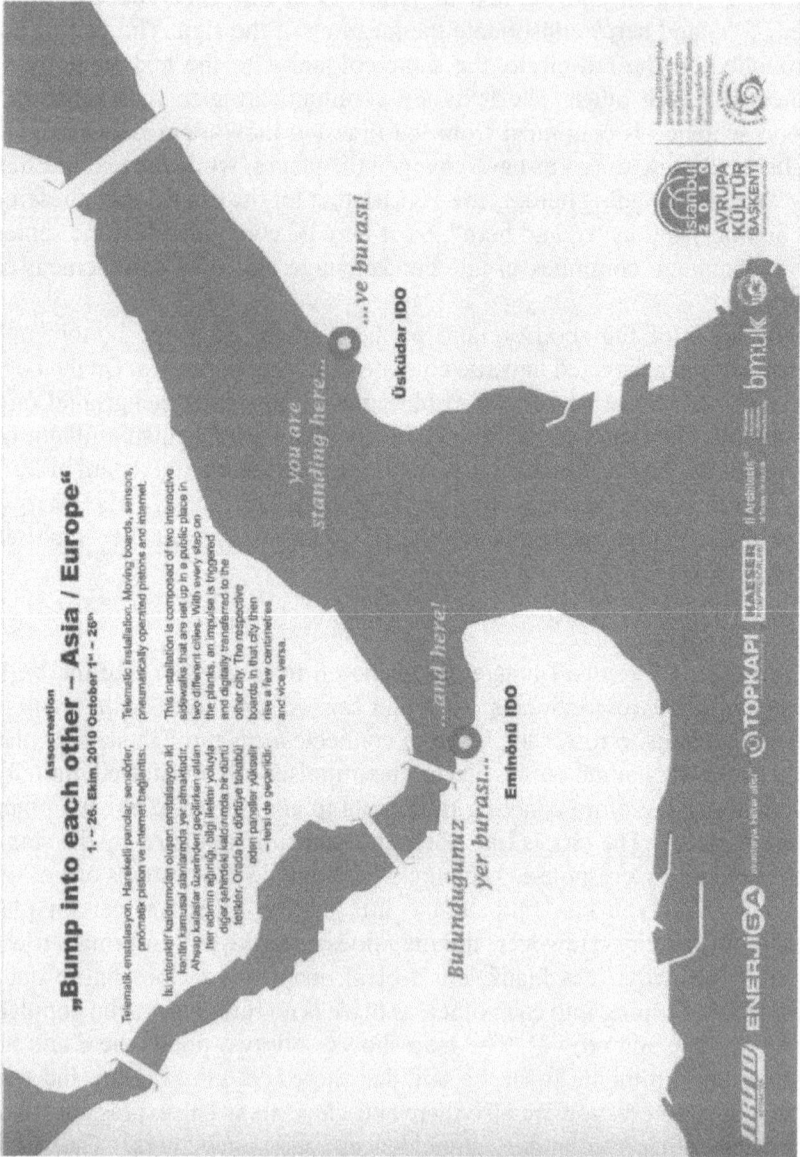

Source: Istanbul 2010 Avrupa Kültür Başkenti Girişim Grubu (2011).

Music and opera

- Türküyem

Figure 24. Poster of Türküyem

Source: Istanbul 2010 Avrupa Kültür Başkenti Girişim Grubu (2011).

1. Form

The designer of the poster is Fikribir. The colour of the background is red changing tone and fading from the top to the bottom. Istanbul 2010 logo is placed on the top right corner this time. On the top left there is the logo of the State Opera and Ballet of Antalya and there are only two logos. This indicates the project do not have international partners or any other supporters.

There is no much of verbal text. The focus is on the title of the project "Türküyem". T and R letters are in capital letters. T is the initial letter; hence it is not surprising but R is also represented in a circle. This is a universal symbol of the logo for "Registered Trademark". Under the title it gives information about the performance, explaining that it is a play with music and dance, "Müzikli Danslı Oyun". Casting is displayed below, but it is so small that almost unreadable. The date and place of the show is mentioned at the bottom right corner.

The gaze of the viewer is centred on the dancers saluting the audience. The word "Türküyem" is like a stage and the dancers are standing on this stage. There are curving leaves overshooting from Türküyem and we see the same pattern, though faded, at the background behind dancers. The posters stand a like theatre décor.

2. Content

The poster give reference to Turkey, the references are not specific to Istanbul. The main references are made to folkloric dance, the multiculturalism across Turkey. Although the clothing style is the show dress, the male clothes can be associated with the traditional dress type in Black Sea region.

The title "Türküyem" is a play on words; "türkü" meaning folk song and "Türkiyem" meaning my country referring to Turkey. "Türküyem" is written with white letters on a red background. Turkish flag is red and the crescent and the star is white. Therefore, the use of red and white colours in the poster gives reference to Turkish flag in a link with the word "Türküyem" in its allusion for "Türkiyem" denoting one's possession of his/her country and connotes patriotic feelings.

The dancers (actors and actresses) are saluting the audience on the stage. The stage is a metaphor for spectacle. Istanbul took the stage in 2010 to showcase its rich history and culture. Culture acted as an engine for branding the city. Istanbul is a microcosm of Turkey and its diversity. Yet the poster is simplistic in the messages given. Basically, it is a poster to promote the show itself rather than branding the city. What makes this poster recognizable as an Istanbul 2010 event is the logo of Istanbul 2010 on the corner. Otherwise it is not different from any other poster designed for the seasonal plays of the State Opera and Ballet.

- Tales of Future - 1 city 1011 Vibrations

1. Form

"1 city 1001 vibrations" is a sound installation project by Sinan Bökesoy, realized through "Tales of Future" project in Istanbul 2010 programme. The poster designed by Ichiro Kojima. The image is placed on a background fading from black from top to white to bottom changing colours and tones. The background is like a frame and the image stands like a framed art piece.

Figure 25. Poster of Tales of Future

Sinan Bökesoy presents

1 city 1001 vibrations

"Tales of Future" sound installation

July 2010 Istanbul Taksim Metro Exhibition Room

Source: Istanbul 2010 Avrupa Kültür Başkenti Girişim Grubu (2011).

The verbal text is placed at the bottom under the image. "1 city 1001 vibrations" is written by giving a vibration effect. The verbal text is in English and cites Sinan Bökesoy as the creator of the project and the title of the project. At the fourth line, the date and place of the event is mentioned. Therefore, we understand that it takes place at a public place, Taksim Metro

Exhibition Room, one of the busiest hubs of public transportation. On the left, there is the logo of Istanbul 2010 in blue colour. At the bottom line other logos are listed.

The project introduces technology to the art. The acoustic sounds of the city are recorded through the microphones installed at Maiden's Tower on the Bosphorus and Sepetçiler Kiosk at Sarayburnu (TimeOut Istanbul, 2011). Therefore, we see Maiden's tower as the main figure in the silhouette of Istanbul. The silhouette depicts historical peninsula together with its minarets to the right. The silhouette is grey and misty. The silhouette is depicted on the waterfront; the water is blue. It is a calm blue and the light is reflecting on the water. On the top of the silhouette and Maiden's Tower, there are lines cutting the image horizontally. The lines are not straight, but they are wavy. They represent the sound-waves recorded through the mics. Three small pictures are placed on the waves, displaying robots and some technological devices.

2. *Content*

At first glance the image has a calming effect, due to the blue colour and misty silhouette of Istanbul. The silhouette is the symbolic representation of Istanbul, which is cited as "1 city" in the verbal text. The sound waves are flying over the sky. They are above the city, although they represent the sounds of the city but the sound is represented not in the city but above the city. The images on the waves stand like the stops of the music. They show robots and technological devices because the recorded sounds are transformed into beats through electronic, even robotic devices in the studio. Therefore, the three small images on the waves refer to the production process in the studio. Therefore, there are two processes of music production. The first stage is acoustic (sounds in the city) and the second stage is electronic (sounds in the studio). "1001 vibrations" connotes the variety of sounds of Istanbul's everyday life: ferries, seagulls, call to prayer and other melodies and beats. Although one should expect the representation of the city vibrating with sounds and rhythms, the city stands dormant at the background. It is just a silhouette of the city not even real face of the city. Thus, the emphasis is not on the city but on the musical process. The technology gives reference to the future due to high speed of innovation. That is why the project is called "Tales of the Future" as the technology and innovation belongs to tomorrow's world in its aim to enhance the present and inventing the new.

Film & documentary & animation

- Ifİstanbul

Figure 26. Poster of Ifİstanbul 2010

Source: Istanbul 2010 Avrupa Kültür Başkenti Girişim Grubu (2011).

1. Form

Ifİstanbul is the International Independent Film Festival of Istanbul, which is organized each year and it was organized for the 9th time in 2010. Therefore, the event is an example of continuous events in the annual cultural agenda of Istanbul and it is not specific to Istanbul 2010 programme as one-time event. It is the same for International festivals of Istanbul organized by Istanbul Foundation for Culture and Arts (IKSV) since the 1970s. The posters of IKSV festivals varying from music to film, from theatre to jazz have been designed around a concept each year and for 2010, the logo of Istanbul 2010 was added to the posters. Since IfIstanbul is a continuous festival as one of the most renowned film festivals of Istanbul together with October Film Festival (Film Ekimi) and International Istanbul Film Festival, the posters have a standard through the series of concepts created in each year. The designers of the poster are Koray Ekremoğlu and Medina Turgul DDB. The logo has been changed through the time as the festival extended first to Ankara and then to Izmir but in 2010 the festival was only in Istanbul and Ankara, therefore we see these two cities on the logo, on top left corner. On the top right corner, the festival dates for Ankara are given with a notice that the festival is taking place for the 9th time. The name of the festival has changed to AFM International Independent Film Festival due to extension to other cities and AFM refers to the sponsoring movie theatre for the festival. Therefore, below the text AFM logo is placed on the right side followed by mybilet logo as the box office and lastly Istanbul 2010 logo (as if it is copied and pasted when it joined the Istanbul 2010 programme) one under the other. Although the name of the festival is changed, the website address could not be changed so easily. "www.ifistanbul.com" is written on the left side of the poster vertically, in very small fonts, almost invisible. On the bottom left part of the image there is a special note written on a red background for promotion tickets for GencTurkcell (Young users of Turkcell, which is a mobile operator in Turkey). It says "buy one and get one free" and the promotion applies only to the screenings on the weekdays before 19.00. The full list of sponsors and partners are given at the bottom of the poster on white background. The background of the poster is blue separated by the horizon line. The sea below is a very dark blue, almost like a night blue and the sky on the upper part is has a lighter tome but still a dark tone of blue a little bit greenish. The slogan of the festival is "Yeni Perspektif" (New Perspective) which is written in 3-D effect and giving a perspective. On the horizon, we see the ship "Titanic" sinking into the sea. Below we see the top of an iceberg and in front of the iceberg there is a rescue boat and the boat is rescuing the iceberg not the sinking ship.

2. Content

Since this a poster for an international festival the signs are intended to signify the concept created for that year of the festival. That is why the theme of Titanic (which is a powerful theme in cinema) is offered through a new perspective in accordance with the verbal text. Thus, the image is strongly linked to the verbal text. The poster invites to give a new look to the image from a different perspective. The meaning signified is unusual because the rescue boat is expected to help the sinking ship but instead it is rescuing the iceberg, which is the cause of the accident. The iceberg has a huge metaphor behind. The top of the iceberg metaphorically signifies that the root is bigger than the surface. The iceberg is at the centre of the image; therefore, the focus is on the iceberg. The theme also has references to Independent film genre. Independent films are unconventional and they have different languages than other genres. Therefore, we cannot have the same look and approach towards independent films and Hollywood films. "Titanic" represents Hollywood cinema. Thus Hollywood cinema is being criticized through breaking the codes and offering a new perspective.

The image has no direct reference to Istanbul. The main reason is that this is a continuous film festival and each year is a new concept is raised for the festival. The poster is designed to communicate the festival concept rather than an effort to adapt to Istanbul 2010 agenda. Thus the festival is also independent from the Istanbul 2010 agenda and its discourses, parallel to the genre of independent films. A second reason is that the festival has extended to other cities and it is not specific to Istanbul. In addition, it should be noted that, the international festivals are not specific to the cities where they take place. They bring the world cinema to the local audience therefore they have an important role in the cultural life of the city. The references can be given to the cities if there is a special programme attributed to the city itself or reference for cinema in a wider context rather than simply promoting the city to an international audience, which would be the aim of Istanbul 2010 in this case.

In sum, the poster should be evaluated independently from the discourses of Istanbul 2010 to be able to understand the codes in the image in a wider context through an approach to cinema and film genres. Yet, I believe the poster establishes a strong link between the word and image in communicating the message. Hollywood cinema is identified with mass culture. Therefore "Titanic" is known to a large number of people. Since the audience is familiar with the story in the image, they message is decoded more easily. Yet it is not a completely direct message. The image encourages the audience to rethink the existing codes in the story and to reinterpret these codes through a new angle. The Titanic image surprises, questions and criticizes.

- "İstanbul'da Bayram Sabahı"

1. Form

"İstanbul'da Bayram Sabahı" is the title of the film written and directed by Mehmet Eryilmaz. The title is kept in Turkish, which means the fest morning in Istanbul. The rest of the text is both in Turkish and in English. The title of film is the focus of attention (big font size and gold colour) in the centre together with the image describing the sunrise over the minarets.

Figure 27. Poster of İstanbul'da Bayram Sabahı

Source: Istanbul 2010 Avrupa Kültür Başkenti Girişim Grubu (2011).

The mosque in the picture is Sultanahmet Mosque or known as Blue Mosque because it has 6 minarets distinguishing it from the other mosques as a unique feature. If we did not read the text, which says morning, we could have interpreted as the sunset. Under the title, there is a description in English:

"LIVING AND FEELING 'THE BAYRAM' IN AN ISTANBUL MORNING". It is written in capital letters as it is written here and it is the second biggest font used after the title. It denotes what the film is about. Right above the title, there is a small text in Turkish, which targets the audience as "for those who misses the tolerance and brotherhood feelings and their continuity in fests. Probably the text is only in Turkish because it targets the audience who already know how "Bayram" feels and who have experienced those feelings. For the rest of the text, Turkish and English words are separated from each other through different colours. On the top of the poster, in the sky over the image Mehmet Eryılmaz is mentioned as the scriptwriter and the director. Below the title on black background the information is given about the "premiere and first screening"; date, place and the begin time. However, some of the information is lost in translation. For instance, the date in Turkish is *"14 Aralık Salı"*, which is translated into English only as December 14, 2010". *"Salı"* which is "Tuesday" is forgotten and the full date with the year is given although Turkish text does not mention the year. Therefore, there are gaps in translation. This brings into minds the museum entrances where the entrance fee is written in words in Turkish and in numbers in English and different fees apply. Yet this problem is worked out in the poster as it is mentioned at the last line of the text at the bottom: "Entrance is free for media members. For the other audiences, invitation card is requested." However, one thing is again forgotten: if it is for all the screenings? It does not make sense because this statement only applies to the premier screening, which is mentioned in the Turkish text, but it goes without question in the English text. It is also noted that the project is realized by "ISTANBUL 2010 / EUROPEAN CAPITAL OF CULTURE AGENCY". The statement is concluded with the Istanbul 2010 logo on the right (bottom corner).

2. Content

The famous Istanbul silhouette with minarets is frequently used in the posters of Istanbul 2010 as we have seen many examples starting with the visual icon by McMillen for "Istanbul Inspirations" campaign. In this film poster we are again face to face with Istanbul silhouette with six minarets but we cannot see the full historical peninsula skyline. It is a close up image of Sultanahmet Mosque, so the image positions the viewer closer to the site where the photography is taken. The representation of mosque is closely associated with the theme of the film. Perhaps even it is a frame shot from the film. The film denotes increasing feelings for tolerance and brotherhood during the fest time. Mosque connotes the community feeling for Muslims where they gather and pray together in the early fest morning, at sunrise time. However, this is practiced by men not women therefore there is gender discrimination in such cultures. Moreover, the mosque denotes Islam and we understand that it is a religious fest time such as Ramadan. The text highlights "tolerance and brotherhood" but there is no other reference to other cultures or religions, although Istanbul is a cosmopolitan city. We only see the close up of a mosque and other parts of the city. A bird (silhouette of a bird) is flying over the dome of the mosque, which is also very common in symbolic representations of Istanbul. If it was the image of the Hagia Sophia, the bird could have represented the messenger or dove figure that connotes Holy Spirit according to Christianity. Hagia Sophia was built as a church and then it was transformed into a mosque. Today it serves as a museum. Whereas Sultanahmet Mosque was built as a mosque in the Ottoman period and still serves as a mosque today. Therefore, the bird figure does not have secondary meanings associated with Christianity but it just entered the snapshot. It can be commented that the messages are direct and simple in this poster but they cannot go beyond being just a cliché. The word and image support each other, whereas the context is described as a Muslim country. If it is not known that the silhouette belongs to Sultanahmet Mosque, it could have been another place instead of Istanbul and any ordinary morning instead of fest morning. The missing elements in the image are supported by the text; therefore, there is a strong link between the two.

Literature

• International Istanbul Poetry Festival

1. Form

The poster is designed by Eray Kula. On the top right corner the event is identified as "INTERNATIONAL ISTANBUL POETRY FESTIVAL" in capital letters both in Turkish (above) and in English (below). "POETRY" is emphasized in bold character. The English text is abbreviated: "INT." for international and "FEST." for festival, which is not a common practice for titles. We see an upside-down image of Galata Tower like a pen. The tower is made of letters. The words are written in Turkish but they do not make sense, as they are not complete in a sentence structure. They function as the stones building the tower rather than building the sentence. The pinpoint draws a way or a river as the ink is blue. The background colour of the poster is white and the text is blue. Istanbul 2010 logo is at the bottom right side of the poster.

Below the logo, the date of the event is written in a box and the theme is stated as "Ireland". Below the box, on the bottom of the poster all the other logos are listed such as Istanbul Metropolitan Municipality and Beyoğlu Municipality. The logo of Beyoğlu Municipality is also represented by Galata

Tower. The web address of the festival ("istanbulsiirfestivali.org") is given at the bottom right corner next to the logos. There is no "www" (worldwideweb) in the beginning of the web address line and the address is in Turkish.

Figure 28. Poster of International Istanbul Poetry Festival

Source: Istanbul 2010 Avrupa Kültür Başkenti Girişim Grubu (2011).

2. Content

The poster has direct references to Istanbul and poetry. Galata Tower has a symbolic meaning for Istanbul as a landmark. By depicting it upside-down the signifier has changed into a pen. There are no historical or cultural connotations between Galata Tower and poetry. The reason for such a representation of the tower as a pen is due to its shape. The tower is represented through words as the building blocks in an effort to establish a metaphoric meaning between the poetry and the tower symbolized as pen. The ink flows like a river when the words are thought as they are flowing in a poem metaphorically. Therefore, the image and text are linked to each other through metaphoric and symbolic meanings in conveying the message. The poetry and Istanbul are the signs that can be easily conferred from the image but there is no direct reference to the theme of the festival, which is "Ireland". If the theme was "Genoa" the representation of Galata Tower would have made perfect sense as it is built by Genoese. But Galata Tower is there only because of its similarity to the pen and most probably due to Beyoğlu Municipality and Galata Tower in its logo. There is no visual reference to Ireland either at the denotative or connotative level. If we force our imaginations the only reference could have been the river drawn by the pen (Galata Tower) representing River Shannon as the longest river in Ireland or River Foyle as the border between the Republic of Ireland and Northern Ireland. Obviously, the only reference to Ireland is made verbally in the text and the context of Ireland is left out of focus in this poster while Istanbul is certainly in focus and Istanbul is signified more than poetry and more than Ireland.

Theatre & performing arts

• Cihangir Insomnia

1. Form

The poster designed by Markus Göbl, shows a wide-open eye with a big pupil and red veins. The eyelashes are depicted as arrows in different directions and there are hundreds of them. On the top right of the eye, in the corner of the poster, there is red big circle like a sun. Inside the circle it is written "/LOVE /PAIN /MUSIC" one under the other and each word starting with a slash. The eye is in the centre of the poster on the yellow background. The background is like wall. There are cracks on the wall one big crack on the left corner above the eye. The colour of the wall is not a pure tone, is a dirty yellow. There is a small moth perching on the wall, below the eye. The two stripes below the moth looks like scotch tape drawing a line on the wall. Below the line, on the left corner "CIHANGIR INSOMNIA" is written in capital bold letters, in black. This is the title of the project. On the bottom right corner, there is the logo of Istanbul 2010. Between the two, there are three lines separating the text from each other. The upper line gives information about the date and place of the performance and contact information. At the line below, there is the web-site address of the project and the small logos of other supporters and/or partners.

Figure 29. Poster of Cihangir Insomnia

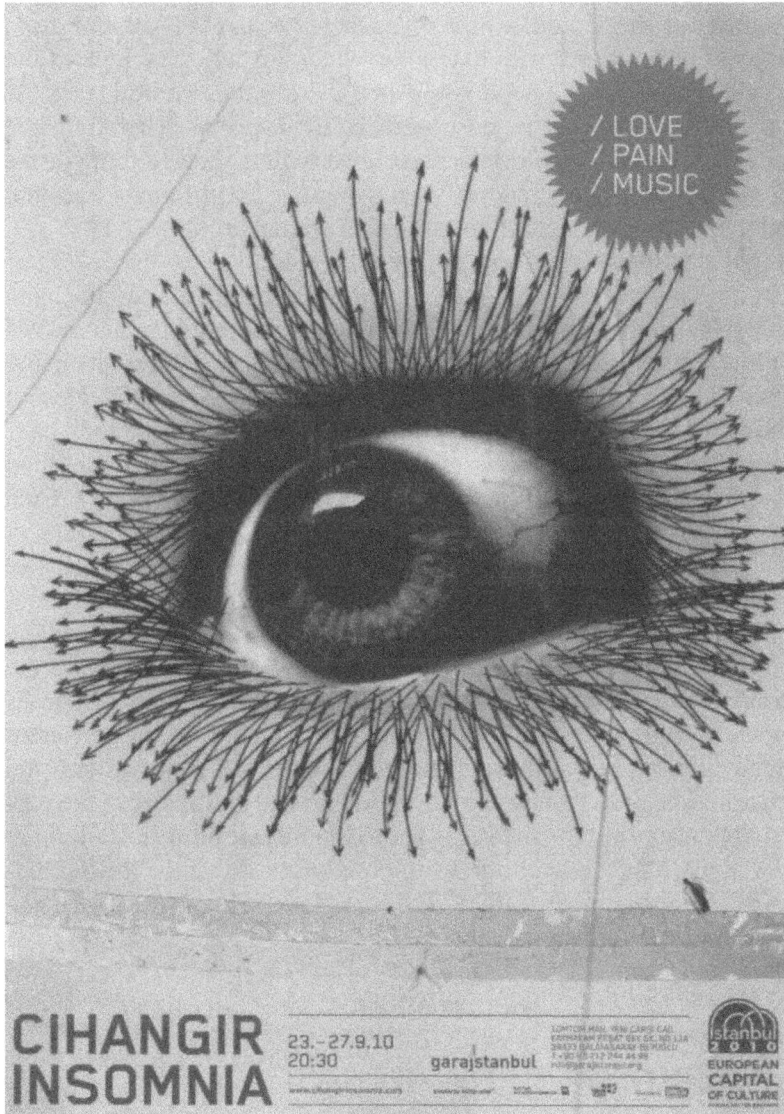

Source: Istanbul 2010 Avrupa Kültür Başkenti Girişim Grubu (2011).

2. Content

The verbal and visual text is closely linked in creating the meaning. The "eye" wide-open is like a sleepless eye in other words a "redeye" signalling "insomnia". The arrows representing the eyelashes are like thorns giving pain. Although the heads of the arrows are pointed out, it is disturbing. Since the arrows pointed out, they could be also associated as a sign of communication or contact with outer world, with exterior or "looking out". The look of the eye is tense and anxious; the pupil is big as if there is a threat or danger. At the denotative level the eye is tense because of insomnia. Therefore, the meaning of "insomnia" in the title is associated with the image through the depiction of the eye. The redeye is a symptom of insomnia, alcohol consumption or even drug use, often associated with nightlife.

"Cihangir" signifies several meanings but I would focus on the district of Istanbul in the city centre (Taksim area), know for nightlife and bohemian way of living. Cihangir has been one of the intense cosmopolitan districts of Istanbul in its history and had been the subject of urban interventions many times. First, the Greek and Armenian populations were cleaned. Then it became home to immigrants from Anatolia and transvestites who took over the emptied houses from the former residents. That time the neighbourhood had a run-down look neglected by the urban planners and government. Then the regeneration started to rehabilitate the area from the marginal groups of people such as the "transvestites" mainly settled down on Pürtelaş Street. The neighbourhood attracted intellectuals and artists due to its centrality and proximity to Taksim and the main pedestrian street of Istanbul, Beyoğlu, which is the symbolic to intellectual life of the city. The newcomers of the neighbourhood gave a bohemian spirit to Cihangir and the rents of houses were increased. Yet there are many places in Istanbul and in different metropolitan cities in the world that have similar stories of gentrification and transformation. The dirty yellow colour of the wall and the cracks on the wall signifies a dilapidated environment. As known, moths are attracted to light in the dark. The moth perching on the wall turned itself up where the big red-point stands like the source of light. The text "love, pain, music" tells the audience what the performance is about.

Traditional arts

• Heritage

1. Form

The poster designed by Cüneyt Özkan. The text is written both in Turkish and in English. On the top, the title of the project "Miras" (Heritage) is written in golden letters and in big font size. Under "Miras", the tittle in English

"Heritage" is given in grey italic letters in a smaller font size. In the centre of the poster, we see an example of calligraphy, most probably written in Arabic, or maybe in Ottoman language. Below the image we read the text: "A Collection from Traditional Turkish Calligraphy Foundation Museum", which is linked to the image above and anchors the meaning that the exhibition is about calligraphy. The English text is written in italics again. Below, there is the logo of Istanbul 2010 and there is no any other logo. All the elements either visual or verbal on the poster are centred.

Figure 30. A Collection from Traditional Turkish Calligraphy Foundation Museum

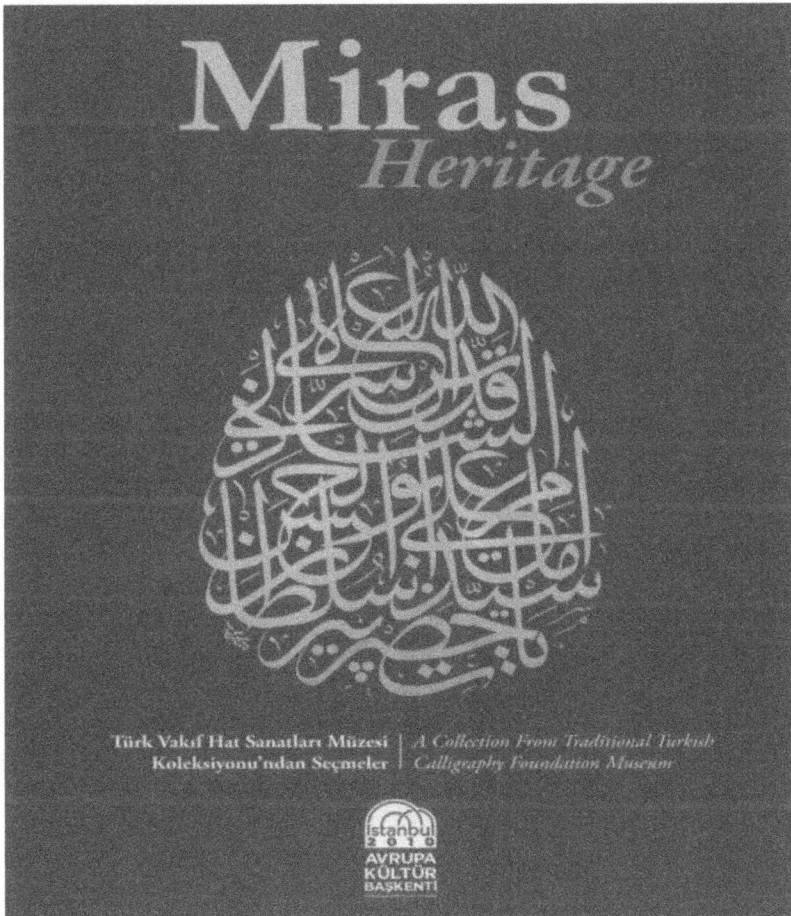

Source: Istanbul 2010 Avrupa Kültür Başkenti Girişim Grubu (2011).

2. Content

The design of the poster is simple as the signs are kept at a very simple level yet they are effective to communicate the main theme. It does not harass the eye of the viewer and does not confuse with redundant details. The message is simple and the design is aesthetical as it reflects a beautiful example of calligraphy art. Therefore, it lets the audience to look and enjoy the art piece on the poster, while giving information only at the fundamental level. The famous painter Andre Lothe comments on the abstractness and beauty of calligraphy as follows:

"I cannot read these writings. It is better that way. So I can enjoy the pure symphony of lines..." (in Eroğlu, 2010: 94).

The image on this poster, which is a calligraphy example, is designed in the shape of an eye drop. It also resembles to fingerprint. A fingerprint is a way of identification and it is unique for each person. Not any two or more people on earth have the same fingerprint. When interpreted through this perspective, the letters signify the ridges on a fingertip.

Most interestingly, the image on the poster is composed in the form of verbal text. As the text is in Arabic Alphabet, the poster is not only in two languages as it has been mentioned initially but it is in three languages.

Calligraphy in Arabic alphabet is often connoted with the Islamic culture and art. The image does not give any reference to the context. It is not depicted on a wall or ceiling of a mosque, etc. The image is depicted on a black background like an art piece. But when the image and text are considered in a link to each other then the viewer would think of Ottoman Turkish Calligraphy as the text connects the meaning of the image with heritage, which is selected from a collection of Traditional Turkish Calligraphy. During the Ottoman period, calligraphy was among the most venerated art forms because the Islamic art denies the representation of God through images (Lewis & Churchill, 2009). Therefore, Islamic art tradition has a strong level of abstraction in meaning. One of the most known examples of such tradition of representation can be seen in Hagia Sophia as a heritage site. As known Hagia Sophia was constructed as a Byzantine church and after the conquest of Istanbul by the Ottomans it was transformed into a mosque and the interior has been changed according to the Islamic traditions. The most extensive restoration of Hagia Sophia was commissioned by Abdülmecid II to Fossati brothers in the 19th century. The mosaics in the upper gallery were cleaned. The iconographic mosaics of the Christianity were not destroyed but they were covered with examples of calligraphy art with Koranic inscriptions and the names of the God and the Prophet. After the foundation of Republic and secularization some of the calligraphy works were kept, while many of them were taken to Museum of Turkish and Islamic Arts. Therefore, this brief information on the history of Hagia Sophia gives an idea for the historical context of calligraphy and its importance as heritage.

Education

• Sulukule Children's Art Workshop Project

Figure 31. Poster of Sulukule

Source: Istanbul 2010 Avrupa Kültür Başkenti Girişim Grubu (2011).

1. Form

The poster designed by Tuncay Köksal/ Lowe Tanıtım for Sulukule Children's Art Workshop Project is very colourful and playful as the target audience is children. Although the verbal text tells "art workshop" in blue colour, we see music notes flying everywhere, they are blowing out from the volcano like figure painted in rainbow colours. Thus it can be understood that the project is mainly about music. Sulukule is differentiated from the rest of the text, which is in purple. Different colours are used to draw attention to Sulukule, which is a historical neighbourhood in Istanbul. The text printed on white background is cutting the volcano into two parts horizontally and the rainbow seems discontinuous. The top of the rainbow volcano is framed and painted on purple-pink background, which stands like another image. Actually this is the logo of the workshop project, which has become part of the image on the poster. The notes are spilling over the frame and flying over the top of the poster. They also get bigger when they spill over the frame to the white background. The logos are listed at the bottom of the poster below the horizontal line where the volcano ends. In the beginning we see Istanbul 2010 logo, and then several art and culture foundations follow consecutively Sulukule Foundation for Culture, which is a local initiative, Istanbul Technical University, Contemporary Drama Foundation for acting and ITU Turkish Music State Conservatory (TMSK) for music education.

2. Content

The meaning of music is strong when we read the image on a contextual basis as well. Sulukule is the neighbourhood in the historical centre of Istanbul, renowned for the Romani people living there and the music industry and culture as a part of their living and traditions. The children learn to play instruments at a very early age, as they are born into a family culture of music. However, apparently this is not a formal education. It is a form of tradition transferred from generation to generation. At the bottom of the poster we see the logo of Istanbul Technical University (ITU) and ITU Turkish Music State Conservatory (TMSK). This signifies the aim of the workshop is to give formal music education to children of Sulukule.

Music is a common language, which is represented with notes flying over the air. The notes are blown out to the air by the volcano representing the creativity. Children are creative they have an imaginative world. This is represented by painting the volcano in rainbow colours. The colourful images are attractive for children. The rainbow is a dream-like figure that appears as a result of diffraction of light in the sky. But this is an extraordinary happening for children as it is visible when there is sun and rain together. The multi-colours of the rainbow represent the polyphony of an orchestra where the music notes are signs of a common language. The children are perceived as the change makers for the future and the importance of the education is highlighted to make the change.

Sulukule is a cosmopolitan district with many voices and colours. The Romani inhabitants of the neighbourhood are the main contributors to its cultural life and development of music industry also in the form of a job. However, as the city transforms, the locality is crushed by the global forces. Sulukule has been recently chosen as the first renewal site. Accordingly, the project implemented by Istanbul Metropolitan Municipality proposes the forceful evictions of the Romani people and creates social exclusion in the area. The art workshop supported by local initiatives, educational bodies and Istanbul 2010 Agency, takes place completely at the opposite side to the urban renewal, in an effort to support culture and education.

Maritime and sports

- Rally of Turkey

1. Form

There are different posters prepared for the Rally of Turkey both in Turkish and in English as it is a mega sports event under the support of Istanbul 2010 event. I have taken the poster in Turkish, printed on the Posters Catalogue by Istanbul 2010 Agency, under investigation.

From top to bottom, the poster changes colours, tones, composition and meanings layer by layer. It starts with a dusty image of symbolic landmarks of Istanbul: Maiden's Tower, Süleymaniye Mosque, Sultan Gate of Dolmabahce Palace, Rumeli Castle and Galata Tower consecutively. The order of these historical and monumental buildings do not represent a geographically order, nor they are on the route of the rally. At the background we see the Bosphorus Bridge, which seems like hung on Maiden's Tower and Galata Tower as its piers. The landscape of Bosphorus at the back is misty and nostalgic. The sun is depicted as either rising or setting just above the Bosphorus Bridge in the middle of the sky. The colour of the image is composed of dusty brown, yellow and orange, which makes the image look like an old representation even nostalgic. Above the Bosphorus Bridge, the slogan is written in big, white, bold capital letters: "The Greatest Rally is in the City of Legends." The slogan is linked firstly to the legendary image of the city and below the symbolic representations of Istanbul. Two race cars are depicted side by side. The light from above falls on the cars as if they are not racing cars but they are show cars presented to the audience on the stage. At the bottom of the poster, in the middle, there is the logo of "Rally of Turkey", above (in the logo) Ministry of Culture and Tourism of Turkey is represented and below the logo the web address is given; "www.rallyofturkey.org".

Figure 32. Poster of Rally of Turkey

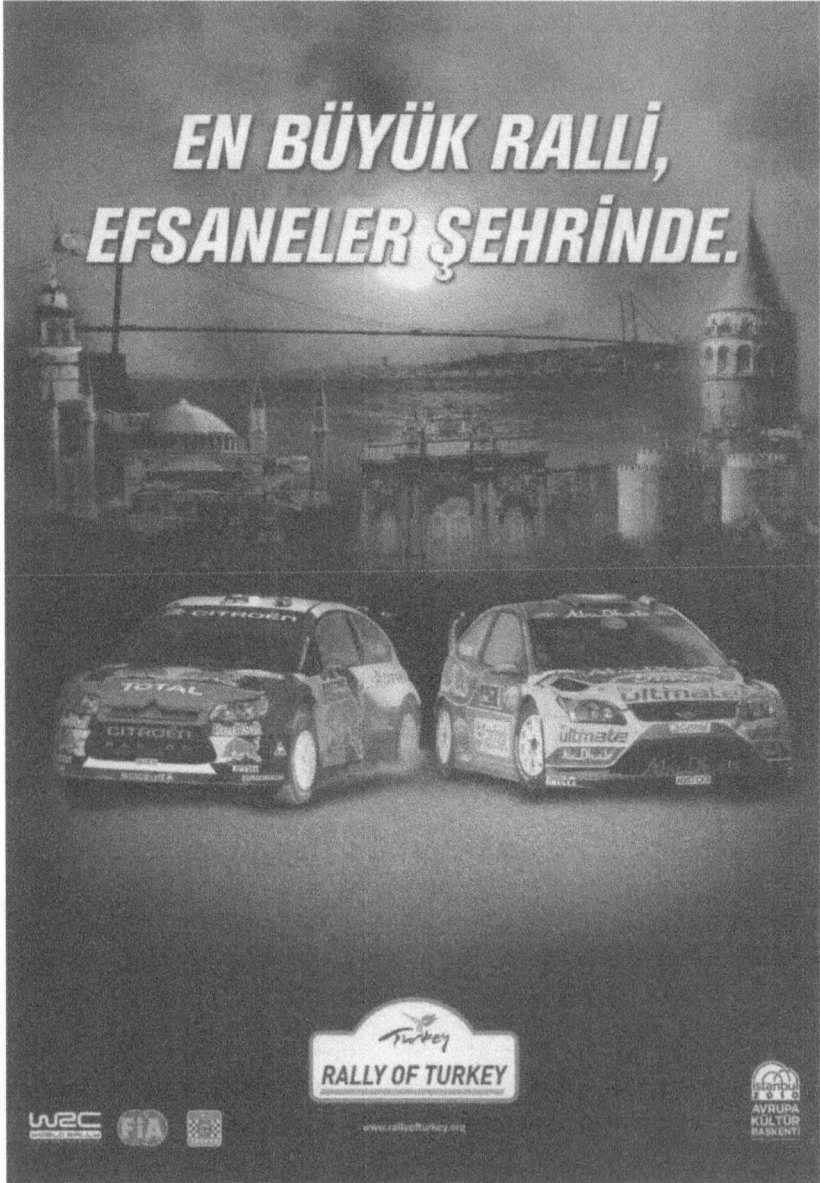

Source: Istanbul 2010 Avrupa Kültür Başkenti Girişim Grubu (2011).

The logo is greater than the other logos listed on the bottom line of the poster. On the right corner there is the logo of Istanbul 2010 Agency, on the left side the logos of WRC (World Rally Championship), FIA (Fédération Internationale de l'Automobile) and TOSFED (Türkiye Otomobil Sporları Federasyonu) are displayed consecutively.

2. Content

At first glance the poster seems bringing the representations of past and modern together through representations of old monuments in the city and the brand new race cars. This seems like a clash and there is something, which does not fit into this picture. The atmosphere created by the colours of brown, yellow, and orange is mystical and nostalgic. It belongs to the old. The cars belong to modern; they are the signs of technology. Therefore, they do not fit into the background image of Istanbul behind. Actually the background image of Istanbul likes a theatre decor, it is not real, the colours are in the tones of watercolour, the sky is dusty brown and it is turbulent it is not blue and calm. The cars at the front stand like they are standing on the stage. The light falling on the cars is like the spotlight. The ground is dusty but the car on the right looks like it does not move at all. They face different directions as if they will start moving in different direction, the car on the right to the right and the car on the left to the left. The car on the left also looks like it does not move but when we look at the tires we see dust is coming out as it is moving on a sandy area.

The verbal text, the slogan, connects the images and layers of meaning to each other. It highlights Istanbul as the "City of legends". That is why Istanbul is depicted like a mystified, historical city through its legendary monuments. The rally is represented through the race cars in the front. The visual opposition between the two is neglected and they are connected through the meaning in the verbal text. Yet the leading actor in this representation is not the city of Istanbul but the cars. The rally is represented as the sports event, as the spectacle in which Istanbul turns into the stage for the spectacle. The mega sports event sometimes may target greater and different segments of audience than the main event itself. This is linked to the culture and popularity of the event in that country. Therefore, the emphasis is given to the rally and Istanbul is presented as the decor of the event. It is also true that mega-events, especially popular sports events are wonderful opportunities to promote the city. Especially sport events that take in the inner city such as marathons, bicycle races etc. offer images for the audience about how the city looks, giving high-angle snapshots of the city. Rally however takes place at a special route outside of the city. Imagine the dust in the historical city of the area and the level of damage to the historical monuments represented on the image if it would take place in the city centre. In that case the city would look like as turbulent as doomsday. Therefore, the representation of Istanbul remains like a layer on the surface.

Parallel events

• Istanbul en Drome

1. Form

The poster designed by Burcu Işık gives a portrayal of Istanbul skyline. But the skyline we see on the top of the poster on a white background (which covers only 1/5th of the whole poster) different from the usual Istanbul silhouette depictions. It does not only represent the look through the historical peninsula, the modern face of the city has entered into the skyline with few skyscrapers in the middle, although they are depicted at a lower height than the historical monuments and minarets. The skyline starts with Bosphorus Bridge on the left and then the three towers of Istanbul, which have become symbolic to the urban representations are depicted, Galata Tower, Beyazıt Tower and Maiden's Tower respectively. Then comes the modern face of the city with modern skyscrapers which are not symbolic for Istanbul (yet) but they can be anywhere in the other modern metropolises of the world. Yet if I am not wrong they are the twin towers of Sabancı Holding (which is one of the biggest capital groups of Turkey) and İş Bankası Building, which was the tallest building of Istanbul till 2010 when the Anthill Residences were built and then "Sapphire of Istanbul" became the tallest building of Istanbul in 2011. Although there is a competition of building the tallest building the representations of these skyscrapers do not look like they are competing to each other. They are depicted at the same level with Haydarpaşa Train Station on their right side. On the right end of the skyline Sultanahmet Mosque is depicted with its six minarets. The shade of the skyline falls like a curtain to the rest of the poster forming a black background. The rest is composed of verbal text printed in white on black colour. Below the skyline, "ISTANBUL EN DROME" is printed in bold capital letters as the title of the exhibition. The small text under the title mentions "ANNEE DE LA TURQUIE EN FRANCE" and "ISTANBUL 2010 CAPITALE EUROPEENE DE LA CULTURE" together. The text is in French as the year 2010 refers to the year of Turkey in France and Istanbul 2010 European Capital of Culture". The rest of the text is also written in French as the exhibition takes place in France in Mairie de Bourg-les-Valence Lyon-France. Then the names of organizers are presented which is followed by the names of Turkish and French artists. Below the date of the exhibition is given. We see the logo of Meke Sanat as the Turkish co-organizer of the event. The other logos are listed at the bottom line of the poster below the logo of Meke Sanat. The logo of Istanbul 2010 is at the end, at the right corner.

Figure 33. Poster of Istanbul en Drome

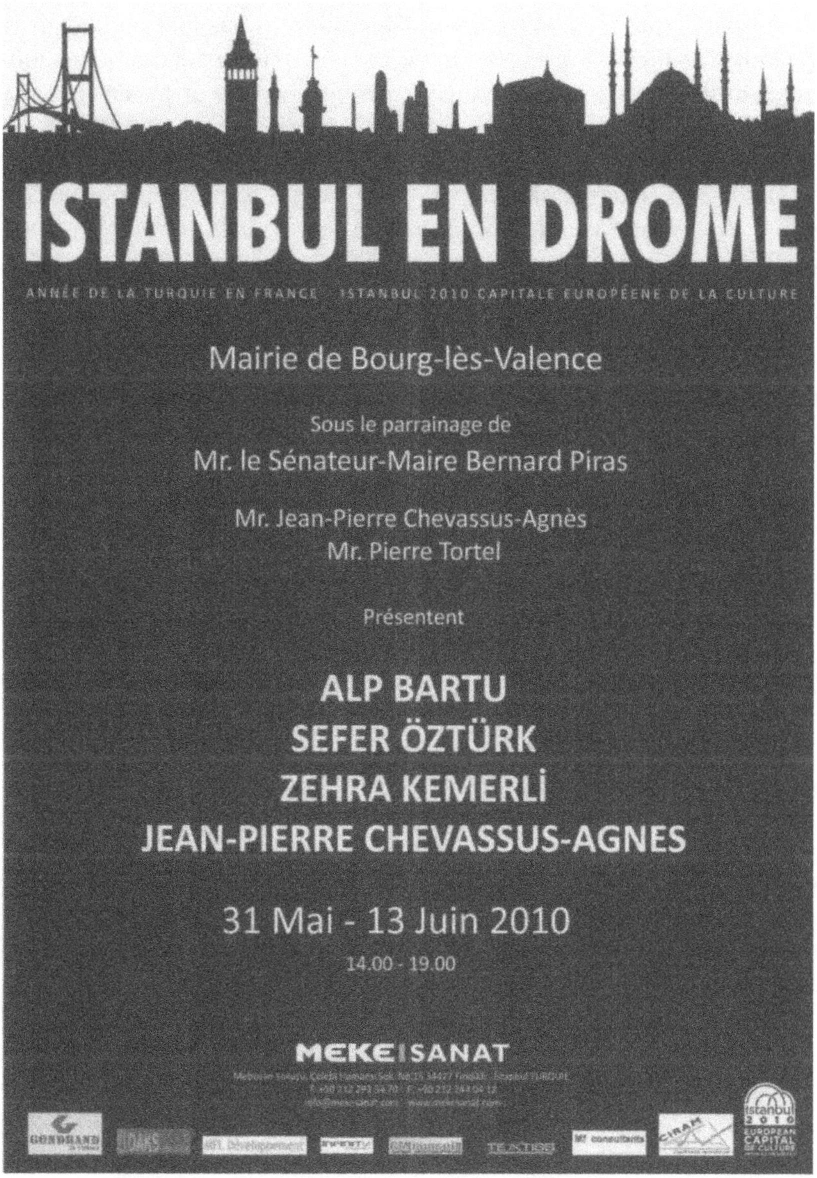

Source: Istanbul 2010 Avrupa Kültür Başkenti Girişim Grubu (2011).

2. Content

As 2010 was the Turkish year in France, the exhibition was organized in an attempt to reinforce the cultural relationships between Turkey and France. In this context the event is not only of international but transnational nature. Yet the image represented on the top of the poster, the Istanbul skyline gives any reference neither to France, nor to the content of the exhibition. The only represented city is Istanbul, although it is not possible to understand the context of this representation from the image. It resembles to the representation of London skyline with rising towers like Tower Bridge, St. Paul, and various modern skyscrapers in any type of promotional poster. Therefore, such representation of Istanbul brings minds the globalization effects leading to marketing cities resembling to each other, which are out of place and out of context. The audience cannot understand if the exhibition is about architecture, or contemporary art or etc. The verbal text is in French because the exhibition was organized in France but it does not also give any reference to the content of the exhibition. The design of the poster is kept at a simple level, so is the text. Nevertheless, the poster is not informative and representative enough to attract the audience to the exhibition as the audience does not have a clue about what to expect from the exhibition.

- Spectres of Trotsky: the Lost Interiors of an Exile

1. Form

The poster is designed on a black background in which we see the image captured by the Irish photographer James Hughes in the middle stretching from left to right. The title of the exhibition "Spectres of Trotsky: the Lost Interiors of an Exile" is printed vertically from top to bottom extending on image. "Spectres of Trotsky" is printed in white and the rest of the title "The Lost Interiors of an Exile" is printed in red colour. The text is in Turkish. On the top left corner of the poster the text starts with "Leon Trotsky" giving reference to the Soviet Communist leader and it follows with "The interior spaces of exile in Büyükada" which gives more information about the exhibition in which Hughes has photographed the interiors of Trotsky house in Büyükada in Istanbul. Below the image, the address of the Istanbul Hatırası Fotograf Merkezi, where the exhibition took place, is given and the logos of the partners and sponsors are listed below. Istanbul 2010 logo is placed on the bottom right of the poster which is reserved like separate place as it is separated by the vertical text dividing the poster. A small and a very interesting detail is the key on the left, below the image, next to the address line. The key is not represented fully, we cannot see where the key leads us, and we cannot see the lock. Only the top of the key is represented which is made of iron and which looks like an old key.

Figure 34. Poster of Spectres of Trotsky

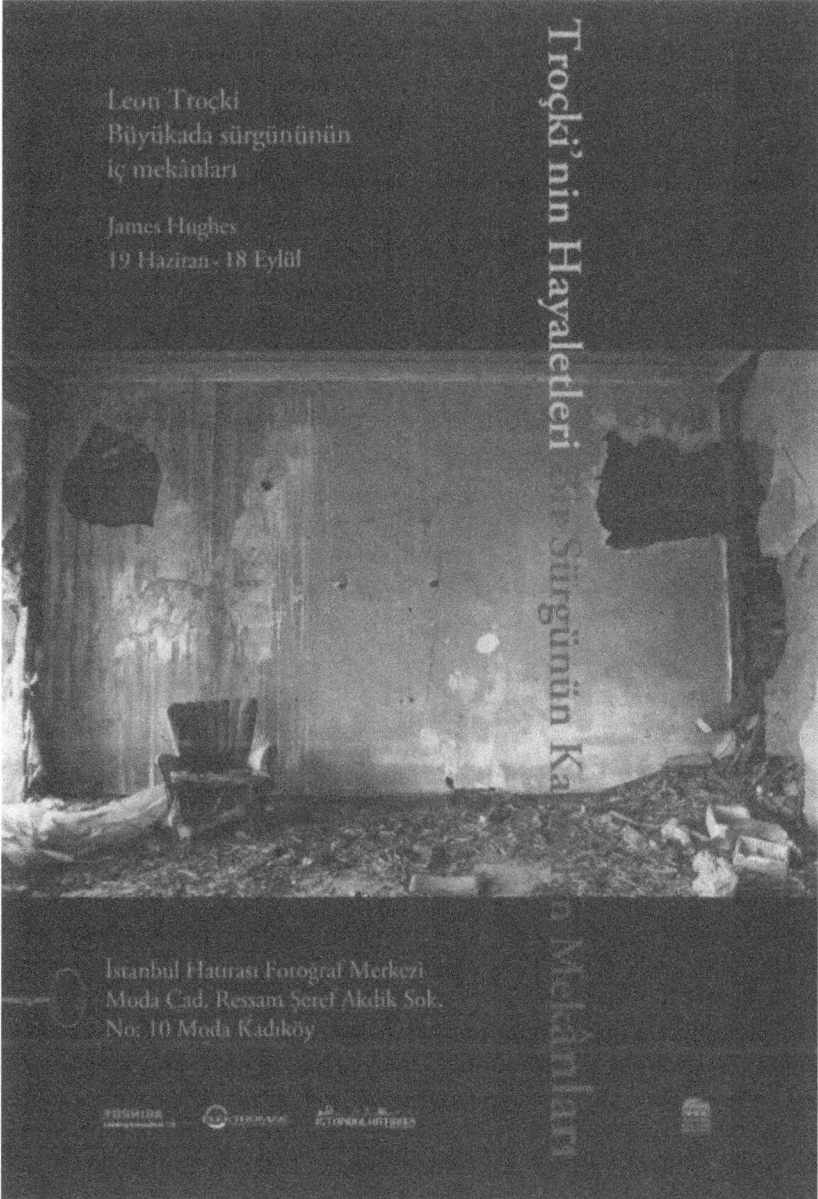

Source: Istanbul 2010 Avrupa Kültür Başkenti Girişim Grubu (2011).

2. Content

If we talk about the context before going into interpretation, it could be appropriate to mention the signs at the denotative level and then relate them to the context. The Soviet Communist leader Leon Trotsky lived in a house in Büyükada (*Prinkipo* in Greek), during his exile years in Istanbul (1929-1933). Therefore, the image shows the picture of the interior of Trotsky House. The room is totally run down and thorn apart, the papers are peeling off from the walls, the room is full of debris on the ground, the room is filled with light from the window (there is no window anymore) on the left. There are holes on the walls and the whole structure is severely damaged. There is a coach on the left side facing towards the audience and it is empty. The whole room is filled with the sense of emptiness, as it is an abandoned place. However, it is also filled with light and memories. It is filled with spectres as we are witnessing the past through the lens of James Hughes. Therefore, Hughes composes the image as well as the narratives by offering a rich story to the audience.

When we look at the image at a deeper level and dig into layers at the connotative level, the photograph gives the feeling of an imaginary place one side and a powerful sense of place and time as a witness on the other. Although it is a lived place and the photographer is documenting the reality, the fiction, fantasy and unreality is mixed into reality in a poetic way. The image reflects powerfully on the identity of place; the time is frozen. In a way, it resembles to the "Ghost Building" project as it demonstrates a run-down building, which is at risk although it still exists as a witness. The similarity is that both invite the audience to imagine; one, to imagine the future scenarios, and the other, the memories of the past.

Hughes offers many layers opening to different worlds. The key at the denotative level is the tool to open the door. There is no visible representation of the door but the key is inviting the audience to enter. It invites to enter the house, to discover the interior spaces. The key is an invitation, which otherwise would be breaking into the house. The interior represents the private life and we are not called to view an ordinary place where ordinary people lived once. We are invited to look at a special place where different people have passed from Ottoman pashas to a Soviet leader. The photo pays a revisit to the past lives through the remnants of a private space. It invites the audience to imagine Trotsky through the surfaces of meaning: the colours, the texture the materials, those have remained and those have perished. Despite the shambles all over the place, there is a grace in the decoration of the room, which offers clues to imagine the past. Therefore, the image shows fragments of past lives through a fragmented space.

- In Between. Austria Contemporary

Figure 35. Poster of in Between. Austria Contemporary

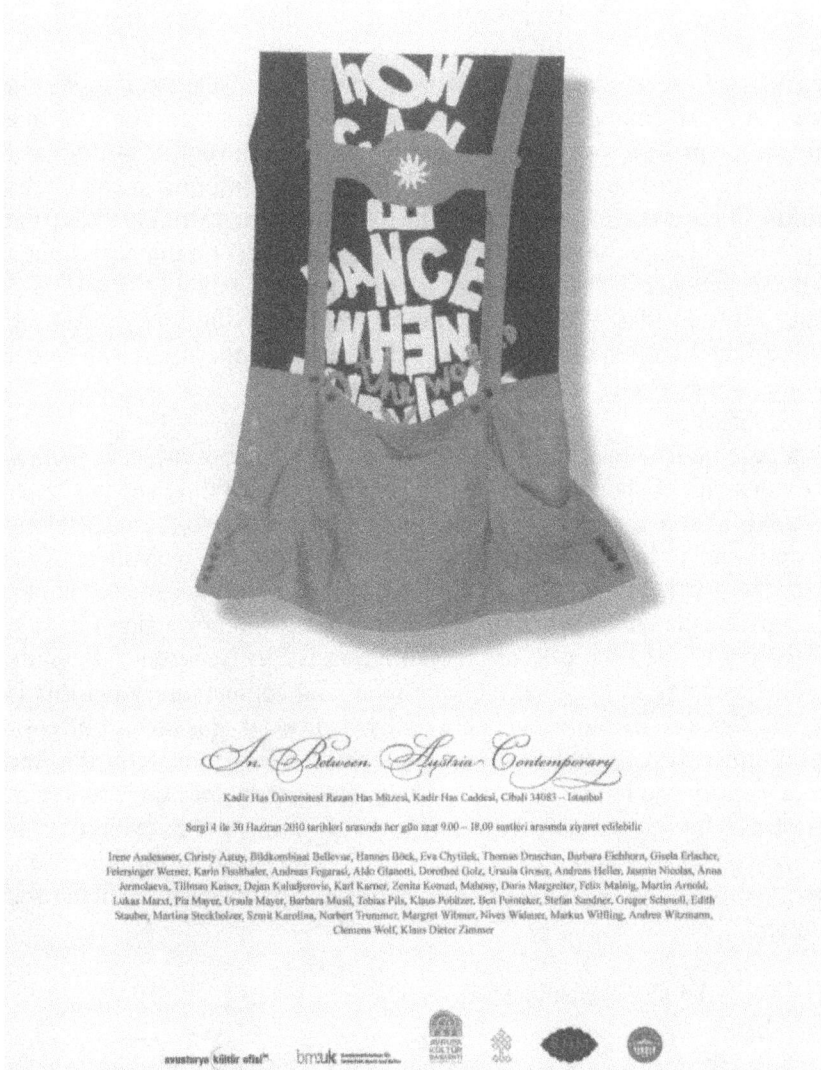

Source: Istanbul 2010 Avrupa Kültür Başkenti Girişim Grubu (2011).

1.   Form

The poster is designed on a white paper. The Austrian traditional dress for men known as "lederhosen" is depicted in green colour, and more than the shorts it looks like a dress for girls. It is not worn it stands like a dress for paper doll. Inside the dress there is a black t-shirt with the words printed on the t-shirt "how, can dance, when, the world…" There is a daisy like a button between the suspenders. Although the dress is exhibited like the costume for a paper doll, the image is like a 3-D image as the shade of the dress falls on the background as if it is exhibited in a shop or a gallery, the light falls from the top left, so the shadow is on the right. The title of the exhibition, "In Between. Austria Contemporary", is written below the image in a font like Edwardian script. The text below the title is written in a very small font and the font type is like Times New Roman. The text gives information about the exhibition; the address and the dates of the exhibition. Interestingly unlike the other posters not only the dates are printed with numbers on the poster but a full sentence is given: "The exhibition can be visited everyday from 4 June to 30 June, between 09.00-18.00". Below, the names of the young Austrian artists are listed and at the bottom line of the poster the logos are given. Everything on the poster is centred.

2. *Content*

Although the costume in the image looks like "lederhosen", it is neither leather, nor a pair of shorts. It is a green costume made of fabric and the lower part is a skirt, yet it can be associated with lederhosen due to the suspenders. The lederhosen is thought as the traditional costume for men in Austria, however the text below says "Austria Contemporary" which seems like an opposition to the image but it is not. "Contemporary" signifies the contemporary art and the title of the exhibition is "In Between". It can be interpreted as being in between the traditional and contemporary but this is only at the surface. The costume is not really traditional, it is an art object or a subject rather than a traditional costume, which offers connotations to the Austrian identity and history as well as the contemporary meanings rooted in the Austrian traditions and Austrian way of living. The exhibition is commissioned and organised by the Austrian Federal Ministry for Education, Arts and Culture, which denotes the Austrian state's promotive role in the arts and culture.

- Antik Aryalar Yarışması "Arie Antiche"
1. *Form*

If we read the poster from top to bottom, first we read the title of the project in Turkish, which means Antique Arias Contest. The title in Turkish is in white, capital letters and below there is the Italian phrase for Antique Arias in quotation marks: "Arie Antiche". If we continue to read through the bottom, we see the date of the contest March 2010 and the logo of Istanbul 2010 below the date. The logo is blue and standing alone in the centre of the page. The image is laid on the background of the poster. We see four females, the two playing the lute (one at the right one at the left, in the front) and the two singing (in the middle at the back). The singing figure is holding a booklet or note sheet in her hands. Below the image, there is the logo of Antik A.S., which is one of the leading art auctioneers in Turkey and the organizer of the event. At the bottom line of the poster, below the logo the contact information of Antik A.S. is given.

Figure 36. Poster of "Arie Antiche"

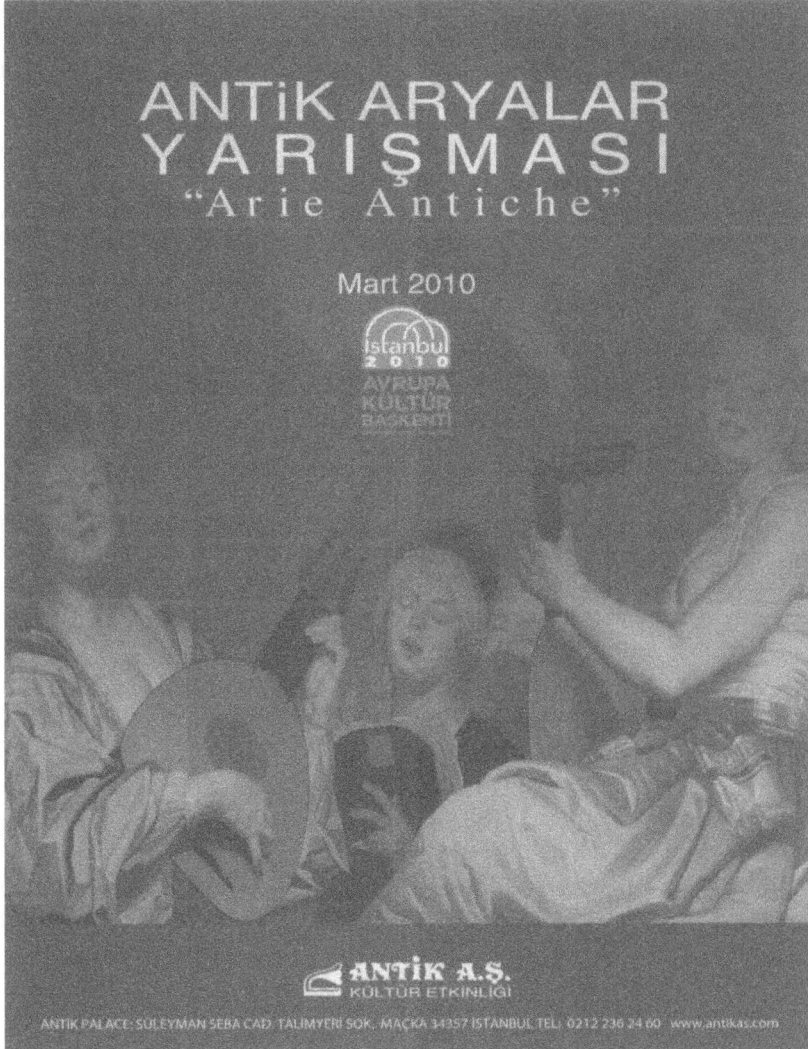

Source: Istanbul 2010 Avrupa Kültür Başkenti Girişim Grubu (2011).

2. Content

As it can be read from the title of the project, it is an opera contest, with a specific concept of "antique arias". Antique arias is mentioned also in Italian, "Arie Antiche" on the poster, however there is not any other reference to Italian partnership in the project although some members of the juries of the contest came from Italy, from renowned institutions.

The word "opera" originates from Italian word for work and defined as "a dramatic work in one or more acts that is set to music for singers and instrumentalists" (Oxford English Dictionary, 2008b). The word "aria" also has its origins in the Italian word for "air", which is defined today as "music a long accompanied song for a solo voice in an opera or oratorio" (Oxford English Dictionary, 2008c). Therefore, as their etymological origins, the music form has references to the Western Culture. The Western art is appreciated by the Republic, as a synonym to modernization. Yet opera, as a western art form, is not very well adopted and well appreciated by the Turkish culture.

If we look at the image to search for anchored meanings between the word and image, we see that the main theme in the image is music. The composition of the image lays out many layers of meanings that are open to contextual interpretation. The image depicts four female figures. Two of them in the front, playing the lute, look western and the one at the back singing looks eastern as she is depicted with turban on her head. Turban signifies the eastern culture and highly represented in the orientalist paintings by Western painters. The lute as an instrument is also attributed to western culture but sometimes it is used interchangeably with "ud" which is presumed as an instrument with eastern origin. Playing ud and singing has been a part of the culture at the Ottoman seraglio, which was represented in the orientalist paintings. If we take the reference for turban and eastern culture, it could be said that the image has references to eastern culture. On the other hand, if we take off western connotations for the lute and opera, it could be said that the image has references to the western culture as playing lute and opera has been part of entertainment life in the west and it was represented in the paintings of the western artists. If we focus on details in the composition, we see that the two females playing the lute are facing to the audience. They are posed with their torsos facing each other and their heads are turned to audience. They look like western figures with their dressing and hairstyles. If we look at the two females at the back, we see the differences in their representation. We can only see the face of the female figure partially so the female holding the book is representative. Their eyes are closed or either they are looking down at the booklet and they are singing or reading. Although we see the facial expression, they are not looking at the audience; they seem they are concentrated in their inner worlds as if they are praying.

The codes in the image can be interpreted differently in different contexts. The image has many references addressing binary oppositions between the East and West. Yet the main theme is the music as the common denominator between the two cultures as well as between the text and the image.

- "Istanbul – Paris – Berlin"

1. Form

On the poster we see three different towers in three different cities. First is the Galata Tower in Istanbul, second is the Eiffel Tower in Paris and third is the TV Tower in Berlin. The towers as iconic structures have become symbolic to the cities. Above the image, over each tower representation we read the names of the cities respectively "ISTANBUL – PARIS – BERLIN" in white capital letters. The text on the poster is in Turkish and below the image it is pointed out that the event is a literature meeting, which takes place at French Cultural Centre in Istanbul. The date is written in black and participants are mentioned together with contributors. The text changes between black and red colour. The bottom of the poster is divided with dashes like a coupon or a ticket, which can be torn down or cut. Below the dashes, it is mentioned that there would be a cocktail at the end of the meeting and RSVP is required for participation. That is why this part is separated like a flyer, which could be presented as a ticket. At the bottom line of the poster the logos of Insitut Français d'Istanbul, Goethe-Institut and Istanbul 2010 are listed representing the three cultural institutions of the three countries. The address of Insitut Français d'Istanbul is given on the bottom left corner as the host of the event. On the top of the poster it has been mentioned that the event is organized "under the auspices of Consulate General of Germany and Consulate General of France". The three institutions taking role in the event are mentioned: Insitut Français d'Istanbul on the occasion of Elysée Treaty, Goethe Institut-Istanbul and Istanbul 2010 ECoC Agency as the proposing parties. Therefore, the event is organized through the contribution of three countries on the theme of three cities: Istanbul, Paris, Berlin in literature.

2. Content

The images of the cities look like sketches on a straw coloured paper due to the background. The straw paper is used for sketching or writing that is why such colour might be chosen for the background. But the images are not sketches; they are old black and white images. We understand they are old due to the fast transformation of cities and the change in their urban texture.

Figure 37. Poster of "Istanbul – Paris – Berlin"

Source: *Istanbul 2010 Avrupa Kültür Başkenti Girişim Grubu (2011).*

New buildings have emerged around Galata Tower, so it does not look like this representation anymore. Giving an old-look to the images might be on purpose as the colour of the background turn them into sepia colour, which feels old and nostalgic. Such representation is a reference to the history.

Tower as a symbol is iconic in the urban representations. It is also metaphoric in its meanings in the literature. Galata Tower is one of the most common symbolic representations of Istanbul. We have seen the use of symbolism for Istanbul through Galata Tower on a poster in a literature event, which was the International Poetry Festival stemming from the metaphoric resemblance between the tower and the pencil. In this poster all three cities are represented through towers as their most powerful symbols. They also represent power in literature, and in history. The rich and royal families competed with each other to build the tallest tower in the city as a means of showing their power, especially in the feudal regimes of the middle ages. Today, the form of the competition has changed, which can be interpreted as the competition between the cities to have the tallest building in the global world. Maybe these towers represented on the poster, were the tallest structures of their times, yet they still remained as monumental structures and symbols of the city through their recognition worldwide. That is why the meaning of the towers is anchored between the text and the image through their representativeness of the cities.

The rest of the text is informative about the event. The event is organized at a high level of bureaucrats under the auspices of French Consulate General. Elysée Treaty represents the reconciliation and friendship between France and Germany, which was signed by The Chancellor of the Federal Republic of Germany, Dr. Konrad Adenauer, and the President of the French Republic, General de Gaulle in 1963 (Benitez, 2013). Istanbul 2010 Agency took the cultural side with two other cultural institutions representing France and Germany. In this context the text is very formal as it is a call to a diplomatic reception and it is informative about the details of the event such date and place, and the participants. However, it does not tell about the three cities. They remain only at the surface, as a representation. They are represented through the images, through the literature ambassadors (novelists), the cultural ambassadors (cultural institutions) and diplomats. It raises the expectation that these three cities are the subject of the talk and they will be talked over the literature works. The novelists Orhan Pamuk, J.-M.G. Le Clézio and Herta Müller are cited, who have won the Nobel Prize for literature. Ahmet Kot, who is the head of Directory of Literature of Istanbul 2010 Agency, is mentioned as a participant along with Harold David and Timour Muhidine.

One last thing to comment on could be the status of the cities. Since the organization of the event has diplomatic references, it should be paid attention that Paris and Berlin share the national capital city status. Istanbul is involved as the European Capital of Culture of 2010 as the whole event is designed in the framework of ECoC 2010.

- Forum Fashion Week

1. Form

When we look at the poster, we see a high-heeled woman shoe made of symbolic buildings brought together from different parts of the world. The high hill is made of Eiffel Tower standing upside down. At the bottom right corner of the poster just under the heel of the shoe, there is the logo of Forum Istanbul, which is presenting itself as the largest shopping mall in Europe. On the bottom left corner there is the logo of Istanbul 2010 together with Elle and Flash Model, the latter two representing the fashion side. The website of the event (www.forumfashionweek.com) is mentioned above the logo of Istanbul 2010. The image is separated into few parts with dashed line and little scissors to be cut into pieces like a coupon in a newspaper or a piece of cloth to be sewed. On the top of the posters "Forum Fashion Week" is written in pink colour. This is the only colour used in the poster as the rest is toned in grey. All the words are separated from each other with dashed lines. The text is placed on a diagonal axis from top left to bottom right corner. The word "week" stands in vertical position next to the words "Forum" and "Fashion" which are written one under the other. The title of the event is followed by some informative text about the event, which is in Turkish: the date, the participants and the parallel events.

2. Content

The high-heeled shoe has a strong denotation for femininity. The ladies room is represented with high heels in public places such as restaurants. The shoe is a fashionable object even it can be at a fetishist level for women. This is closely linked with the commodity fetishism in Marxist terminology. Women tend to buy objects even they will not wear or use them. That is why fashion objects have greater sign value than their use value. Just the idea of possession of that object signifies the power and status. When the incentive behind buying and/or possessing is the desire then it becomes a fetish object. This is the basic idea behind the advertisements to motivate the desires of people. The desire is provoked by the devil in the metaphoric sense (although in the middle ages it was taken literally). The image offers similarities with the poster of the film "The Devil Wears Prada", where we see a red, heeled shoe and the heel is the fork of the devil. Red is the colour of desire and fork represents the devil.

Figure 38. Poster of Forum Fashion Week

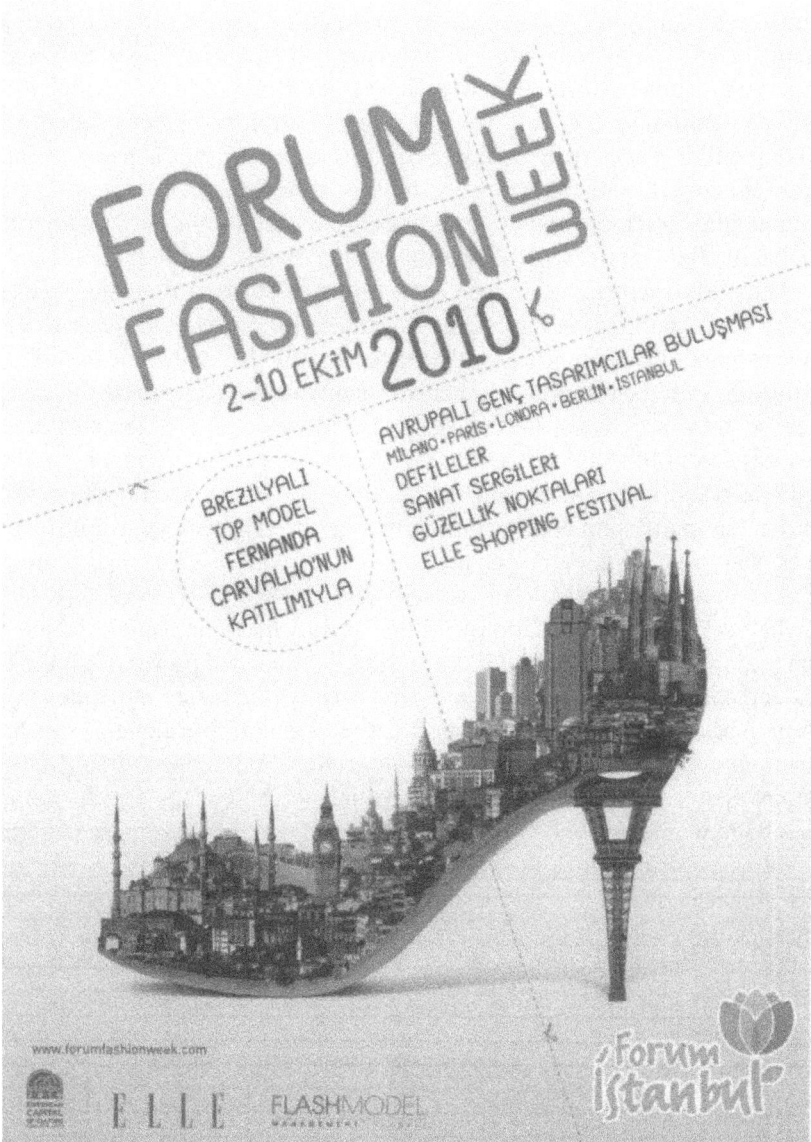

Source: Istanbul 2010 Avrupa Kültür Başkenti Girişim Grubu (2011).

In the poster of the fashion week the codes are not so salient. There is no red colour, and no fork of the devil. The shoe is rather connoted as a design object. The design can be interpreted as fashion design, while the urban texture embedded onto the shoe in which the buildings have become the elements building the show leads to the interpretation as architectural and urban design. The monumental buildings are laid on top of each other ranging from Sultanahmet Mosque to Big Ben, from Ritz Carlton Istanbul to La Sagrada Familia, from Galata Tower to Eiffel Tower, no matter what they are old or modern. They are merged into the urban fabric in the shape of a woman shoe. When we look at carefully to this urban fabric, we see that the monumental structures and tall buildings are placed on the surface on top of the macro urban fabric, which gives the feeling of the city rather than focusing on symbolic structures one by one. This type of formation also underlines the meaning of a palimpsest city as the layers are formed on top of each other. Towers and tall buildings are on the surface as the denotative meanings refer to meanings on the surface. Another comment may be they are on the surface because they are rising to the sky. The towers are visible from multi-perspectives in the city. The tall buildings carry a secondary meaning of the desire to reach God in the gothic sense, through the towers and pinnacles. It is reflected to different architectural forms in different periods, for instance it takes the form of minarets in mosques. The modern skyscrapers are tall because there is no space left in the city and the city grows vertically. But it can be also interpreted according to the orders of capitalism in which the competition for the tallest building signifies the financial power of a city. Yet, it is depicted all these structures are supported by the macro structures in the urban fabric, without the city beneath they cannot rise alone. They have meanings attributed to the cities, without New York there would not be Empire State, without Istanbul there would not be Galata Tower, without Paris there would not be Eiffel Tower and vice versa, because these structures became symbolic to the cities that they are located in.

Both the shoe and the city are represented as feminine in linguistics terms. The shoe is a woman shoe, which reinforces the meaning of female. We refer to the cities using "she" pronoun. Therefore, there are cross-references between the representation of fashion, city and the female character. The target audience of the poster are not only women or fashion lowers but also those who have interest in the city and culture. Laying the city on a woman shoe reflects an aesthetical design, but creates a chaotic urban structure at the same time. It is not a flat city. There are ups and downs. This corresponds to the description of Istanbul, it is a city of desires; it is beautiful and unique, and it is crowded and chaotic.

The qualities of Istanbul have made Istanbul attractive for visitors, therefore ranked among the fashionable places in the world, even taking its place as a "style city" in the contemporary world through fashion, design, art and architecture. Yet we see that the heel of the show is depicted with Eiffel tower alone, different from the other structures forming the shoe figure. The first is reason is the form of Eiffel Tower, which fits into the form of the heel, referring to the rule of resemblance. Another reason is more on the contextual level, as Eiffel is accepted to be the capital city of fashion it is placed as the main supporting element and it stands alone.

A last comment, which could be made, is related to the symbolic buildings representing different cities in the urban fabric presented on the shoe figure. There is the multiplicity of cities and the coexistence in this figure, therefore a cosmopolitan urban fabric is created through the multiple meanings and multi-cultural structures. While symbolic structures catch the eye of the viewer whereas they do not leave each other in the shade, they are in harmony. We can see the parallel line stretching diagonally between the minarets of Sultanahmet Mosque and the towers of Sagrada Familia. It points out a harmonious hybrid structure. As a matter of fact, Istanbul has been formed by this hybrid and multi-cultural structure through the historical accumulation of different eras ranging from Byzantian churches to Jewish synagogues and Ottoman mosques.

In sum the symbolic language of the poster offers meanings related to fashion and consumption on the surface anchoring the text, but when looked deeply underneath and to the meaning layers, it offers a rich text composed of urban and cultural signs with references to Istanbul, underlining the meaning of Istanbul as a "world city".

Chapter 5: Istanbul in between

The analysis and the findings rest on a careful reading and description of the posters. The analytical framework here is built on "city-image-spectacle" triad, while the related methodologies for each step of analysis are schematized in the Figure 39. The multi-method framework is useful in my analyses and methods complement each other. I used textual analysis (Semiotics), contextual analysis (discourse analysis), and structural analysis (thematic analysis).

The analysis demonstrates how these multiple methods are utilized towards answering the research question. The analysis of the data is conducted by applying different qualitative methods in different phases of the analysis. Therefore, firstly it is provided clarification on which method applies to which step of the analysis and how.

Figure 39. Analytical framework applied to city marketing

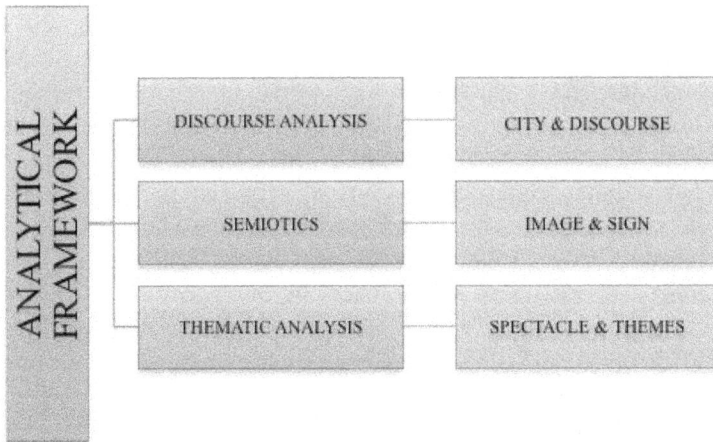

Table 7 demonstrates the threefold structure of the analysis methods according to the research objectives. It also shows which method is useful at which stage with respect to the level of analysis. Accordingly, the information and meaning derived through description of the form and interpretation of the content of the posters are done by applying semiotics and discourse analysis. This is followed by another task - building codebooks, or simply coding. Theming or thematic analysis follows coding through the application of themes to the chunks or actual texts and linking them with the conceptual and contextual framework.

Table 7. Classification of analysis methods according to the objectives

Type of analysis	Methods of analysis	Level of analysis	Objectives
Textual analysis	Semiotics	Form	Description of the signs on the denotative level
Contextual analysis	Discourse analysis	Content	Interpretation of meaning at contextual level
Structural analysis	Thematic analysis	Latent (Themes)	Discovery of the meaning units that make up a communication

Reading the cultural codes is not easy when the cultural accumulation and context of Istanbul is taken into account. Familiarization with the cultural codes, signs and discourses paves the way to step into the next level in research: selecting the appropriate tools and analysing the data.

Visual Qualitative Methods

In contemporary cultures, visual means (i.e. symbols, logos, trademarks, etc.) have become more important than ever because of "increasing reliance on visual aspects of communicative interactions and the increasing frequency with which visual metaphors are employed..." (Konecki, 2011: 131-2). Mirzoeff (1998: 4) claims the postmodern is ocularcentric due to the visually designed and constructed communicative interactions rather than the knowledge that is articulated visually. In this regard, the term visual culture tells us about how images look and how they are looked at.

When talking about brands, visual representations have indisputable importance for making the brand more communicational (Begoll, 2006: 4). The visual analysis of the images is increasingly gaining recognition by the researchers, though still rarely used in comparison to other qualitative methods based on solely text. Visual analysis has a number of advantages, depending on the aim of the research, in comparison to the observation or written or spoken speech in deciphering the relationships and interactions between the social actors and the site of the image.

Although there is a growing interest for the visual in many disciplines, image-based research has been largely overlooked even in some visual intensive fields such as marketing and advertising (Prosser, 1998; Belk, 2006). This may be explained by the lack of systematic approaches to code and categorize visual qualitative data and the high degree of subjectivity in capturing visual meanings. I mainly used both theoretical concepts and analytical methods in an effort to tackle image-based research. I also hoped to contribute to this particular field by providing a qualitative model for understanding the image-making process for places in city branding.

A qualitative in-depth analysis of the meaning expressed in a sample of posters deemed more appropriate than content analysis, a possibly useful quantitative method for theory testing. The process of image-making is critical for my analysis rather than the process of reception where a large set of data can be collected and analysed for the statistics of the audience. That is why I refrain from repeating the type of image studies done by place marketing organizations via large surveys of the perceptions of the audience. In addition, I evaluated the meaning according to context as quantitative methods might fail to offer an insightful approach (Blaxter et al., 2010: 230). As it has been stressed that a text is open to different possible readings, quantitative methods are unable to reveal the relationship between negotiated and oppositional readings (Şahin & Baloğlu, 2011: 75). According to Deacon et al. (2007: 20-1) "various approaches to textual analysis start where content analysis leaves off". Content analysis is quantitative and descriptive in its aim to "manifest content of communication" (Berelson, 1952: 18), whereas visual (textual) analysis is qualitative and usually interpretive in its aim to reveal latent meanings in some cases through questioning "what text really means" and "how meanings are organized" (Jensen, 2002: 119). The deconstruction of the text allows "to look for hidden subtexts" and "to explore deeper meanings or multiple meanings" through a good rhetoric (Bernard & Ryan, 2010: 4).

The whole idea can be explained through the study of rhetoric in its concern to reconstruct the contextual means by taking in its core that the text is created in a context by the producer in an attempt to convince the audience (Alasuutari, 1995: 95). According to Wigan (2009: 255) the behaviour can be affected by the visual impression, such as through posters. Van Leeuwen (2004: 8) coined the term "communicative act" instead of "speech act" referring to the multimodality of the posters "in which all the signs combine to determine its communicative intent". As a communicative act, branding is concerned with discursive processes determining the communicative content. The meaning is communicated through the code, which has a generally agreed meaning depending on the level of connotation (Lacey, 2009: 23-4). In some cases, the powerful subjects could impose the codes through dominating the meaning (Buck-Morss, 2004: 24). As the value of signs depends on a wider context, the code cannot be analyzed on its own as the meaning is dependent on the context and the message (Lacey, 2009: 31).

Benjamin (2002) imagines the city as a multi-layered space composed of layers of meaning to be uncovered. In this context, the meaning is an "interface between personal experiences and memories, and dominant meanings and values" (Savage & Warde, 1993: 123). Thus in the cityscapes, the texts and meanings are dispersed with codes and discourses circulating around them (Jørgensen & Phillips, 2002). Everyday meanings and practices are interconnected to the codes created in the texts and messages given by the media, inherent in the branding and imaging strategies. I show how the communication of these messages or signs creates an impact on the people's perceptions or everyday meanings.

Burn & Parker (2003: 3-5) argues that multimodality is crucial in the visual analysis of images as none of the methods are sufficient alone. The methodological tools provide "a systematic approach" and description of data to be used for analysis. Therefore, a hybrid methodology is required by the nature of data as well as selecting analytical tools that can answer research question better than a mono-method. Semiotics is a useful tool in providing the "abstract systems of codes structuring the meaning production", while the critical part of the research is the interpretation of codes. Semiotics applies to "the image itself as the most important site of meaning" (Rose, 2001: 72), while discourse analysis is used to supplement the model of analysis in order to have a more rigorous framework. Discourse analysis is helpful in investigating the meaning in Istanbul narratives and in "revealing experiential image patterns in qualitative data" (Şahin & Baloğlu, 2011). Thematic analysis is employed to analyse patterns originating from the codes and messages. The use of language and symbols is essential in creating a code system for the brand to be associated within the minds of the audience. This is the marketing function, which aims to create a standard brand language that "speaks for the brand" (Oswald, 2012: 46). Nonetheless, there is one crucial element, which is highly significant in the interpretation of brand language, in other words signs. That is the culture. The reason why the sign systems have two levels of meaning as denotation and connotation can be explained by the function of these sign systems in that specific cultural context.

Thus, the image itself, as the site where the meaning is made, and the modalities used for critical understanding of the images are crucial for the interpretation of the content and messages. The different levels of meanings could have been only interpreted through the analysis at contextual level. Therefore, it is crucial to (de)/(re)-construct the possible meanings by paying attention to the cultural context. Accordingly, the first step is the exploration and the description of the coded signs in the text through semiotic analysis. Then, the initial reading of the text is extended through shared meanings in the cultural context merging into discourse analysis. Finally, it comes evaluating the meaning by drawing meaningful patterns from the codes to the themes.

Semiotics:

"Semiology" and "Semiotics" are used interchangeably and addressed as the "science of signs". I preferred to use the term semiotics and adopted a framework used by Peirce instead of Saussure's linguistic use. Peircean semiotic tradition establishes links between the sign, the user of the sign and the object referring to the external reality. In this model, as the signifier becomes the *"representamen"*, the signified becomes *"interpretant"*. Interpretant refers to a mental concept related to the "user's cultural experience of the sign" in which the meaning is dependent on the reader, therefore it is not fixed (Crow, 2010: 23). Berger (2004) notes that the arbitrariness of the relationship between signifier and signified lead to variety in meaning. In other words, signs can mean anything we agree that they mean, and they can mean different things to different people.

The focus of the analysis is neither the intended meanings by the producer, nor the perceived meanings by the audience. It is what the text signifies and communicates along with the discourses of Istanbul 2010 with respect to city imaging. Accordingly, the object of semiotics is the sign, not the phenomenal real, as Magritte[1] suggests (Torczyner, 1977: 71). While analysing the posters visually, my intention is not judging the quality of the images according to aesthetic criteria. The objective is to figure out what the images tell about the city, based on what type of discourses and sign systems. That is why semiotics is an essential tool in understanding how the signs transfer meanings within the image or through complex systems of urban, social, cultural, political and ideological contexts (Rose, 2001; Vanolo, 2008). Semiotics works towards "the appreciation of the text that reshape accepted ideas and at the same time reacting against the manipulative exploitation of received opinion" (Scholes, 1982: 14). Text is not only recognized as words and linguistic elements but the "text" as defined in media studies: any object (artefact) that contains information (Lacey, 2009: 14). Thus the analysis identifies the structural components of the text, and investigates how they communicate the message. Scholes (1982: 15-16) identifies a text as "open, incomplete and insufficient" that assigns the analyst "to speculate about what went on before the decision to stop writing, and what might have gone afterward..." The analytical model draws the relationship between the design elements and the meaning in text. This attempt is towards looking beyond the visible meanings on the surface and unravelling the second meanings with respect to the cultural codes and social means.

In this framework, the object of analysis is text. Text refers to any object that contains information (Lacey, 2009: 14). It is not solely a written material. It may take the form of an image or a combination of words and images as in the case of posters, chosen for this research. The message is embedded in a social situation, which is called context (Lacey, 2009: 27). Context is crucial in "understanding and explaining the impact of the various texts" (Wodak,

---

[1] *"Ceci n'est pas une pipe":* French for "This is not a pipe"

2006: 5). Contact, on the other hand, refers to the channel of communication, in other words "the medium used to convey the message". McLuhan (1964) states, "the medium is the message", which can be regarded as a simplistic point of view for the communication process. Nevertheless, it clearly illustrates the manner in the reception of information affected by the medium in translating the meaning of the message (Lacey, 2009: 28). Message is the information sent by the addresser to the addressee, although the message could be interpreted differently by the receiver than the intended meaning by the sender.

Moreover, cultural background makes a difference in the reception of messages and interpretation of the images (Short, 2012: 42). City image is subjective. Therefore, it changes from one person to another. There is difference between a person who is born into the culture of a city and an outsider who views that city as the collective symbols and memories (Schweitzer et al., 1999). Barthes (1977: 26-7) suggests the amplification of text to the image that the message given by the text loads the image with culture and imagination or in some cases producing a new signified through imagination. It is the same for media texts or for any kind of text produced no matter what the context is (Deacon et al., 2007: 145-6).

Lévi-Strauss has originated the term floating signifier in the 1950s to denote signifiers without referents, in other words signifiers that do not have agreed meanings or that do not refer to any actual object (Lechte 1994, 26-7, 64, 73). Barthes (1977: 39) suggests especially non-linguistic signs as such. They are so open to interpretation leading to floating chain of signifiers. The polysemous character of the images make them open to interpretation, in which the viewers can choose some floating signifiers with a connoted cultural meaning and ignore other (Wetherell et al., 2001: 788-9). The nodal point refers to the sign around which a given discourse is organized. When the sign is open to different meanings it takes the name "floating signifier", which become the "object for struggle between discourses for the attribution of meaning" (Laclau and Mouffe, 1985: 113).

In case the floating signifiers refer to a space of representation, the mental construction of the imagined space might be influenced by the myths. The myth can be understood as "a principle of reading of a given situation, which bears no relation of continuity with the dominant structural objectivity" (Laclau, 1990: 61). Therefore, myth is recognized as "a form of ideology", in the second order semiological system (Barthes, 1975: 123) that builds upon denotative signs. Jung (1964) explains it through what he calls as archetypes: "arche" in Greek signifies "beginning, origin, cause, primal source principle"; it also signifies "position of a leader, supreme rule and government" (in other words a kind of "dominant"): "type" means "blow and what is produced by a

blow, the imprint of a coin ...form, image, prototype, model, order, and norm",
or in the figurative, modern sense, "pattern underlying form, primordial form"
(Stevens, 2003). In this framework, myths can be interpreted through a "broad
understanding of a culture's dynamics" (Rose, 2001: 91). Recognizing the
recurring patterns in myths and the way in which the meaning unfolds shape
our understanding of contemporary cultures.

Symbols are contextually significant as they allow the emergence of
themes (Whitmont, 1969). The role of symbols is vital to the individual and
collective imagery in two ways: "attracting all with whom they come into
contact, and awakening them to the heritage of the collective unconscious"
(Ryan, 2002: 80). Lacan's orders of "symbolic" and "imaginary" may be
aligned with Jung's archetypal theory. According to Lacanian theory "the
symbolic order patterns the contents of the imaginary" (Samuels, 1985: 40).

In this context, the methodology works beyond the interpretation of
compositional elements in the image. Therefore, it is not simply descriptive.
The visual interpretation takes place at two levels: the signs on the surface,
such as images, words, fonts, colours create a brand image or brand
personality for the product, whereas there are hidden meanings at the
underlying level interpreted by the audience (Beasley, 2002). Cobley & Jansz
(2010: 24) mention three kinds of interpretants employed by Peirce: the
immediate one corresponds to the "correct understanding of the sign", the
second one, which is dynamic, is the "direct result of the sign" and the last
one, the final interpretant, is given as the rare result of a sign. In this research,
the immediate intrepretant corresponds to the signs at the denotative level.
The dynamic interpretant reveals the dynamic relationship between the
signifier and the signified, while the final interpretant specifies the signified
through the given codes in the context. Accordingly, the description of the
posters enables the researcher to talk about immediate interpretants leading to
more meanings to be produced through dynamic and final interpretants at the
connotative level. From this point of view, interpretative research plays a vital
role for the analysis of the visual signs, as Peirce (1965 [1931]) argues "the
socially available semiosis contains all of the available possible worlds at a
given moment and in a given society". The case of Istanbul ECoC 2010
constitutes a good basis for the contextual framework of the methods to be
tapped "at a given moment and in a given society" as stressed in this
argument.

Barthes (1977) identifies three levels of messages: "the linguistic (the few
recognizable words in the ad), the denoted image (exactly what has been
photographed), and the connotative image". The meanings at the denotative
level are innocent and factual meanings irrespective of the cultural
background of the reader whereas the meanings at the connotative level refer

to the culturally assigned meanings (Barthes, 1967). Duncan & Duncan (1992) stress the role of underlying structure of the text in determining function of the text and the plurality of the meaning in cultural texts (Duncan & Duncan, 1992). Hall (1980: 112) describes this situation in advertising practice: *"Every visual sign in advertising connotes a quality, situation, value or inference, which is present as an implication or implied meaning, depending on the connotational positioning."*

Hall (1980) analysed the image formation process through the communication model of encoding/decoding, which draws beyond information sources and draw links between the possible meanings through a semiotic analysis. The semiotic analysis is interested in the communication model not only in terms of transmission of messages between the sender and receiver but in terms of interpretation of the signs and how the meaning is created. Thus, it disregards the belief that consumers passively consume places according to the dominant messages. On the contrary they are actively reading the messages and making the meaning, which in the end affect their perceptions, choices and decisions (Lacey, 2009: 14). The consumption takes place when we take the sign for what it signifies. According to critical marketing theory what is consumed is not the product but its image in the sense of meanings of the images and signs based on a code system of consumption (Goldman, 1992).

Hall (1980: 107) demonstrates the communication as a circular process of production, circulation, distribution/consumption, reproduction, which are connected to each other and each represents a single moment in the whole circle. In the communication process, the product is defined as the "message". For a message to be meaningful or effective, it needs to be meaningfully decoded. Hall (1980: 109) puts it this way: *"It is this set of decoded meanings which 'have an effect', influence, entertain, instruct or persuade, with very complex perceptual, cognitive, emotional, ideological or behavioural consequences."*

In this framework, the codes operate as "a set of practices familiar to users" by creating meaningful systems and making discourses intelligible (Hall, 1980: 131). Codes are helpful in "limiting the range of possible meanings" (Turner, 1992: 17). Thus, they make it easier to interpret the signs by "simplifying the phenomena" (Gombrich, 1982: 35). The key is pinning down the most appropriate signified for a certain signifier and thus identifying the relevant codes for making the sense of the text as a whole.

Hall (1980: 134) explains this by the transformation of the sign into a multiple "connotative configurations". There is the "dominant cultural order" in a society, which is formed by dominant or preferred meanings shared among the community members. Signs are transferred through codes in the "wider structures of meaning" that takes the form of "dominant codes, ideologies, myths or referent systems" (Rose, 2001: 92, 99). The meaning making process and the way we view the world is influenced by the categorizations, ideologies and myths.

Figure 40. Encoding/Decoding messages

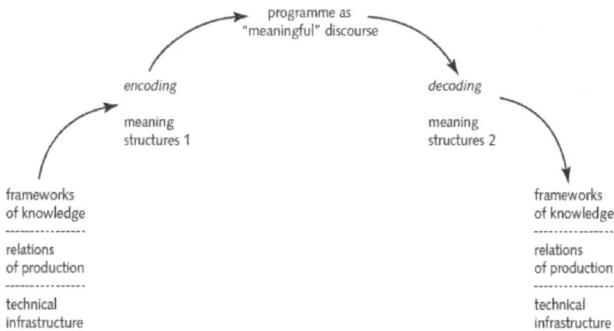

Source: Hall (1980)[2]

Evans & Hall (1999: 1) assert that much of the cultural and media studies rest upon theoretical works of Barthes, Benjamin, Baudrillard and Foucault and their concerns for the visual varying from "spectacle", "reproduction of the image", "simulacrum", and "politics of representation". The city is represented through "image and text" (Barthes, 1977) in the realms of discourse and practice. The meanings are constructed through "discourses, symbols, metaphors and fantasies" (Hubbard, 2006: 59-60). Studies of meaning evolve from semiotics with an effort to interpret messages through signs and patterns of symbolism. When interpreting the semiotic construction of the social reality, the cultural codes are important as they are the keys to the production, dissemination and manipulation of the meanings attached. In this framework, the study opposes to the unlimited semiosis (not in the theory but in the practice of my analysis here) as Eco (1976, 68–9) suggested, because the meanings are tied to the relationship between knowledge and power in the formation of the discourse.

Discourse Analysis:

Discourse is defined, in Foucauldian terms, as "an entity of sequences, of signs, in that they are enouncements (*énoncés*)" (Foucault, 1972). The enouncement in this definition refers to the statement as an abstract construct

---

[2] 'Encoding/Decoding' / originally published as 'Encoding and Decoding in Television Discourse' in 1973.

of linkages between (and among) objects, subjects through sign language but not only in the sense of a unit of semiotic signs. Therefore, the discursive formation describes the communication process to produce discourses highly influenced by power and knowledge.

Discourse analysis can be explained, in its simplest form, as the analysis of meaning patterns (Jørgensen & Phillips, 2002: 12). Discourse analysis involves an "analysis of the ways in which discourses constitute the social world" (Mason, 2006). Fairclough (2005) suggests that the term "discourse" designates semiotic elements, what he calls as "semiosis" while as a second meaning to discourse. He proposes "a category for designating particular ways of representing particular aspects of social life" (Fairclough, 2005).

Fairclough (2001: 122) underlines the "social means" in production and defines the practices of production with respect to productive activity, means of production, social relations, social identities, cultural values, consciousness and semiosis. According to Fairclough (2011), the social structures create shared codes in the form of norms that are dominant in the society and cannot be broken by single individuals but only society and time. Advertising and communication are framed according to these rules for their messages to be understood correctly but also they break away from the norms in an attempt to be more provocative and interesting, therefore more striking (Leach, 2005: 126). According to Rose (2001: 6) "images offer views to the world" as they reflect a position and convey a message, and/or impose a meaning. On the other hand, images are never innocent as "they are never transparent windows on to the world" (Rose, 2001: 2).

Kress and van Leeuwen (2001) comment on the signification, which is influenced by production-reproduction-interpretation processes. There are four strata defined by Kress and van Leeuwen (2001) in an attempt to explain the system of signification. According to their definition discourse is "knowledge of reality" in which every single sign in the text is a part of. The discursive context might be different from the context that the text is produced. The "choice of mode" whether the text is written or visual refers to the design of the text, while "choice of medium" refers to the production. Lastly, they mention distribution, which has become hard to distinguish from production and design in the digitalized media world (Burn & Parker, 2003: 7-8).

Cook (2001) describes advertising as a discourse itself in terms of both text (the ad itself) and context (based on the shared knowledge, needs, desires, imaginaries, narratives and discourses that the audience respond to meanings created by the ad). According to Holloway (2004: 265) the aim of an advertisement is "to inform, to persuade and to remind", in accordance with the AIDA principle in marketing, which is "attracting Attention, creating

Interest, fostering Desire and inspiring Action". Therefore, advertisement is recognized as a form of communication aimed at "convincing people to buy" (Berger, 2004: 71). Levin shows us in his video work[3] that images create messages aimed at consumption. In this context, the city imaging encourages us to "buy" through positive and attractive images, which is defined in a broad fashion through "city selling" concept (Ashworth & Voogd, 1990). Nevertheless, the "consumed" is not the city itself but its image; it is the perception, and eventually it is the experience. Advertisers use subliminal messages in order to affect on the subconscious world of the consumers. The subliminal messages are buried in the message, therefore cannot be perceived right away by the conscious mind.

The production of symbols is related to meta-language while interpretation of symbols is linked to social interaction process (Albayrak & Suerdem, 2008). The scope of analyses here is limited to the "text or discourse immanent critique", which implies to "a detailed text analysis on all levels of discourse" (Wodak, 2006: 8-9). The social and political goals and functions of discursive practices or the change of behaviour/action, transformation are beyond the scope of this book and requires audience analysis. Critical social scientists might have concerns directed towards "being too close to the text [...]" or "too distant, out of fear of being accused of being 'too subjective' or 'too political" (Wodak 2005). Nevertheless, Critical Discourse Analysis (CDA) should go further than a pure deconstruction of meaning in the text and should evaluate the contents more than giving description (Wodak, 2006: 11-2).

The steps involved in a critical research start with the deconstruction of complexity and uncovering the contradictory readings. Following the interpretation of the meanings; alternative meanings, "possibly subversive and innovative meanings" are created (Wodak, 2006: 12). Fairclough (1995: 59) proposes a three dimensional framework for CDA with an aim to investigate "social situations in which texts are produced and consumed and social processes at large (Jensen, 2002: 106). The text is at the core as the object of analysis at the micro level. The analysis of discursive practice develops around the text. Lastly, social practice is investigated through socio-historical conditions and the framework to capture broader meanings as the macro-level analysis (Fairclough & Wodak, 1997: 258). Although the three dimensional model for analysis (see Fig. 41) introduced by Fairclough (1995: 59) has been influential, it is criticized by Hodge (2012: 6) that "meanings at

---

[3] Exhibition: Video Vintage, Centre Pompidou Paris - Survey of video art from 1963 to 1983 in the Centre Pompidou. The selection includes 70 video works by about fifty artists such as Vito Acconci, Sonia Andrade, Samuel Beckett, Les Levine, Bruce Nauman, Nam June Paik (8-02-2012 to 7-05-2012)
*Notes taken by the author, 08.02.2012, Paris.

levels above the text will come only from the prejudices of the analyst", thus higher level meanings require a more extensive model. I kept the analysis at the micro-level only. The scope of analysis is not extended to meso and macro levels of discursive and social practice as these two levels are beyond the focus and the scope.

Apart from the above-mentioned concerns, CDA has been mainly used for linguistic analysis of texts. Kress & Van Leeuwen (2001) can be cited among the scholars who introduced the visual analysis to CDA, therefore providing a multi-modal framework (Wetherell et al., 2001: 779-780).

Figure 41. Three dimensional framework for CDA

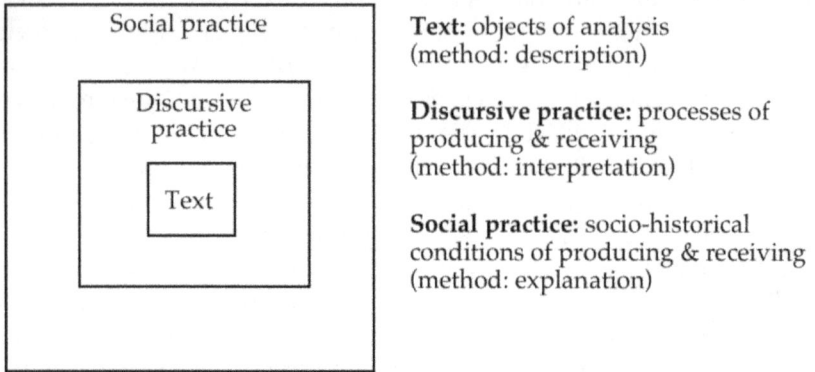

| Social practice |
| Discursive practice |
| Text |

Text: objects of analysis (method: description)

Discursive practice: processes of producing & receiving (method: interpretation)

Social practice: socio-historical conditions of producing & receiving (method: explanation)

Source: Fairclough (1995: 59)

Fairclough's (1992) concepts of interdiscursivity and intertextuality appear to be key concepts in understanding the way that meanings are attributed. Intertextuality points the meanings carried by more than a single text (Rose, 2001: 136), while interdiscursivity refers to "how a text is constituted by a combination of other language conventions (genres, discourses and styles)" (Wu, 2011: 97-9). Interdiscursivity is adapted to advertising by pointing out "ever-increasing use of multi-media, explosion of information technology, multi-disciplinary contexts of the world of work, increasingly competitive professional (academic as well as business) environment, and the overwhelmingly compulsive nature of promotional and advertising activities" (Wu, 2011: 102).

The discourses defined under the strategic objectives of ECoC 2010 denote the power relations and the meanings behind. The image and discourses are the tools of city marketing communication produced and used by global and local actors. The social dimension is taken under consideration only through context defining the production of images and the shared meanings in the society. In the case of ECoC, EU has a cultural agenda functioning for "improving mutual knowledge among Europeans..." (Morley

& Robins, 1995: 3). In this context ECoC can be thought of a cultural tool as well as a political and promotional tool. The analytical part of the research is designed in with an aim to find answers to the questions such as "what discourses are present for ECOC 2010" in the selected posters. The answer is sought to the main question in defining the effects of discourses created and used by Istanbul 2010 in the posters.

Thematic Analysis

The conceptual tools are useful in classifying and comparing the essential features of the phenomena under investigation (Dey, 2005: 100). The qualitative information provided by the examination of form and content of the posters has been useful for familiarizing with the data and generating initial codes. Yet, explicit codes are necessary in order to organize our data to identify and develop themes. This may be a list of themes that follow a "pattern found in the information that at minimum describes and organizes the possible observations and at maximum interprets aspects of the phenomenon" (Boyatzis, 1998: 4). The interpretation of the data adheres to the "hermeneutical procedures of context definition, the construction of patterned similarities and differences, and the use of relevant social and material culture theory" (Denzin & Lincoln, 1998: 127). We can start with identifying pure forms on the first layer of the image. The "conventional stratum consisted of symbolic or 'coded' meanings" lays at the second layer (Howells, 2009: 123).

Reading is an interaction between the text and the reader. In this process, there are different stages such as decoding, responding, comprehending, critiquing and analysing (Walsh, 2006). The meaning does not only occur in one specific text but within a number of contexts including "the genre and purpose of the text as well as the interest and purpose of the reader", thus both production and reception sites (Walsh, 2006: 25). Systems of meaning are analyzed by looking at cultural and communication products and events as signs, and then by looking at the relationship among these signs. Thus, it is essential for this research that the researcher is conscious about cultural messages and language used in the images to be able to interpret the meanings. As a native to Istanbul, my role as a researcher plays a key role in the analysis and contributes to the value of the research. Bernard & Ryan (2010: 257) stress the importance of familiarity with the language and local culture for hermeneutic analysis, which otherwise would result in lack of capability to see the "connections among symbols". The social conditions and cultural practices are recognized as effective factors both shaping and being shaped by social inclusions and exclusions. The cultural meanings produced by those practices and processes need to be addressed by critical approach.

Visual codes:

The angle, the perspective and the proximity are influential in an image for the perception of the object in focus. For instance, close-ups allow a more intimate relationship, while being able to show only a part of it not in full body by re-framing and attracting the attention to some parts if the object is not so small (Kress & van Leeuwen, 2006). The panoramic photos are taken from a distance to show a wide area the relationship of the object between its surroundings.

When we look at the signs through a deconstructivist approach we can understand the relationship between the signifier and the signified in the image. Minarets, mosques and Topkapı Palace being the signifiers that connote historicism and orientalism as the silhouette image can be associated with the Western gaze. In the past, the first look to Istanbul was taken from the same angle by the Westerners arriving to the city by the sea. The ferryboats are still important means of public transportation in everyday life. On the other side, the ferries connote the geographic crossing between Asia and Europe or crossing the Bosphorus. Topkapı Palace, Hagia Sophia and the whole skyline stands for a representation of the past world with connotations to the city's imperial power.

There are different opinions among scholars, who appraise different sorts of modality. Some pay attention to the compositional parts whereas others are concerned in the social effects of an image's meaning, thus pay attention to the social modality. Kress and van Leeuwen (2006: 177) argue that compositional elements such as colour, size, perspective as well as cultural factors are effective on the "salience" of the image to attract viewers' attention. According to Scollon & Scollon (2003: 91), socio-cultural context is more effective than the technical features of the image; in fact, what is in the image and to what extend it represents the reality depends on the viewers' interpretation affected by context, society and culture. It should be noted that texts offer new texts "by linking different subtexts, images, symbols, icons and pictures to each other" (Wodak, 2006: 3). According to Wodak (2006: 3) this leads to a "heteroglossia" in the Bakhtinean sense where a mixture of voices is combined through hypertexts, introduced into the concept of "hyper modality".

Kress & van Leeuwen (2006) argue that producers aim to create a mental image that the viewers make sense of the text. The shared codes and meanings are effective in the communication and understanding of the messages. The compositional features of the image are shaped by the social values in the perception of intended meanings. The close-ups or long shots have different effects according to the intimacy and social relations. Horizontal or vertical angles affect on the level of the involvement of the audience. The position of the camera and angle represents the relation of power, in which the high angle stands for higher rank. The colour elements such as contrast, hue, saturation, and brightness mark the truthfulness of the images. Advertising often uses bright colours, which reduces the credibility but increases the attractiveness of the images. All of these aspects are coded within the image by the producer. Nevertheless, it should be noted that the receiver has his/her own individual way of perception and a socio-cultural background and may respond differently to the images than the intended meaning.

From Codes to Themes...

There are several approaches to the coding process. When the researcher holds a theory and formulates the indicators of evidence to support this theory, it is called "theory driven coding". Coding can also be done by using the secondary data and knowledge, which are available through the prior researches. However, this type of "research driven coding" requires inter-rater reliability due to the direct use of ready made codes. The research might be inductive in its approach towards drawing on the meanings in "data driven coding". Codes are provided through the interpretation of each single unit of data analysed (Kawulich, 2004: 99).

Coding is a crucial step in qualitative analysis, followed by developing themes within the raw data, which may include taking frequencies, identifying co-occurrence and displaying relationships within and between the groups of codes. In my analyses, the codes were listed on an Excel sheet in order to search for a pattern between them by counting the frequency of each code. This was done by "COUNTIF" function in Excel and not by "FREQUENCY", because the data is not coded as numbers but words (such as culture, history, heritage, city, mosque, bridge, etc.).

Table 8. Frequency of codes

Keywords	Frequency (f)	Keywords	Frequency (f)
Istanbul	25	Modern	8
Culture	18	Heritage	7
History	16	Spectacle	7
Monument	15	Nostalgia	5
City	15	Bridge	4

As shown in Table 8, the name "Istanbul" appeared very frequently in the posters. It is either coded as a word in the verbal text or represented through iconic symbols, synecdoche images and/or panoramic views. The total number of posters included in the analysis is 32. Thus, 25 stands for a high frequency value, which means that a large share of the posters speak about Istanbul. The second most frequent code appearing in the posters is "culture", which is identified in more than half of the posters. Since the ECoC event has a focus on culture, cities showcase their cultural assets and they brand themselves through cultural events.

Calculating the frequency of occurrence helps the researcher to spot repeating ideas. However, the codes with the highest frequency rates should not be understood as a sign of prevalence. It is important to pay attention how codes combine to form over-reaching themes in the data with an aim of focusing on broader patterns and integrating coded data with proposed themes.

Dey (2005: 45-47) approaches to categorization as a "method of funnelling the data" through "breaking up data & bringing it together again" and "laying down the conceptual foundations for analysis". Classifying the codes into the thematic groups provides "practical reasoning" and a reasonable "basis for comparison. Redefining categories allows a more rigorous conceptualization, which should be "guided by research objectives" (Dey, 2005: 47).

Coding is described to be a heuristic[4] and an exploratory process leading the researcher "from the data to the idea, and from the idea to all the data pertaining to that idea" (Richards & Morse, 2007: 137). Therefore coding is not just the act of labelling but also linking the ideas. The process of coding data includes looking for patterns and themes. It is important to identify patterns and to group the data accordingly, because this is what gives the theory specificity (Kawulich, 2004: 99). De Santis & Ugarriza (2000: 362) defined a theme as "an abstract entity that brings meaning and identity to a recurrent experience and its variant manifestations". Interpretative analysis of texts is interested in finding out how they are related to one another (Bernard & Ryan, 2010: 4). Bernard & Ryan (2010: 54) note that analysing texts involves:

1. Discovering themes and sub-themes
2. Describing the core and peripheral elements of themes
3. Building hierarchies of themes or codebooks
4. Applying themes – attaching them to chunks of actual texts
5. Linking themes into theoretical models

For the first stage - discovering the themes - a comprehensive technique is applied by looking at both the form and the content of the posters. The patterns related to the form such as colour or compositional elements are given through the description of the posters. The sub-themes and deeper meanings are investigated through the content by using an interpretive approach. This can be thought of a familiarization process of the researcher with the data and

---

[4] heuriskein (ancient Greek) and heurisricus (Latin): "to find out, discover" (Romanycia & Pelletier, 1985: 48)

preparing the raw information for coding, which can be simply called as the transcription of the data. The challenge lies at "drawing the richness of the themes from the raw information without reducing the insights (Boyatzis, 1998: 14). The process of transcribing the form and the content of the data is a crucial step.

Although the emphasis is on the image in the posters in order to attract the attention of the viewer and to convey the message visually, the main objective of the posters is giving information about the event or product, which is the goal of advertising. The posters fulfil the main function of informing the public and at the same time they focus on the Istanbul images and symbolic representations to a large extent. Yet the symbolic representation cannot go beyond being only a cliché in most of the cases. Istanbul silhouette, Galata Tower, Maiden's Tower, Bosphorus Bridge, mosques and minarets, churches and cross have become cliché symbols for the Istanbul representations. Birds, water and waterfront, sky, sunset and sunrise are also usual depictions.

The silhouette is one of the most frequently used images when we evaluate the posters on the basis of the selected sample and/or perhaps even throughout the population of posters used in Istanbul 2010. The silhouette of Istanbul has become a cliché image, but on the other hand has gained brand value by being the visual icon of the city through the promotional campaign of Istanbul 2010. The silhouette image either takes the form of a photographic image, generally depicted in the sunset, or a graphic and iconic image. No matter what the situation is, both of the cases offer symbolic meanings as the emblem of Istanbul.

Galata Tower is another example to the most frequently used images together with the silhouette, as a part of the silhouette or alone itself. Galata Tower, which is one of the leading symbols for multicultural heritage of Istanbul, has become a synonym to Eiffel Tower symbolically. Towers are prone to be symbols of the cities in the form of synecdoche representations (representativeness of the whole through focusing on the parts). Towers are also visible structures through different perspectives "in" the city. Therefore, they offer a powerful urban imagery. They are not only effective signifiers through their physical features but also they propose different meanings based on metaphors. If we remember of the poster of International Poetry Festival, Galata Tower is represented as a pen composed of letters. This kind of representation is based on resemblance in the form of appearance (Langer, 1951: 67). Moreover, phallic meanings are associated with towers at connotational level. Towers have become symbols of power in the feudal system of the middle ages, when the rich and powerful families competed to erect the tallest tower in the city as a sign of power. In today's globalized world, cities are competing with each other to have the tallest building as a sign of capitalist power. The new high-rise buildings are added to the city skyline coupling with the historical tall buildings. Another reason why towers are symbolic is because they are tall. Towers are the places to look at the cities from above, to have the panoramic view of the city. In a similar vein, most of the posters give a panoramic portrait of the city either offering a silhouette from afar or a bird's-eye shot from above. This is one of the most usual types in touristic representations with an aim of imaging the city as a whole rather than focusing on one single frame. Viewing the city from afar and above represents the depictions of Istanbul and its silhouette like the engravings of the 19th century on one side, and tautological images commonly used in place branding on the other. The city dumps, non-places, poverty and crime are neglected, while the city is presented by its positive images to attract people.

The analysis results are summarized according to the themes, which are found to be following meaningful patterns. The themes appear into 3 categories by drawing parallelism with the triad of spectacle-city-image, which has been used in the structure of conceptual and contextual framework of this research. The spectacle is linked to cultural consumption where the cityscapes become the theatre decor. The urban transformation can be read through the historical monuments symbolizing the city. This is the second category, which is exemplified through the slogan of rediscover. The city image is explained through the contrasts portraying Istanbul as a city in-between (East-West, old-contemporary, etc.). The sub-themes and deeper meanings are also discussed under these categories:

1. The spectacularization of culture: "The stage is yours Istanbul"
2. Transformation of the city from past to present: "Now is the time to Rediscover!"
3. The dialectics of city imaging: Istanbul in between...

Table 9 indicates which stratum has a direct link with which thematic category in accordance with the theoretical concepts. These categories also comply with the strata, which were defined before for the classification of the second data set of the posters. As presented earlier, Istanbul 2010 put the emphasis on three areas: "tourism and promotion", "urban transformation" and lastly "culture and arts" (Istanbul 2010 ECoC Agency, 2011: 13). If we evaluate the images on a thematic basis with respect to these sub-groups (strata), each stratum can be assigned to one of the thematic categories inferred from the analysis. Art and culture apply to the theme of spectacle, urban transformation applies to the theme of rediscovering the discourses on the city from past to present, and lastly tourism and promotion apply to the theme of marketing the city image through a dialectic discussion of unity and fragmentation.

Table 9. Thematic categories and subthemes

Theoretical concepts	Brand & Image	Spectacle	City
Strata	Tourism & promotion	Culture and Arts	Urban Transformation
Themes	The dialectics of city imaging: Istanbul in between...	The spectacularization of culture: "The stage is yours Istanbul"	Transformation of the city from past to present: "Now is the time to Rediscover!"
Subthemes	Patterns: silhouette, domes & minarets, dynamism, continuity, change, collective memory	Patterns: commodity fetish, theatricality, authenticity, standardization, art, culture, mobility	Patterns: bridge, diversity, cosmopolitan, tolerant globalization, self-orientalism, monument, heritage
	Contrasts: Orient/ Occident new/ old past/ contemporary continuous/ discontinuous destruction/ reconstruction	Utterances: "Inspiring city" "A city of four elements"	Utterances: "Diver-city" "Palimpsest city" "Meeting point between East & West" "Mosaic of cultures" "Cradle of civilizations"
	Symbols: - synecdoche: silhouette, Galata, water/waterfront - totalizing : panorama, bird-eye - metaphor	Denomination: projected city cool city creative city contemporary metropolis	Denomination: Capital city European city World city global city

Furthermore, no matter which category they belong to, some posters of the events are different from the rest in their design and in their intended meanings. The posters of continuous events such as festivals can be given as example. IfIstanbul, for instance, has been held since 2002 and it is expanding with the participation of other cities (Ankara and Izmir). IfIstanbul has a different cultural agenda and concept than Istanbul 2010. These kinds of posters were intended to promote the event rather than focusing on the image of Istanbul and promoting the city. On the other hand, if we think they are not one-time events and they are continuous, their aggregated impact could be greater in making the image of Istanbul. Also it should be taken into consideration that they are international events, promoting the city to a wide audience, plus they have a certain target audience who has become frequenter of the event.

In this framework, the posters in each group have diverse characteristics. Their meanings are shaped according to the patterns drawing upon the common and different meanings within and between the groups. Defining the strata for data and adopting the thematic groups for analysis adhered to the programme catalogue of Istanbul 2010 projects is found to be appropriate and consistent in order to infer meanings based on the group characteristics.

On the other hand, sometimes the lines separating the categories and meanings as the lines separating past and present becomes blurred, since the links cannot be separated from each other with sharp lines. That is why the themes should form clear patterns to avoid a significant amount of overlap. The important point in answering the research question is to identify how the themes fit together and convey a story about data set. The study takes data-driven inductive approach of Boyatzis (1998) by drawing upon the recurring themes in the posters. The themes are incorporated through deductive approach into its structure with the information available from conceptual and contextual framework. Now, we will look closely at the themes identified into three categories.

Thematic Categories

1. The spectacularization of culture: "The stage is yours Istanbul"

This category is about the spectacle; in other words, it concentrates on the meanings created by ECoC as an example of mega-event. The spectacularization of the culture refers to the critical theory on consumer culture, in which the culture becomes the commodified object represented through the mechanisms of the spectacle. In this respect, Istanbul 2010 is the stage for the materialization of the discourses directed towards the cultural production, which turns commodity fetish into romanticized images and/or phantasmagorias of the Istanbul myth. Istanbul is presented to the world with its historical landmarks as a symbol of the rich culture and history. The restoration projects are paid a greater attention under the programme of Istanbul 2010 in an urge to revitalize the image of Istanbul through the monuments of the glorious past of the imperial capital. The imperial identity is still visible in its monuments that have reached today. However, the preservation of the past and the imaging strategies accompanying these practices only led to creation of floating chain of signifiers. What does heritage represent for the inhabitants of Istanbul, what does it represent for the Europeans? How much did the posters tell us about our own heritage, how much did they tell to the Europeans about the common heritage? Whose heritage is this and to whom it is signified, through which signs? What is the meaning of all this as a matter of imagined and lived space?

Culture and heritage appear as a common theme in the posters. Heritage sites and historical landmarks, which are shown abundantly in the images created for Istanbul 2010 event prove that. Even one of the posters that belongs to the exhibition is entitled "Heritage". If we extend the meaning of heritage, we can find similar patterns throughout the cultural representations of Istanbul. One of the themes is "mosaic of cultures". The ancestors of the city have left their marks in the built environment, which is still full of signifiers rendering the history to the contemporary everyday life, maybe in the most interactive way. Istanbul has been the capital of three empires hosting different nationalities, different ethnicities, and different religions which contributed making Istanbul a "cosmopolitan" city. The image of Istanbul as a cosmopolitan city is represented through churches, mosques and synagogues side by side. This refers to what Istanbul was once, perhaps until the end of the Ottoman Empire. Nevertheless, today's Istanbul is predominantly Muslim and Turkish along with the diminishing minority groups and increasing numbers of refugees and immigrants mostly from the Middle East. The minorities, refugees, and undocumented migrants however do not find their way onto the marketing plans. They are better kept out of sight. The lived space and the imagined one (imposed by the promotional campaign) contradict in this regard.

Whereas, multi-cultural urban structure of Sulukule has attracted the attention of Istanbul 2010 Agency as a part of Istanbul image. The cultural accumulation and Romani traditional music are represented by a colourful rainbow erupting from a volcano on the poster. The eruption is also a sign of energy diffusing into different colours in the light spectrum. Colourful elements of Istanbul images are transformed into monochrome and standard images under the effect of globalization and governmental politics. In this respect, Istanbul becomes a battlefield of the clash between the differences and homogenizing urban development processes through "over-imposed visions". The colourful image of Sulukule is trapped in colourless TOKI (housing estates) in the real urban life through urban evacuation. There is a constant and rapid urban transformation. However, this transformation takes place according to the ideological frameworks of the ruling government, yet with a lack of planning. The urbanization has been criticized for massive destructions and erasing the traces of the past and memory of the city. This increases the contradiction between the lived space and imagined space.

One of the dominant discourses for Istanbul is "the meeting point between East and West" symbolized through the Bosphorus Bridge connecting Asia and Europe. The pervasive use of the image of the Bosphorus Bridge in Istanbul representations supports this discourse. On the other hand, according to Yüksek (2011: 57) any bridge built on the Bosphorus separates the two shores from each other and alienates to each other instead of bringing them closer. Simmel (1994) proposes that the objects need to be separated in order to come together and create an interaction through the concepts "bridge and door". Bridge has a representational value not only because of its function connecting the two different sides that are separate from each other but also because of making this relationship visible. The meaning of bridging is extended into global networking; therefore, it does not have only two ends.

The messages communicated by the posters are parallel to the discourse streamlines such as "meeting of civilizations", "cultural bridge-cultural dialogue", "cultural richness" through the representations of historic, cosmopolitan and palimpsest city. Some of the posters such as "Palimpsest Istanbul", "Ghost Buildings" and/or "Istanbul 1910-2010" were intended to draw the attention to the lost meanings that are not allowed to pass through the layers of history.

Accordingly, the lived space transforms itself into imagined space as the urban cultural assets and the cityscapes are transforming into a theatre decor marketed to spectators. On the other hand, the real city opposed to the imagined city is no more livable for the locals, who suffer the everyday life, overcrowding, traffic, high cost of living, and unemployment. The next step is to "rediscover" different meanings attributed to Istanbul in its transformation from past to present.

2. Transformation of The City from Past to Present: "Now is the Time to Rediscover!"

The posters for domestic promotion campaign invite the viewers to rethink the past and "rediscover" the meaning of heritage by heavily relying on the representations of heritage sites. The intention is to offer a new perspective to the centuries old monumental structures (by showing them in different places rather than their original places in Istanbul) and to surprise the viewers, which is a common trick in marketing. Nevertheless, these posters came under criticism suggesting that they are falsified and/or touristified images. Moreover, the theme "Now is the time to rediscover" and how it is represented through images of Galata Tower, Haydarpaşa and Hagia Sophia remain controversial due to the contraposition between the emphasis on the historical value of the objects at the discourse level and the current urban transformation projects of the government at the actual level. Ataturk Culture Centre (AKM) in Taksim Square (replaced by the image of Haydarpaşa in one of the posters) is face to face with demolition. Haydarpaşa shares the destiny of AKM through a mega urban regeneration project. Moreover, due to the risk of demolitions, heritage can be interpreted as the heritage in danger. It is so, not only in terms of imagined space but also in terms of lived space. According to "ICOMOS World Report 2008-2010 on Monuments and Sites in Danger", the heritage is at risk at the Historic Areas of Istanbul (Debold-Kritter, 2010).

Apart from the domestic promotion campaign, the majority of the posters present the image of Istanbul vibrating with art and culture. In doing so, culture and arts are recognized as the engines for culture-led urban transformation. The main motivation is "generating the transformative energy to build the capacity" (Rampton et al., 2011: 77, 81), whereas how Istanbul 2010 used this energy is questionable. The initial idea of participative and democratic structure anticipating the bottom-up transformation of the city and its image is left behind. The participative voice is kept behind the images, but even this "participative"ness proposes banal images through a top-down mechanism of decision-making. The public policies heavily rely on urban mega-projects to re-create the city image, where the top-down mechanisms become more visible. Therefore, it can be argued that this energy did not flow bottom up due to organizational change. But it can be said that the projects and the promotional messages intended to increase the participation and enrich the number of participants by making art and culture accessible to a wider audience. The idea behind the projects such as "Portable Art" can be given as an example.

Culture and arts as one of the strategic areas of Istanbul 2010 concentrate on creative industries and creative labor. This objective is directed towards making the image of Istanbul into a creative city. The borders are removing, and the networks connecting the cities to each other are expanding through international projects. ECoC is an example of a European network based on culture. Therefore, some of the projects are joint organizations by other European cities and ECoCs either the same year 2010 (Essen and Pécs) or past/future ECoCs (Warsaw 2016). These projects, such as "In Between. Austria Contemporary", "Divercity. Learning from Istanbul", and/or "Golden Routes", facilitate the mobility of artists.

Intercity networks do not only facilitate flows of people but also flows of images. Istanbul 2010 programme is intended for a re-signification of Istanbul. Most of the symbolic images and visual representations concentrate on Istanbul (f=25), which tell us Istanbul is the main actor. Istanbul is not positioned in association with the marketing strategies of other European cities through a common vision of ECoC. Yet, the partnerships are based on cultural and artistic networking that reflects positively on the international communication of the event.

The international projects should be evaluated by taking the visual and cultural codes and their meanings in the cultural context of the partner cities. Defining the target audience is important for contextual meanings. National and international projects are different from each other in their use of symbols and language due to the different meanings created in different contexts. Thus, when analysing the posters, the meanings are interpreted in a wider context. An example can be given by the poster of "Divercity. Learning from Istanbul", in which the illusionist leitmotiv does not only include connotations to the spectacle in Turkey but also in Poland and the visual culture in the 1970s. In this sense, the symbolic representations gain new meanings in different contexts or their meanings are strengthened through the shared meanings. Therefore, intercontextual meanings are as important as the contextual meanings in order to interpret the codes according to what they represent in different cultures and how they relate to Istanbul.

Some of the posters, although they do not give direct references to Istanbul image at the denotative level, they offer a rich text through its own systematic of signification. The poster of "If Istanbul 2010" is a good example of this kind. The rescued object is not the ship but the iceberg in this picture. While the rich culture and history represent the lower part of the iceberg; the visible part on the surface is composed of the signs and structures developed by the cities resembling to each other in the globalizing world. Thus the heritage and historical roots are the sources of a powerful image rather than what is copied and inserted into the city image from the Western world. Such representation is a result of the intention to offer a different perspective to the conventional perceptions. Maybe it is the right approach to the preservation of the heritage, not only to preserve its past meanings but also to attribute new meanings to make it more understandable by the new generations. Although the set of signifiers could be the same, their signifieds could have gained new meanings in the new global cultural and political order.

The new globalizing image of Istanbul, no more presents the colours of the city. They are stuck between the high-rise buildings gazing the city above. Istanbul is depicted as a modern city with skyscrapers like New York and Hong Kong in the poster of Istanbul 1910-2010. Istanbul strives for a Western look like most of the European and World Cities by adding skyscrapers, tall business plazas and shopping centres in contrast to the silhouette with domes and minarets. The landscape of Istanbul in the globalization process is changing parallel to the standardization of its image of any global city that can be found elsewhere in the world.

Since the colours of Istanbul are fading into the monochrome image of the city, Istanbul image is transforming into a monophonic symphony of the city. These kinds of images are generally used in the posters telling about the urban transformation. On the other hand, the posters about the heritage represent Istanbul with the qualities that do not exist today or they have lost their meaning. They represent nostalgia, thus the signs of heritage are signified by fading colours and sepia tones. According to Soysal (2010) the exhibitions about cultural heritage are natural extensions of the urban gentrification and beautification projects. They stand as empty signifiers of the heritage directed at place marketing purposes. The new values gained over the commodification of culture transform into marketing tools blessed with bright and vivid colours in contrast to the pastel colours and sepia tones representing the historical landmarks.

This is highly related to the discourses about the gentrification and Istanbul as a "projected city" by governors. According to Esen (2011: 456) the modern city shaped by the urban planners and governors is waiting its time to show itself, but for now it is still in the shadow of Orientalist paradigms. Istanbul cannot get rid of the Orientalist gaze of the Westerners to the city, or maybe it does not want to get rid of it... It desires to get advantage of the mystified image. It can be said that Istanbul depicts itself from a Western eye[5], reorienting itself through the Westernization myth. Representations of the historical sites and monuments are heavily used throughout the posters, reflecting the historicist approach and mystifying Istanbul's oriental images through the Western gaze.

When we look at the posters, we see that Istanbul is on the way of Ottomanization rather than Westernization through historicizing the city and celebrating the glorious past through the representations of monumental structures. However, imaging and building projects differ from each other in that sense. Istanbul in the Ottoman era can be characterized by the image of an imperial capital and the building projects by the ruling elite to show this image through monuments. This was done through the creation of a network of significant buildings in the programme of a collective enterprise of the ruling elite. Such practice proposes "a range of meanings to a diverse set of users and audiences" as a synonym to "resignification" of Constantinople referring to the set of signifiers of the new cultural and political order (Kafesçioğlu, 2009: 130).

The poster of the exhibition of "Armenian Architects of Istanbul in the Era of Westernization" is an example of such resignification. It is a powerful image that belongs to the past, to the Ottoman era, but it also gives reference

---

[5] Paul MacMillen has been the creative director of international promotion campaign of Istanbul 2010, who is Irish but leaving in Istanbul for more than 30 years therefore claims himself to be a local of Istanbul.

to the Westernization period. The Greek and Armenian architects of the Ottoman period are remembered and revisited through the historical buildings such as Dolmabahçe Palace. Although Dolmabahçe reflects a distinct Western influence in its architectural style, it would be more accurate to express it as a masterly interpretation of Western impressions in a synthesis with the Ottoman style (Republic of Turkey Ministry of Culture and Tourism, 2005). The Western values are imported in the late Ottoman period in order to integrate with Europe. Westernization in the Republican era was directed towards the same goal but the meaning of Western was underlined as a contrast to Eastern. Therefore, it was addressed to break off with the Ottoman period and Oriental representations in the programme of nation building. Therefore, this poster offers rich codes to the city in transformation. As the city is transformed, its population, its buildings, the sites and the meanings are transformed as well. Istanbul was cleared from its multi-ethnic communities to a larger extent after the population exchange took place. The religious buildings such as churches and synagogues have lost their communities and these representations have become empty signifiers of today.

The transformation is a continuous process, as the society transforms, cities transform and they become spaces of representations through the change in meanings and representations of space. The transformation in the representation of Istanbul is made visible through the effort of connecting the past with the future. The history and modern coexist together in Istanbul. The discourses of urban transformation found in the posters of "Istanbul 1910-2010", "Ghost Buildings" and "Palimpsest Istanbul" supports these meanings by showing Istanbul is a multi-layered city in which the modern is established on the remnants of the past. Istanbul is a dynamic city transforming itself at a rapid pace. This energy was claimed as the key element of transformation in the promotion campaigns.

The question, which needs to be asked here, is the change brought by Istanbul 2010 in terms of its impact on the transformation of Istanbul's image. The assumption on the signification level is that, mega-events such as ECoC became a strategic tool to make Istanbul's image more visible in the international arena in accordance with Istanbul's aspiration to re-position itself as a global city. Today, what describe Istanbul have become these controversies and chaotic structure built on multiple layers of the palimpsest city. Talocci (n.d.) claims "the high speed, through which these clashes and the consequent urban transformations happen, makes semiotic reading particularly significant". Aydınlı (2001: 22) takes the contrasting pairs such as "continuity and change" by means of "both opposing but complementary concepts in a world where global issues and local values are put on the agenda". Such understanding connotes urban environments surrounded by contradictions through the interplay between the global and the local.

3. The Dialectics of City Imaging: Istanbul in between...

Batur (1996: xxi) comments, "narrating Istanbul is like weaving a tangled web", which indicates a high degree of complexity. In this book, the image of Istanbul is explored as "a narrative through its dialectics" (Aydınlı, 2001: 23) that can be experienced in its social and cultural contexts. The emphasis is on the integrity of meaning, since the meaning exists in the web of polarities in everyday life. Dondis (1973) posits understanding of meaning through contrasting pairs; "if there would be an understanding of hot without cold, high without low, sweet without sour". The importance of contrasting pairs has been recognized not only as a way of "clarifying the content of visual communication" but also in "creating a coherent whole" (Aydınlı, 2001: 23). In addition, contrast adds dynamism to the composition of an image or work of art in general sense through "tensions and resolutions, balance and unbalance, rhythmic coherence making it not a precarious yet continuous unity" (Langer, 1957). In this description the meaning of contrast is understood not only in terms of dichotomies and/or dualisms but rather in the sense of contrasting elements complementing each other in the unified whole. Istanbul is a continuous city when it is read through its history; but the continuity is cut through destructions and re-constructions. The continuous urban change brings discontinuity to the images to be read on the same axis of meanings. It needs constant re-interpretation of the signs at the contextual level. Therefore, Istanbul is portrayed through the images of contrasts by moving back and forth through the dynamic interplay between the continuity of historical events and discontinuity of collective memory and shared meanings.

The poster of Palimpsest Istanbul portrays the city under construction through this kind of interplay. Its signifiers (construction site, the transportation hub, the old port, the mannequin) and its signifieds (urban change, everyday life, consumption, commodity fetishism, heritage) tell us the tide between the past and present and its meanings. The exhibition of Ghost Buildings and its poster tells this story through the animated images of the historical buildings, which are not existing anymore, and asking the questions "what if?". Today, many people ask "What is this building used to be?" when passing by. In most of the cases, most of the people find it difficult to remember what was there before. Those who are not native to Istanbul do not know about its past although they have a blurred image of it. Another reason is that the city is changing at a great pace and the urban spaces become alike. While the urban collective memory of the city is being erased, the references of the city image are disappearing both physically and in the minds of the people. It refers to ephemerality of the spectacle and the city image in the urban memory.

The story of image-making for Istanbul, with respect to urban transformation and construction, is reflected on the "visual representations and their texts" by bringing contradictory and complementary layers of meaning together (Akpınar, 2003: 169).

> *"Despite the rhetoric of sudden change and a shift towards Westernisation (with the connotation of Americanisation), the discourse of Turkishness-Ottomanism-Islamism became more and more dominant. And as a result, Ottoman works of arts - mosques, in particular - became of primary importance... To tell the story of the urban reconstruction in the city of Istanbul is, in fact, unveiling its many layers and revealing their contradictory features, and responding to the cultural work of representations of urban space, which offer us specific and visual practices for approaching the spatiality of the city." (Akpınar, 2003: 194-5)*

Yıldırım (2008) studied the engravings of Istanbul as the visual texts by mapping the layers of meanings in search of the collective memory of the city of a certain time-period. A similar method of reading the city is applied to this research, not through engravings but through posters. Nevertheless, there are similarities that can be drawn easily between both. As mentioned before, the research relies on subjective methods in its interpretation of the meaning. However, it should be noted here that the city image is a product of collective memory and therefore it can be told and understood through shared meanings, which shows us the importance of the cultural context in making sense of the images. Culture, defined as making sense of the world (Hall, 1997: 2), is an integral part of branding a place, which involves cultural exchange (Anholt, 2005: 140).

The representations of historical landmarks (i.e. Eiffel Tower, Tower Bridge, etc.) are shared through collective imagination. The urban space is full of images, which provide meanings and internalization of the information to the viewer. According to Tanyeli (1997: 83), neither demographic information nor economic data could have been useful as the image of Eiffel Tower in internalizing Paris. The architectural images are easy to perceive, that is why they are the most common elements in the image of the city. However, the images do not exist by themselves in the form of single floating signifiers. Urban spaces are complex systems and therefore their images are part of this system shared among the community members (Tanyeli, 1997: 83).

Istanbul cannot claim its national capital status but leans on being cultural capital or financial capital of Turkey especially in the aftermath of the neo-liberalist politics of the 1980s. Istanbul sets off as a global city due to its strategic location as the finance centre and being the largest city of Turkey. One of the crucial aspects shared by global cities is the attractiveness and being the hub for mobilities. Istanbul became the hub for the Anatolian migrants because of the industry and employment opportunities after the 1950s, and now it continues to be the hub for expats and foreign employees of the multinational companies. However, the newcomers to the city push the old inhabitants out. The migration in the end creates a loss of urban memory and discontinuity of the city image. The newcomers do not recognize and appreciate the existing urban culture and the worst is that they do not claim it as their culture. They do not claim Istanbul as their city of origin, and therefore the city becomes unpossessed. The discontinuity of the image is not related to the encoding but to the decoding. The codes are continuous maybe, but the people reading them are far from interpreting the meanings.

Today, a number of images, sounds, global-local icons of the city are merging into the same picture, which makes the urban experience and the images of the city temporary, transitory, transitional and transformational. The city is transforming, so do images. The transformation enables the creation of new scenarios and reinterpretation of the existing meanings. Yürekli & İnceoğlu (2011: 214) mark the characteristics of Istanbul as follows: "continuous change, temporary usage of space, contradictions, incompleteness, ambiguity, heterogeneity, being unpossessed". The last one is linked to the sense of belonging. This multi-layered city is home to people with different origins. Istanbul is a city of unexpected encounters; it is a city of dichotomies between the East and the West. Thus Pamuk (2003) notes that the state of in-betweenness creates alienation and Istanbul remains unpossessed as anyone wants to possess it but no one claims its possession. Şenay (2009: 83) claims the imagined past of the city for the inhabitants of Istanbul that served as a common denominator on the collective memory and sense of pride, "although most of them are not born there or had lived there".

It is no more possible to know who is originally from Istanbul or what does it mean "to be from Istanbul". It is no more possible to know Istanbul (Batur 2010). It is no more possible to define the city with respect to what we call Istanbul today by thinking its past. Its image could be influenced by media, the perceptions of people could be shaped but today's Istanbul cannot be delineated by the old discourses of its 2500 years of past (Kuban, 2010b: 414, 418).

Dutton & Dukerich (1991: 547) argue that identity is dependent on image. Moreover, the identity of a city and its brand is substantially embedded in its context (Kornberger, 2010: 93). As a matter of fact all these binary oppositions and multiplicities are reduced into one single message in the international promotion campaign: "Istanbul, the most inspiring city"... However, Istanbul Inspirations has adopted an over pretentious strategy. Ancient past and history of Istanbul is conveyed through empty signifiers in the touristic images of the historical monuments. City branding strategies should be consistent in the use of brand image in order to create a coherent message in the minds of the audience and to provide the match between the intended and the perceived meanings. Otherwise the message would not be conveyed truly and the city image would be somewhat different than the one designed by the image-makers.

Obviously Istanbul has a strong identity rooted in its past, but the meanings inferred from the messages reflect on the city Istanbul is at the crossroads where the past meets the future, East meets West, and the mystic meets the modern. That is why the analysis takes a holistic approach through reading the codes as a narrative directed towards the interpretation of the fragmented components of a whole (Aydınlı, 2001: 23). Nevertheless, when the messages are evaluated at the strategic level to city branding, the fragmented components do not lead to uniformed whole and a coherent message. The multi-layers of meanings diffuse into multi-messages standing on top of each other in a chaotic structure. Therefore, the outcome of the analysis shows that each poster is consistent in the intended messages for their specific cases but when they are taken as a whole the only element integrating them together is the logo of Istanbul 2010. Different messages are produced through different representations of Istanbul concentrating on different eras, different values and communicating through different code systems. In this framework the polysemious structure of images and their subjective interpretation may lead to a variety of meanings in which the receivers get confused.

Istanbul's image swinging between floating signifiers

Place marketing is about the particular meanings attached to a place (what it is and what it should be) through signs. Cities create symbols, signs, icons through images and discourses in the production of urban representations. City branding involves "urban imaginary" and "urban representation" in which symbolic meaning is created through the symbolic economy of the city, in Zukin's (1991, 1996) terms "the landscapes of power". In the globalizing world, cities are in competition to integrate with world economies and this necessitates making themselves more visible and recognizable through symbolic language of the urban representations. Mega-events are the instruments for effectively marketing and communicating the city image. Another point to be highlighted is the element of culture. Hall (1997: 2) underlines the role of culture in "production and exchange of meanings… thus culture depends on participants interpreting meaningfully what is around them." There is a certain image of Istanbul in the minds of the people, which is created through shared meaning. In addition, ECoC is a cultural event in which the image of the city is materialized and communicated widely to the different segments of the society.

Branding Istanbul through ECoC 2010 is a unique opportunity for international visibility. The benefits of the brand do not, however, flow automatically. This means; "the opportunity is there and it is up to the city to make the best use of it" (European Commission, 2010). The key to the success for city imaging lies in stressing the unique features of the city, although globalization works in the opposite way through homogenization. A city, which has a lot to offer something for everyone, is different from a city where everyone can find similar things to other cities. Istanbul has a lot to offer to visitors. The diversity makes Istanbul attractive as its biggest competitive advantage in branding strategy. Istanbul positions itself by putting forward the diversity and cultural pluralism through Istanbul 2010.

The symbolic language in the posters includes signs for city of Istanbul and image of Istanbul, but these symbols do not construct a common language of signs. The messages are produced at different levels through different chain of signifiers. There is a difference in the international and domestic advertising campaign of Istanbul 2010. The international campaign shows the mystified image of the Ottoman Palace (Topkapı) and minarets in the silhouette image. This image represents Western gaze through Orientalist images. It does not offer something new but asks the Westerns to "remember" of this beautified and turistified image. The domestic campaign, on the other hand, asks not only "remember" but also to "rediscover". The images invite us to look from afar to the city of Istanbul, whereas the messages encourage "being part of this unique experience"[6]. We cannot see what the city really is, if we only look at it from a distance. On the other hand, we could be part of the change as Istanbul 2010 tells us to look and to "rediscover". That is why the verbal message is so important, however it does not anchor well with the image therefore does not lead to a powerful message for the audience.

The images of Istanbul pile up in videos and posters to show the city in every aspect in which everything becomes mishmash and the message gets lost in the chaos. It becomes hard for the audience to read the images especially if they are not familiar with the cultural codes. Moreover, adding everything into a single image ends up being chaotic and makes the place somewhere you can find everything. But this feels not special, not original and even ordinary as the cities started to resemble each other more and more.

---

[6] Slogan of Istanbul Inspirations promotion campaign.

Therefore, instead of focusing on the unique elements and stressing the competitive advantage, it creates generic images that are hard to remember and distinguish from each other.

When one thinks of the historical ties of Istanbul and the layers of city image built on thousands of years, it would be unfavourable to expect that the city image could be solely affected by a contemporary mega-event. For this reason, it could be claimed that the main discourse of Istanbul 2010 and the major strategies for city imaging is adding the "new" without cutting its roots with the "old". While Istanbul is depicted as a mystified city through Orientalist representations, this image is coupled with the high-rise buildings promising a financially powerful city, no different from the leading global cities today. In this context, Istanbul seems like a city between the past and contemporary, in which the heritage is represented as a commodifiable object. The heritage has become a mean of "public consumption as nostalgia" (Soysal, 2010: 302) through the restoration and renovation projects supported by Istanbul 2010 programme. The urban transformation of run-down areas and heritage sites into archaeological parks and conversion of old buildings into cultural venues and museums are such examples. This has become the point of issue that has started with decisions taken by local authorities imposed into urban and cultural politics and continued with Istanbul 2010 rather than being a process that started with Istanbul 2010.

The marketing campaign for Istanbul 2010 announces that "stage belongs to Istanbul" while inviting the audience to "re-discover" the culture and heritage in an attempt to create "a brand name for the city" (Soysal, 2010: 302, 307). The marketing and branding objectives centre around the city image improvement, the multicultural aspects and values come forward "to attract the attention of the world's public opinion" (Bilsel & Arıcan, 2010: 217). This is about branding Istanbul on the international platform and placing Istanbul on the cultural map of Europe. The strategic location of Istanbul is emphasized through culture and art networks, which is similar to the global networks and mobilities: *"Istanbul is now a centre for culture and arts, not only locally, but also internationally... The city is developing as a crossroad on the world's art and culture circuit." (Çolakoğlu, n.d.)*

Whether the contemporary art is inserted in the marketing strategies, it is not possible to dominate historical representations. It is so rooted in the past that these images are not subjected to change in a short period of time. ECoC should be considered as an opportunity to open to door to impact on the perceptions of people. Istanbul 2010 acts as a propaganda tool in shaping mental maps through the images (Akpınar, 2003: 152-3). In this framework, city imaging should be seen as a part of the systematic city branding strategy. Branding during Istanbul 2010 is part of a wider and comprehensive city branding strategy, which has to be consistent but also diverse in a way to be able to emphasize distinctive aspects and the importance of city as Istanbul 2010 among other brand features. Accordingly, the communication campaign needed to be "able to brand such a complex programme" (Rampton et al., 2011: 67). The effectiveness of media and promotion campaigns in creating awareness both in the country and abroad cannot be denied. Despite the broad use of communication channels and success in creating awareness, it cannot be said so for communicating the message. People know "there is something called Istanbul 2010 but not sure what it is exactly" (Sevin, 2010). This mainly stems from the lack of focus in branding and communication. The point of origin where Istanbul 2010 started, and the point of destination where it arrived, differentiates between the objectives and achievements.

Nevertheless, one of the main critical aspects about image-making strategy of Istanbul stems from the cliché statements of old-new and East-West as the examples of binary oppositions. Istanbul has been perceived as a meeting point between East and West. If we put it another way, this perception is intensified, overemphasized and imposed to consumers – buyers of the city image. The skyscrapers, added to the silhouette of Istanbul with minarets, increased the tension between the binary oppositions such as East-West, old-new, Islam-Modern. This "dialectical image" is converted into a marketing tool by annexing other adjectives such as "diverse", "cosmopolitan", "tolerant", etc. The discourses of a city are highly related to its representations and vice versa. The bridge metaphor can also be understood as a link between the past and the present in cliché terms. The geographical location of Istanbul stands out both as a unique feature of its image and as a significant factor to attract the attention of world economy and to join the list of global cities.

The complexity of city marketing can be clearly seen, when the city and its image are accepted as a text that can be read in different ways. When all the concepts of "discourses, symbols, metaphors and fantasies" are applied to urban contexts, the city is recognized as interplay between coding and decoding the meanings interactively through a dialogue with urban spaces (Donald, 1992: 422). Barthes (1975: 92) recognizes city as a discourse in which "discourse is truly a language".

When the image making process is considered through the analysis results appearing in three themes, recommendations can be provided as follows in line with the themes:

1. Authenticity

There is a matter of theatricality and authenticity. Istanbul is presented as a stage for various cultural events to take place during the year of 2010. The main decor is depicted as the heritage sites with an aim to signify the importance of heritage. On the other hand, the radical urban transformation and mega architecture projects in pursuit of having a global city image leads to complexities and controversies in this process. The spectacle is created and communicated through the images of monumental sites exposed to viewers, which are unlikely to exist in the near future as they are face to face with demolition according to the new political and economic order. The link between the representation and meaning of heritage is problematic due to the use of empty signifiers and connection with the context. Heritage is represented in accordance with the symbols and meanings in the context of self-orientalism through the discourse of "remembering the past", however creating touristified images in the end.

2. Transparency

The matter of authenticity can be also linked to the organization of the event and the failure in bottom up approach. The project should be inclusive and participative. Nevertheless, this is not possible without effective communication and transparency. This increases the tension between the decision makers as the authoritative figures and the stakeholders.

3. Communication of the messages

Communicating the messages effectively and consistently can be raised as the last comment and recommendation, as the whole branding process is recognized as a matter of communication process through encoding and decoding the messages. The anchorage between encoding and decoding is essential for the continuity of codes in order to grasp the meanings through dialectics of the images. The image of a contemporary city pleading to be European is coupled with exotic images offering a Western gaze to the city, in an effort to turn this image into marketable object. However, such practice is based on the assumption for unconditional acceptance of brand propositions by the viewers. I suggest taking a more careful approach to brand identity and brand authenticity for creating the brand image in a response to match the expectations and the perceptions.

Conclusion

In this work I have focused on the communication process aimed at influencing the perceptions about Istanbul's image, rather than concentrating on the end results of the mega-event itself. This is an attempt to draw a model for analysis by using visual qualitative methods. One central idea around hosting mega-events is the motivation and strategic vision in building an international city image. According to Nadeau et al. (2011: 237), the significance of international perceptions for the host country reflects to "tourism, revenue generation, export/import issues and investing decisions". As noted previously imaging and re-imaging activities may be applied to the industrial urban centres in the form of urban regeneration in order to erase the negative perceptions of urban decay. However, there is a paradox brought by this city re-imaging panacea, which is "recursive" and "serial mass production" of identical city places across space (Boyer, 1990: 96).

The image of the city, constructed by the spectacle, travels through "the present" as imagined, "the games" as reality, and "the future" as utopia during different stages of the event. The reality as the object of representation never materializes, "as the sky is never quite as blue, the grass as green…" (Rice, 2012: 99). Yet, the experience makes the reality richer through the cognitive, haptic and phenomenological processes in the lived space. Therefore, the semiotic image and the messages cannot be totally controlled by the producer, as the receivers will add their own meanings and reinterpretations. "The image remains a speculative hybrid of these multiple authors, viewers and users […] But what does remain of the image? Legacy…" (Rice, 2012: 99).

Istanbul 2010 is an example for city branding which is a continuous process with strategic implications. From a visually critical perspective, one should respect the fact that Istanbul could not be represented with a single image, but only through a collection of images. This collection should be consistent at least in its cognate and opposite meanings. This necessitates well orchestrated good curatorial skills. Otherwise the result can be a chaotic image perplexing the audience. Identifying an image through binary oppositions is a powerful way of generating meaning; as "the meaning of dark is relative to the meaning of light; form is inconceivable except in relation to content" (Chandler, 2007: 91). Yet, the image of Istanbul moves between the opposite ends, but could not reach an agreement. Brand identity is the backbone of a strong brand value. Hence, the first step in creating a consistent branding strategy for Istanbul is to have a clear vision. Symbolic language of the posters includes extensive signs to represent Istanbul and its image. Istanbul 2010 had an impact on Istanbul image, but this impact was not an outcome of an effective branding strategy, because the place branding activities for Istanbul 2010 are found to be lacking a common language.

Studies dealing with mega events and related visual materials are a challenge in its entirety. Availability and access to materials is a barrier. Perhaps more conclusive analyses are possible with complete sets of materials in other mega events and of course more time allowed for such research is always desirable. Long term analysis of these effects might lead to different understandings.

City branding, by its very nature, is a multidisciplinary field of study. As a researcher with background in tourism and marketing as well as in history of architecture, I tried to bring together a wealthier mix to substantiate my inevitably subjective interpretation. This has also allowed me to apply visual qualitative methods to marketing researchin an effort to analyse visual materials through the use of multimodality. This is also an invitation for further research examining visual materials. With ubiquitious internet and digital materials rapidly expanding, new forms of communication available to wider audience may warrant and enable new forms of visual qualitative analyses. This book is only offering a form of analysis over a selected set of materials. Hence I acknowledge the possibility of many other ways in which this case or similar other cases could have been analysed. While cautioning the readers, I would like to underline that a more comprehensive understanding of the mega events' impact on city image can be possible with multi sited research gathering information and views from the sites, agents, audiences and with triangulation of all.

References

Aaker, D. A. (1996). *Building strong brands*, New York: Free Press.
Aaker, D. A. and Joachimsthaler, E. (2000). *Brand leadership*, London: Free Press.
Abbas, A. (2003). *Cinema, the city, and the cinematic*. In L. Krause & P. Pietro *(Eds.), Global Cities: Cinema, Architecture, and Urbanism in a Digital Age* (pp. 142–156). New Brunswick, New Jersey: Rutgers University Press.
Adanalı, Y. A. (2011). De-spatialized space as neoliberal utopia: Gentrified İstiklal Street and commercialized urban spaces. *Red Thread, 3*. Retrieved from http://www.red-thread.org/en/article.asp?a=50
Akpınar, İ. (2003). *The rebuilding of Istanbul after the plan of Henri Prost, 1937-1960: from secularisation to Turkish modernisation* (Unpublished doctoral dissertation). University College London, London, UK.
Akpınar, İ. Y. (2011). *Remapping the mid-20th century urban demolitions: representation of the rebuilding of Istanbul.* [Exhibition catalogue], History and Destruction in Istanbul: Ghost Buildings (pp.174-183). Istanbul: Şan Ofset.
Aksoy, A. (2009). Istanbul's choice: Openness. *Istanbul: City of Intersections*, LSE Cities, Urban Age Conference Publication, London. Retrieved from http://lsecities.net/media/objects/articles/istanbuls-choice
Aksoy, A. (2010). İstanbul: Dilemma of direction. *Europa Nostra*. Retrieved from http://www.europanostra-tr.org/files/file/Asu%20Aksoy_Istanbul_Dilemma%20of%20Direction.pdf
Aktaş, G. (2006). *Marketing cities for tourism: developing marketing strategies for Istanbul with lessons from Amsterdam and London* (Unpublished doctoral dissertation). Bournemouth University, UK.
Alasuutari, P. (1995). *Researching culture: Qualitative method and cultural studies*, London: Sage.
Albayrak, R. S. & Suerdem, A. (2008). *Toward a new approach in social simulations: Meta- Language.* Retrieved from mabs2008.dcti.iscte.pt/revised_for_pre_proceedings/Albayrak.pdf
Amin, A. & Thrift, N. (Eds.). (1994). *Globalisation, institutions, and regional development in Europe*. Oxford: Oxford University Press.
Anatolia News Agency (2009, July 12). Istanbul 2010 commercial campaign launched. *Hurriyet Daily News*, 12th July. Retrieved from http://www.hurriyetdailynews.com/default.aspx?pageid=438&n=istanbul-2010-reklam-kampanyasi-2009-12-04
Andersson, M. (2010). Provincial globalization: The local struggle of place-making. *Culture Unbound, 2* (pp. 193–215) Linköping University Electronic Press. Retrieved from http://www.cultureunbound.ep.liu.se/v2/a12/cu10v2a12.pdf
Andreoli, E. (1996). The visible cities of São Paulo. In I. Borden, J. Kerr, A. Pivaro, & J. Rendell (Eds.), *Strangely Familiar: Narratives of Architecture in the City* (pp. 62-66). London: Routledge.
Anholt, S. (2005). *Brand new justice: how branding places and products can help the developing world*. Oxford: Elsevier Butterworth-Heinemann.
Anholt, S. (2007). *Competitive identity: The new brand management for nations, cities and regions*. London: Palgrave Macmillan.
Anholt, S. (2010) *Places: Identity, image and reputation*. London: Palgrave Macmillan.
Annibal-Iribarne, J. (2003). Some thoughts on cities – Visions and plans. In L. Krause & P. Pietro (Eds.), *Global Cities: Cinema, Architecture and Urbanism in a Digital Age* (pp.177-184). New Brunswick, New Jersey: Rutgers University Press.
Appadurai, A. (1990). Disjuncture and difference in the global cultural economy. In M. Featherstone (Ed.), *Global Culture: Nationalism, Globalization and Modernity* (pp. 295-310). London: Sage.
Appadurai, A. (1996). *Modernity at large: Cultural dimensions of globalization*. Minneapolis: University of Minnesota Press.
Applbaum, K. (2004). *The Marketing Era From Professional Practice to Global Provisioning*. New York: Routledge.
Ashworth, G. J. (1992). Is there an urban tourism? *Tourism Recreation Research, 17* (2), 3-8.
Ashworth, G. J. (2008). *Can we, do we, should we, brand places? [Or are we doing what we think and say we are doing?]* In: INPOLIS, 1st international conference: "Marketing Cities: Place Branding in Perspective", Berlin, December 4-6. Retrieved from http://www.inpolis.de/inpolis-projektdetail_1_en.html

Ashworth, G. J. & Kavaratzis, M. (2009). Beyond the logo: Brand management for cities. *Journal of Brand Management, 16*(8), 520-531.

Ashworth, G. J. & Kavaratzis, M. (Eds.) (2010). *Towards effective place brand management: branding European cities and regions.* MA: Edward Elgar.

Ashworth, G. J. & Voogd, H. (1988). Marketing the city: concepts, processes and Dutch applications. *Transport Planning Review, 59*(l), 65-79.

Ashworth, G. J. & Voogd, H. (1990). *Selling the city: Marketing approaches in public sector urban planning.* London: Belhaven Press.

Askegaard, S. (2006). Brands as a global ideoscape. In: J. Schroeder & M. Salzer-Mörling (Eds.), *Brand Culture* (pp. 91-102). London: Routledge.

Avraham, E. (2004). Media strategies for improving an unfavorable city image, *Cities, 21*(6), 471 - 479.

Aydınlı, S. (2001). Continuity and change in the image of the Istanbul. *EDRA, 32*, 22-26.

Babalık, F. (2010). *İstanbul 2010 Avrupa Kültür* Başkenti'nin *ilham veren ilkleri* [CD]. İstanbul: İstanbul 2010 Avrupa Kültür Başkenti.

Bağış, E. (2010). "Europe without Istanbul unimaginable". Interview by B. Aydın, *Istanbul 2010: "Colour", 4* (Autumn), 26- 29.

Bal, M. & Bryson, N. (1991). Semiotics and art history. *The Art Bulletin, 73*(2), 174-208.

Balibrea, M. P. (2001). Urbanism, culture and the post-industrial city: Challenging the 'Barcelona Model'. *Journal of Spanish Cultural Studies, 2*(2), 187–210.

Baloğlu, Ş. & McCleary, K. W. (1999). A model of destination image formation. *Annals of Tourism Research, 26*(4), 868-897.

Barthes, R. (1967). *Elements of semiology.* London: Jonathan Cape.

Barthes, R. (1975). *Mythologies.* Paris: Seuil.

Barthes, R. (1977). *Image/Music/Text.* New York: Noonday.

Batur, A. (1996). Designing an exhibition for Istanbul. (J. Alguadis, Trans.). In A. Evin (Ed.), *Istanbul-World City,* Istanbul: History Foundation Publications.

Batur, E. (2010). *İstanbul ansiklopedisi.* İstanbul: Doğuş Grubu İletişim Yay. ve Tic. A.Ş.

Baudrillard, J. (1981 [1972]). *For a critique of the political economy of the sign.* St. Louis: Telos Press.

Baudrillard, J. (1994 [1981]). *Simulacra and simulation.* Ann Arbor: University of Michigan Press.

Baudrillard, J. (1996). *The system of objects.* London: Verso.

Baudrillard, J. (1998 [1970]). *The consumer society: Myths* and *structures.* Thousand Oaks, California: Sage Publications.

Beasley, R. (2002). *Persuasive signs: The semiotics of advertising.* Berlin: Walter de Gruyter GmbH & KG.

Beaumont, P. (2012, July 7). How Qatar is taking on the world. *The Guardian,* Retrieved from http://www.guardian.co.uk/world/2012/jul/07/qatar-takes-on-the-world

Beaverstock, J. V., Smith, R. G. & Taylor, P. J. (*1999*). A roster of world *cities. Cities, 16*(*6*), *445-458.*

Begoll, M. (2006). *Absolut ads. A critical analysis of an advertising phenomenon* [Research Paper]. Retrieved from www.discourse-analysis.de

Belk, R. W. (2006). *Handbook of qualitative research* methods *in marketing.* Aldershot, UK: Edward Elgar Publishing Ltd.

Benitez, J. (2013, January 22). Text of the Elysee Treaty (Joint Declaration of Franco-German Friendship). *Atlantic Council.* Retrieved from http://www.acus.org/natosource/text-elysee-treaty-joint-declaration-franco-german-friendship

Benjamin, W. (1979). *One-Way street and other writings,* (E. Jephcott & K. Shorter, Trans.). London: New Left Books.

Benjamin, W. (1999). Surrealism: The last snapshot of the european intelligentsia. In M. W. Jennings, E. Howard, & G. Smith (Eds.) *Selected Writings, 2*(1), (pp. 207-221). Cambridge, MA: Harvard University Press.

Benjamin, W. (2002). *The arcades project.* (H. Eiland & K. McLaughlin, Trans.). In R. Tiedemann (Ed.) New York: Belknap Press.

Bennett, T. (1995). *The birth of the museum.* London: Routledge.

Berelson, B. (1952). *Content analysis in communications research.* Glencoe, IL: Free Press.

Berger, A. A. (2004). *Deconstructing travel: Cultural perspectives on tourism.* Walnut Creek, CA: Altamira Press.

Berger, J. (1972). *Ways of seeing.* London: Penguin.

Bernard, H. R., & Ryan, G. W. (2010). *Analyzing qualitative data: Systematic approaches,* Thousand Oaks, CA: Sage Publications.

Besson, E., & Sutherland, M. (2007). The European Capital of Culture process: Opportunities for managing cultural tourism. *PICTURE Position paper, 5.* Retrieved from http://ecoc-doc-athens.eu/attachments/416_Besson,%20E.%20M.%20Sutherland%20Opportunities%20for%20mana ging%20Cult.ural%20Tourism.pdf

Beyazıt, E., & Tosun, Y. (2006). *Evaluating Istanbul in the process of European Capital of Culture 2010* [PDF]. 42nd ISoCaRP Congress. Retrieved from http://ecoc-doc-athens.eu/attachments/1201_Evaluating%20Istanbul%20in%20the%20Process%20of%20European %20Capital%20of%20Culture.pdf

Beyoğlu Güzelleştirme ve Koruma Derneği (n.d.). *Beyoğlu müzikle başkadır.* Retrived from http://www.beyoglu.org.tr/

Bianchini, F. (1993). Remaking European cities: the role of cultural policies. In: F. Bianchini & M. Parkinson (Eds.) *Cultural Policy and Urban Regeneration: The West European Experience* (pp. 1–21). Manchester: Manchester University Press.

Bianchini, F. (1999). The relationship between cultural resources and urban tourism policies: Issues from European debates. In D. Dodd & A. van Hemel (Eds.), *Planning Cultural Tourism in Europe: a Presentation of Theories and Cases* (pp. 78-90). Amsterdam: Boekman Foundation.

Bilsel, C., & Arıcan, T. (2010). Istanbul 2010 European Capital of Culture: An impetus for the regeneration of the historic city, *Rivista di Scienze del Turismo, 1*(2), 215-241.

Black, D. R., & Van Der Westhuizen, J. (2004). The allure of global games for 'semi-peripheral' polities and spaces: A research agenda, *Third World Quarterly, 25* (7), 1195-1214.

Blaxter, L., Hughes, C., & Tight, M. (2010). *How to research.* Milton Keynes: Open University Press.

Boland, V. (2011, June 27). Istanbul: Something for the urban global elite. *Financial Times.* Retrieved from http://www.ft.com/intl/cms/s/0/12fe9f02-a070-11e0-a115-00144feabdc0.html#axzz3yxWtJDSf

Boorstin, D. J. (1961). *The image, or what happened to the American dream.* London: Weidenfeld and Nicolson.

Boorstin, D. J. (1992). *The image: a guide to psuedo-events in America.* New York: Vintage Books.

Borden, I., Kerr, J., Rendell, J., & Pivaro, A. (2001). *The unknown city: Contesting architecture and social space.* Cambridge, MA: MIT Press.

Bourdeau-Lepage L., & Huriot J.-M. **(2006). Megacities vs. global cities: Development and institutions.** *ERSA conference papers,* 1-19.

Bourdeau-Lepage, L., & Huriot J.-M. (2005). The metropolis in retrospect: Permanence and change, *Recherches Economiques de Louvain, 71*(3), 257-284.

Bourdieu, P. (1977). *Outline of a theory of practice.* Cambridge: Cambridge University Press.

Boyatzis, R. E. (1998). *Transforming qualitative* information: *Thematic analysis and code development.* Thousand Oaks, CA: Sage.

Boyer, M. C. (1990). The return of aesthetics to city planning. In D. Crow (Ed.) *Philosophical Streets* (pp. 93-112). Washington, DC: Maisonneuve Press.

Bozkuş, Ş. B. (2012). Putting Istanbul on the map of art world: Analysing Istanbul 2010 Cultural Capital of Europe. *ATINER'S Conference Paper Series,* No: MDT2012-0075, Athens.

Brenner, N. (1998). Global cities, global states: Global city formation and state territorial restructuring in contemporary Europe. *Review of International Political Economy, 5*(1),1-37.

Bridge, G., & Watson, S. (2000). *A companion to the city.* Oxford, UK: Blackwell.

Bristow, G. (2010). Resilient regions: Re-'place'ing regional competitiveness. *Cambridge Journal of Regions, Economy and Society, 3*(1), 153–167.

Bryman, A. (1999). The sisneyization of society. *Sociological Review, 47*(1), 25-47.

Buck-Morss, S. (2004). Visual studies and global imagination. *Papers of Surrealism, Summer*(2). Retrieved from http://www.surrealismcentre.ac.uk/papersofsurrealism/journal2/acrobat_files/buck_morss_article.pdf

Burgess, J. A. (1982). Selling places: Environmental images for the executive. *Regional Studies, 16*(1), 1-17.

Burgess, J., & Wood, P.(1988). Decoding docklands. In J. Eyles & D. Smith (Eds.). *Qualitative Methods. Human Geography* (pp. 94–117). Totowa, N.J: Barnes & Noble.

Burn, A.,& Parker, D. (2003). *Analysing media texts.* London: Continuum.

Calvino, I. (1997 [1972]). *Invisible cities.* London: Vintage.

Canclini, N. G. (2001). *Consumers and Citizens: Globalization and Multicultural Conflicts* (G. Yúdice, Trans.). Minneapolis: University of Minnesota Press.

Carpenter, E. (1972). *Oh, What a blow that phantom gave me!* New York, Chicago, San Francisco: Holt, Rinehart & Winston.

Carr, S., Francis, M., Rivlin, L. G., & Stone, A.M. (1992). *Public Space*. Cambridge: Cambridge University Press.

Castells, M. (1989). *The informational city: Information technology, economic restructuring, and the urban-regional processes*. Oxford: Basil Blackwell.

Chandler, D. (2007). *Semiotics: The basics* (2nd ed.). London: Routledge.

Clarke, D. B. (2008). The ruins of the future: On urban transience and durability. In A. Cronin. & K. Hetherington (Eds.), *Consuming the Entrepreneurial City: Image, Memory, Spectacle* (pp. 127–142). New York: Routledge.

Clifton, R., & Maughan, E. *(2000). The future of brands*. New York: New York University Press.

Close, P., Askew, D., & Xu, X. (2007). *The Beijing Olympiad: the political economy of a sporting mega-event*. London & New York: Routledge.

Cobley, P., & Jansz, L. (2010). *Introducing semiotics: A graphic guide*. London: Icon books.

Colomb, C. (2012). *Staging the new Berlin: Place marketing and the politics of urban reinvention post-1989*. London: Routledge.

Cook, G. (2001). *The discourse of advertising*. London: Routledge.

Council of the European Union (2007, May 24-25). *Council Conclusions on the contribution of the cultural and creative sectors to the achievement of the Lisbon objectives*. Education, Youth and Culture Council meeting, Brussels. Retrieved from http://www.consilium.europa.eu/ueDocs/cms_Data/docs/pressData/en/educ/94291.pdf

Cox, W. (2012, March 5). World urban areas population and density: A 2012 update. *New Geography*. Retrieved from http://www.newgeography.com/content/002808-world-urban-areas-population-and-density-a-2012-update

Crace, J. (2002, August 14). Urban ambition, *The Guardian*. Retrieved from http://www.guardian.co.uk/society/2002/aug/14/communities.localgovernment

Crampton, J. W., & Krygier, J. (2006). An introduction to critical cartography. *ACME: An International E-Journal for Critical Geographies, 4*(1), 11-33.

Crawshaw, C., & Urry, J. (1997). Tourism and the photographic eye. In C. Rojek, & J. Urry (Eds), *Touring Cultures: Transformations of Travel and Theory* (pp. 176-195). London: Routledge.

Crow, D. (2010). *Visible signs: An introduction to semiotics in the visual arts*. London: AVA Publishing.

Currid, E. (2006). New York as a global creative hub: a competitive analysis of four theories on world cities. *Economic Development Quarterly, 20*(4), 330-350.

Çelik, Z. (1998). *19. yüzyılda Osmanlı başkenti: Değişen İstanbul* İstanbul: Tarih Vakfı Yurt Yayınları.

Çolakoğlu, N. (n.d.). *Istanbul 2010 ECOC A multi-layered and multi-faceted project* [PowerPoint slides].

Dailymotion (2009, Dec. 22). *İstanbul 2010'a Hazırlanıyor* [Web-Video] Retrieved from http://www.dailymotion.com/video/xbljlb_ystanbul-2010-a-hazyrlanyyor_news#.UYe4LCsRBAt

Davis, S. B. (2002). *Media space: An analysis of spatial practices in planar pictorial media* (Unpublished doctoral dissertation). Middlesex University, UK.

De Castro, J. L. (1999). The other dimension of third-level politics in Europe: The congress of local and regional powers of the council of Europe. *Regional & Federal Studies, 9*(1), 95-110.

De Certeau, M. (1984). *The practice of everyday life*. Berkeley: University of California Press.

De Chernatony, L. (1999). Brand management through narrowing the gap between brand identity and brand reputation. *Journal of Marketing Management, 15*(1), 157-179.

De Santis, L. & Ugarriza, D. N. (2000). The concept of theme as used in qualitative nursing research. *Western Journal of Nursing Research, 22*(April), 351-372.

Deacon, D., Murdock, G., Pickering, M., and Golding, P. (2007). *Researching communications: A practical guide to methods in media and cultural analysis* (2nd ed.). London: Hodder Arnold.

Debold-Kritter, A. (2010). Threats to the World Heritage in the Changing Metropolitan Areas of Istanbul. In C .Machat, M. Petzet & J. Ziesemer (Eds.), *Heritage at Risk, ICOMOS World Report 2008–2010 on Monuments and Sites in Danger* (pp.175-179). Berlin: hendrik Bäßler verlag. ISBN 978-3-930388-65-3. Retrieved from http://www.icomos.org/risk/world_report/2008-2010/H@R_2008-2010_final.pdf

Debord, G. (1994 [1967]). *Society of the spectacle*. New York: Zone Books.

Denzin, N. K., & Lincoln, Y.S. (Eds.). (1998). *Collecting and interpreting qualitative materials.* Thousand Oaks, CA: Sage.

Derudder, B. (2006). On conceptual confusion in empirical analyses of a transnational urban network. *Urban Studies, 43*(11), 2027-2046.

Dey, I. (2005). *Qualitative Data Analysis: A user-friendly guide for social scientists.* London: Routledge.

Donald, J. (1992). Metropolis: the city as text. In R. Bocock & K. Thompson (Eds.), *Social and Cultural Forms of Modernity* (pp. 417-461). Cambridge: Polity.

Dondis, D. A. (1973). *A primer of visual literacy.* Cambridge, MA: The MIT Press.

Duncan, J., & Duncan, N. (1992). Ideology and bliss: Roland Barthes and the secret histories of landscape. In T. Barnes & J. Duncan (Eds.), *Writing Worlds: Discourse, Text and Metaphor in the Representation of Landscape* (pp. 18-37). London and New York: Routledge.

Durkheim, E. (1965). *The elementary forms of religious life.* (J. W. Swain, Trans.). New York: The FreePress.

Dutton, J. E., & Dukerich, J. M. (1991). Keeping and eye on the mirror: Image and identity in organizational adaptation. *Academy of Management Journal, 34*(3), 517-554.

Eco, U. (1976). *A theory of semiotics.* Bloomington: Indiana University Press.

ECOTEC (2009, Nov.). *Ex-Post Evaluation of 2007 and 2008 European Capitals of Culture Final Report.* Birminhgam: ECOTEC Research and Consulting Ltd.

Eeckhout, B. (2001). The "Disneyification" of Times Square: Back to the future? In K. F. Gotham (Ed.), *Critical perspectives on urban redevelopment* (pp. 379–428). New York: Elsevier.

Eisinger, P. (2000). The politics of bread and circuses: Building the city for the visitor class. *Urban Affairs Review, 35*(3), 316-333.

Ekinci, Y., & Hosany, S. (2006). Destination personality: An application of brand personality to tourism destinations. *Journal of Travel Research, 45*(2), 127-139.

Erciyes, C. (2010, Dec. 23). 2010 Kültür Başkenti rüzgar gibi geçti gitti. *Radikal.* Retrieved from http://www.radikal.com.tr/hayat/2010-kultur-baskenti-ruzgar-gibi-gecti-gitti-1033677/

Eroğlu, M. (2010). Introducing the Turkish Foundation Museum of Calligraphic Arts Collection Heritage. *Istanbul 2010 - Colour, Autumn*(04), 94-95.

Erten, S. (2008). *Spatial analysis of mega-event hosting: Olympic host and olympic bid cities* (Unpublished doctoral dissertation). Middle East Technical University, Ankara.

Esen, O. (2011). İstanbul'dan öğrenmek. In: Y. Köse (ed.), Ayşe Dağlı (trans.), *İstanbul: İmparatorluk Başkentinden Megakente* (pp. 455-488). İstanbul: Kitap Yayınevi.

Espelt, N. G., & Benito, J. A. D. (2005). The social construction of the image of Girona: A methodological approach. *Tourism Management, 26*(5), 777-785.

Essex, S., & Chalkley, B. (1998). Olympic Games: Catalyst of urban change. *Leisure Studies, 17*(3), 187-206.

European Commission (1994, Dec. 14). *Lisbon 94 - European City of Culture.* Ref: IP/94/1218. Retrieved from http://europa.eu/rapid/press-release_IP-94-1218_en.htm#PR_metaPressRelease_bottom

European Commission (2010). Celebrating 25 years of European Capitals of Culture. *Summary of the European Commission Conference.* March 23-24, Brussels. Retrieved from http://ec.europa.eu/culture/documents/conclusions_ecoc.pdf

European Commission (2011, Jan. 17). European Capitals of Culture. *European Commission Culture.* Retrieved from http://ec.europa.eu/culture/our-programmes-and-actions/doc413_en.htm

European Commission (2014, Dec.). European Capitals of Culture 2020 - 2033 Guide for cities preparing to bid. *European Commission Culture.* Retrieved from http://ec.europa.eu/programmes/creative-europe/actions/documents/ecoc-candidates-guide_en.pdf

European Communities (2009). *European Capitals of Culture: the road to success from 1985 to 2010.* Luxembourg: Office for Official Publications of the European Communities. Retrieved from http://ec.europa.eu/culture/pub/pdf/ecoc_25years_en.pdf

Evans, G. (2003) Hard branding the cultural city – From Prado to Prada. *International Journal of Urban and Regional Research, 27*(2), 417–440.

Evans, G. (2005). Measure for measure: Evaluating the evidence of culture's contribution to regeneration. *Urban Studies, 42*(5), 959 – 983.

Evans, G. (2011). Cities of culture and the regeneration game. *London Journal of Tourism, Sport and Creative Industries (LJTSCI), 5*(6), 5-18.

Evans, J., & Hall, S. (Eds.) (1999). *Visual culture: The reader.* London: Sage.

Eyice, S. (1980). *Tarih içinde İstanbul ve şehrin gelişmesi*. Atatürk Konferansları VII'den ayrıbasım. Ankara: Türk Tarih Kurumu Basımevi.

Fairclough, N. (1992). *Discourse and social change*. Cambridge: Polity Press.

Fairclough, N. (1995). *Critical discourse analysis: The critical study of language*. London: Longman.

Fairclough, N. (2001). Critical dicourse analysis as a method in social scientific research. In: R. Wodak & M. Meyer (Eds.). *Methodas of Critical Discourse Analysis* (pp. 121-138). London: Sage.

Fairclough, N. (2005). Critical discourse analysis. *Marges Linguistiques, 9*, 76-94.

Fairclough, N., & Wodak, R. (1997). Critical discourse analysis. In: T. Van Dijk (Ed.) *Discourse Studies: A Multidisciplinary Introduction*, Vol. 2 (pp. 258-284). London: Sage.

Falkheimer, J. (2006). When place images collide: Place branding and news journalism. In: J. Falkheimer, & A. Jansson (Eds.). *Geographies of Communication: The Spatial Turn in Media Studies*, (pp. 125-138). Gothenburg: Nordicom.

Farias, I., & Stemmler, S. (2006). Deconstructing 'Metropolis'. critical reflections on a eruopean concept. *CMS Working Paper Series*, No. 004-2006. Berlin: Center for Metropolitan Studies, Technical University Berlin, *Retrieved from* http://www.metropolitanstudies.de

Firat, F. A., & Venkatesh, A. (1993). Postmodernity: The age of marketing. *International Journal of Research in Marketing, 10*(3), 227–249.

Font, X. (1997). Managing the tourist destination's image. *Journal of Vacation Marketing, 3*(2), 123–131.

Foster, H. (Ed.). (1988). *Vision and visuality*. Seattle, WA: Bay Press.

Foucault, M. (1972). *The archaeology of knowledge and the discourse on language*. New York: Pantheon Books.

Foucault, M. (1974 [1966]). *The order of things*. London: Routledge.

Freely, J. (1996). *Istanbul: The imperial city*. Penguin Books: London.

Fretter, A. D. (1993). Place marketing: A local authority perspective. In G. Kearns & C. Philo (Eds.). *Selling Places: The City as Cultural Capital, Past and Present* (pp. 163-174). Oxford: Pergamon.

Friedmann, J. (1986). The world city hypothesis. *Development and Change, 17*(1), 69–83.

Frisby, D., & Featherstone, M. (2000). *Simmel on culture, Selected Writings*. Sage: London.

Galtung, J., & Ruge, M. (1981). Structuring and selecting news. In: S. Cohen & J. Youn (Eds.). *The Manufacture of News* (pp. 52-63). London: Constable.

Garcia, B. (2004). Cultural policy and urban regeneration in Western European cities: lessons from experience, prospects for the future. *Local Economy, 19*(4), 312-326.

Garcia, B. (2005). Deconstructing the city of culture: The long-term cultural legacies of Glasgow 1990. *Urban Studies, 42*(5/6), 841–868.

Gartner, W. C. (1993). *Image formation process. Journal of Travel & Tourism Marketing, 2*(2/3), 191-215.

Getz, D. (2005). *Event management and event tourism* (2nd ed.). New York: Cognizant.

Gill, S. (1990). *American hegemony and the trilateral commission*. Cambridge, UK: Cambridge University Press.

Gold, J. R., & Ward, S. V. (Eds.). (1994). *Place promotion: The use of publicity and marketing to sell towns and regions*. Chichester: John Wiley & Sons.

Goldman, R. (1992). *Reading ads socially: Sociology of culture/cultural studies*. London: Routledge.

Gombrich, E. H. (1982). *The image and the eye: Further studies in the psychology of pictorial representation*. London: Phaidon.

Gonzalez, J. (1993). Bilbao: culture, citizenship and quality of life. In: F. Bianchini & M. Parkinson (Eds.). *Cultural policy and urban regeneration: the West European experience* (pp. 73-89). Manchester: Manchester University Press.

Gospodini, A. (2004). Urban space morphology and place identity in European cities: Built heritage and innovative design. *Journal of Urban Design, 2*(9), 225-248.

Gotham, K. F. (2005). Theorizing urban spectacles: Festivals, tourism and the transformation of urban space. *City, 9*(2), 225-246.

Gotham, K. F., & Krier, D. A. (2008). From the culture industry to the society of the spectacle: Critical theory and the Situationist International. In H. F. Dahms (Ed.). *No Social Science without Critical Theory (Current Perspectives in Social Theory, Volume 25)* (pp.155-192). Bingley, UK: Emerald.

Gould, P., & White, R. (1974). *Mental maps*. Harmondsworth: Penguin Books.

Greenhalgh, P. (1988). *Ephemeral vistas: The Expositions Universelles— Great Exhibitions and World's Fairs, 1851-1939*. Manchester: Manchester University Press.

Gunn, C. A. (1988). *Vacationscapes: Designing tourist regions* (2nd ed.). New York: Van Nostrand Reinhold.

Gümüş, K. (2010). "Creating Interfaces for a Sustainable Cultural Programme for Istanbul". Interview by Hulya Ertas. In: *Architectural Design, Special Issue: Turkey: At the Threshold, 80*(1), pp. 70–75.

Güvenç, M. and Ünlü-Yücesoy, E. (2009). Urban spaces in and around Istanbul. *Istanbul: City of Intersections*, LSE Cities, Urban Age Conference Publication, London. Retrieved from: http://lsecities.net/media/objects/articles/urban-spaces-in-and-around-istanbul

Haarmann, A. (2005) The urban self. In P. Oswalt (Ed.). *Shrinking Cities* (vol. 2), (pp. 772-776). Interventions, Ostfildern: Hatje Cantz Verlag.

Hall, C. M. (1989). Hallmark tourist events: Analysis, definition, methodology and review. In G. J. Syme, B. J. Shaw, D. M. Fenton, & W. S. Mueller (Eds.). *The Planning and Evaluation of Hallmark Events* (pp. 3-19). Avebury, England: Aldershot.

Hall, C. M. (1992). *Hallmark tourist events: Impacts, management, and planning*. London: Belhaven Press.

Hall, C. M. (1994). *Tourism and politics: Policy, power and place*. London: John Wiley.

Hall, S. (1980). Encoding/Decoding. In Hall, D. Hobson, A. Lowe, and P. Willis (Eds.). *Culture, Media, Language, Working Papers in Cultural Studies, 1972–79* (pp. 128-138). London: Hutchinson.

Hall, S. (1997). Representation: Cultural representations and signifying practices. London, Thousand Oaks, California: Sage in association with the Open University. ISBN 9780761954323.

Hansen, M. H. (2006). *Polis: An introduction to the* ancient *Greek city-state*. Oxford: Oxford University Press.

Harvey, D. (1989a). *The condition of postmodernity: An enquiry into the origins of cultural change*. Oxford: Basil Blackwell.

Harvey, D. (1989b). From managerialism to entrepreneurialism: The transformation of urban governance in late capitalism. *Geografiska Annaler, 71B*, 3-17.

Harvey, D. (1991). The urban face of capitalism. In J. F. Hart (Ed.). *Our changing cities* (pp. 51- 66). Baltimore: Johns Hopkins University Press.

Harvey, D. (2012, May 10). *Rebel cities: The urbanization of class struggle*, LSE Cities and Department of Geography and Environment public lecture. LSE, London.

Harvey, D. (2013). "Urban Class Warfare: Are Cities Built for the Rich?" Interview by C. Twickel. *Spiegel*. Retrieved from: http://www.spiegel.de/international/world/marxist-and-geographer-david-harvey-on-urban-development-and-power-a-900976.html

Häußermann, H., & Siebel, W. (Eds.). (1993). Die politik der festivalisierung und die festivalisierung der politik. *Festivalisierung der Stadtpolitik* (pp. 7-31). Opladen: Westdeutscher Verlag.

Hein, C. (2010). The European Capital of Culture Programme and Istanbul 2010. In D. Göktürk, L. Soysal, & İ. Türeli (Eds.). *Orienting Istanbul: Cultural Capital of Europe?* (pp. 253-266). London: Routledge.

Hem, L. E., & Iversen, N. M. (2008). How to develop a destination brand logo: A qualitative and quantitative approach. *Scandinavian Journal of Hospitality and Tourism, 4*(2), 83-106.

Hiller, H. H. (1999). Toward an urban sociology of mega-events. In R. Hutchison (Ed.). *Constructions of Urban Space (Research in Urban Sociology, Volume 5* (pp.181-205). Greenwich, CT: JAI Press.

Hiller, H. H. (2000). Mega-events, urban boosterism and growth strategies: An analysis of the objectives and legitimations of the Cape Town 2004 Olympic Bid. *International Journal of Urban and Regional Research, 24*(2), 439-458.

Hodge, B. (2012). Ideology, identity, interaction: Contradictions and challenges for critical discourse analysis. *Critical Approaches to Discourse Analysis across Disciplines, 5*(2), 1-18.

Holcomb, B. (1994). City make-overs: Marketing the post-industrial city. In J. R. Gold & S. V. Ward (Eds.). *Place Promotion: The Use of Publicity and Marketing to Sell Towns and Regions* (pp. 115-131). Chichester: John Wiley & Sons.

Holloway, J. C. (2004). *Marketing for tourism*. Essex: Pearson Education Limited.

Horkheimer, M., & Adorno, T.W. (1991 [1944]). *Dialektik der Aufklärung. Philosophische Fragmente*. Frankfurt am Main: Fischer.

Hospers, G.-J., & van Dalm, R. (2005). How to create a creative city? The viewpoints of Richard Florida and Jane Jacobs. *Foresight, 7*(4), 8-12.

Howells, R. (2009). *Visual culture*. Cambridge: Polity Press.

Howes, D. (Ed.). (1996). *Cross-cultural consumption: Global markets local realities*. London & New York: Routledge.

Hubbard, P. (2006). *City*. New York, NY: Routledge.
Istanbul 2010 Avrupa Kültür Başkenti Girişim Grubu (2011). *İstanbul 2010 Avrupa Kültür Başkenti Ajansı Projeleri Afiş Seçkisi*. İstanbul: İstanbul 2010 Avrupa Kültür Başkenti Ajansı. ISBN: 9786058815360
Istanbul 2010 ECoC Agency (2011). *Istanbul 2010 AKB Kentsel Projeler ve Kültürel Miras Projeleri (2008/2010)*. In A. Sengozer (Ed.). İstanbul: İstanbul 2010 Avrupa Kültür Başkenti Ajansı.
İBB Kentsel Dönüşüm Müdürlüğü (2010). *Craddle of civilizations: Collective memory/ Spatial continuities*. Istanbul: FSF Print House.
İnankur, Z. (2010). *Batının gözünden İstanbul. In Bizantion'dan İstanbul'a Bir Başkentin 8000 yılı*, Sabancı Üniversitesi Sakıp Sabancı Müzesi, 5 Haziran-4 Eylül.
Jacobs, J. (1969). *The economy of cities*. New York: Random House.
Jacobs, J. (1984). *Cities and the wealth of nations*. New York: Random House.
Jamieson, K. (2004). The festival gaze and its boundaries. *Space and Culture, 7*(1), 64- 75.
Jenkins, O. H. (1999). Understanding and measuring tourist destination images. *International Journal of Tourism Research, 1*(1), 1–15.
Jenks, C. (1995). *Visual culture*. London: Routledge.
Jensen, K. B. (2002). *A handbook of media and communication research: Qualitative and quantitative methodologies*. London: Routledge.
Jones, P., & Wilks-Heeg, S. (2004). Capitalising culture: Liverpool 2008. *Local Economy, 19*(4), 341-360.
Jørgensen, M. W., & Phillips, L. J. (2002). *Discourse analysis as theory and method*. London: Sage.
Jung, C. G. (1964). *Man and his symbols*.Garden City, N.Y.: Doubleday. ISBN 0-440-35183-9.
Kafesçioğlu, Ç. (2009). *Constantinopolis/ Istanbul: Cultural encounter, imperial vision, and the construction of the Ottoman capital*. University Park: Pennsylvania State University Press.
Kalandides, A. (2007). Fragmented Branding for a Fragmented City: Marketing Berlin. Conference paper presented at the *Sixth European Urban & Regional Studies Conference: Boundaries and Connections in a Changing Europe*, Roskilde, Denmark, September 21st to 24th, 2006.
Kalergis, D. (2008). The Role of Architecture In Culture-Led Urban Regeneration Strategies. In L. Malíková & M. Sirák (Eds.). *Regional and Urban Regeneration in European Peripheries: What Role for Culture?* (pp. 21-34). Bratislava: Institute of Public Policy.
Kapferer, J.-N. (1997). *Strategic brand management: Creating and sustaining brand equity long term*. London: Kogan Page.
Kaplan, M. D., Yurt, O., Guneri, B., & Kurtulus, K. (2010). Branding places: Applying brand personality concept to cities. *European Journal of Marketing, 44*(9), 1286-1304.
Karaman, O. (2008). Urban pulse – (re)making space for globalization in Istanbul. *Urban Geography, 29*(6), 518-525.
Kavaratzis, M. (2004). From city marketing to city branding: Towards a theoretical framework for developing city brands. *Place Branding, 1*(1), 58–73.
Kavaratzis, M. (2005). Branding the City through Culture and Entertainment, paper presented at the *AESOP 2005 Conference*, 13-18 July, Vienna, Austria. Retrieved from http://aesop2005.scix.net/data/papers/att/378.fullTextPrint.pdf
Kavaratzis, M., & Ashworth, G. J. (2005). City branding: An effective assertion of identity or a transitory marketing trick?, *Tijdschrift voor Economische en Sociale Geografie, 96*(5), 506-514.
Kawulich, B. B. (2004). Data Analysis Techniques in Qualitative Research. *Journal of Research in Education, 14*(1), 96-113.
Kaya, Ö. (2010). *Cumhuriyet'in vitrin şehri 3 devirde Istanbul*. Istanbul: Küre Yay.
Kearns, G., & Philo, C. (Eds.). (1993). *Selling places: The city as cultural capital, past and present*. Oxford: Pergamon.
Keller, K. L. (2003). *Strategic brand management: Building, measuring, and managing brand equity*. Upper Saddle River: Prentice Hall.
Keyder, Ç. (1993). *Istanbul'u nasıl satmalı? Ulusal kalkınmacılığın iflası*. Istanbul: Metis Yayınları.
Keyder, Ç. (2009). Istanbul in a Global Context [PDF]. *Istanbul: City of Intersections*, LSE Cities, Urban Age Conference Publication, London. Retrieved from http://lsecities.net/media/objects/articles/istanbul-in-a-global-context
Keyder, Ç. (Ed.). (1999). *Istanbul: Between the global and the local*. Lanham: Rowman & Littlefield.
Keyder, Ç., & Öncü, A. (1994). Globalization of a third world metropolis: Istanbul in the 1980s. *Review, 17*(3), 383-421.

Kipfer, S., Schmid, C., Goonewardena, K., & Milgrom, R. (2008). Globalizing Lefebvre? In
  K. Goonewardena, S. Kipfer, R. Milgrom, & C. Schmid (Eds.). *Space, Difference, Everyday Life:*
  Reading Henri Lefebvre (pp. 285-305). London and New York: Routledge.
Kirezli, Ö. (2011). Museum marketing: Shift from traditional to experiential marketing, *International*
  Journal of Management Cases, Special Issue: CIRCLE Conference, 12, 173-184.
Klaic, D. (2010). Culture shapes the contemporary city. *EUROZINE*. Retrieved from
  http://www.eurozine.com/articles/2010-06-22-klaic-en.html
Kohli, C., & Thakor, M. (1997). Branding consumer goods: Insights form theory and practice. *Journal of*
  Consumer Marketing, 14(3), 206-219.
Konecki, K. T. (2011). Visual grounded theory: A methodological outline and examples from empirical
  work, *Revija Za Sociologiju, 41*(2), 131–160.
Koolhaas, R. (2000). Whatever happened to urbanism? In M. Miles, T. Hall, & I. Borden (Eds). *The City*
  Cultures Reader (pp. 327-329). London: Routledge.
Koolhaas, R., Chung, C. J., Inaba, J., & Leong, S. T. (2002). The Harvard Design School Guide to
  Shopping. *Harvard Design School Project on the City 2*, New York: Taschen.
Kornberger, M. (2010). *Brand society: How brands transform management and lifestyle*. Cambridge,
  New York: Cambridge University Press.
Kotler, P. (2000). *Marketing management* (The Millennium Edition). Upper Saddle River: Prentice Hall.
Kotler, P., Haider, D. H., & Rein, I. (1993). *Marketing places: Attracting investment, industry, and*
  tourism to cities, states, and nations. New York: Free Press.
Krautheimer, R. (1983). *Three Christian Capitals: Topography and politics*. Los Angeles, CA.:
  University of California Press.
Kress, G. R., & van Leeuwen, T. (2001). *Multimodal discourse: The modes and media of contemporary*
  communication. London: Arnold.
Kress, G. R., & van Leeuwen, T. (2006). *Reading images: The grammar of visual design* (2nd ed.).
  London: Routledge.
Kuban, D. (1998). *Kent ve mimarlık üzerine İstanbul yazıları*. Istanbul: YEM Yayın.
Kuban, D. (2010a). *Konstantinopolis-İstanbul'un destanı tarihi*. [Article in the Exhibition Catalogue of
  Bizantion'dan İstanbul'a Bir Başkentin 8000 yılı, Sabancı Üniversitesi Sakıp Sabancı Müzesi, 5
  June-4 September 2010]. İstanbul: Mas Matbaacilik.
Kuban, D. (2010b). *İstanbul bir kent tarihi Bizantion, Konstantinopolis, İstanbul*. İstanbul: Türkiye İş
  Bankası Kültür Yay.
Kurtarır, E., & Cengiz, H. (2005). *What are the dynamics of creative economy in Istanbul?* Paper
  presented at the 41st ISoCaRP Congress. Retrieved from
  http://www.isocarp.net/data/case_studies/650.pdf
Lacan, J. (1977). *Seminar XI: The four fundamental concepts of psychoanalysis* (A. Sheridan, Trans.). J.-
  A. Miller (Ed.). New York, London: Penguin.
Lacey, N. (2009). *Image and representation: Key concepts in media studies*. Basingstoke: Palgrave
  Macmillan.
Laclau, E. (1990). *New reflections on the revolution of our time*. London: Verso.
Laclau, E., & Mouffe, C. (1985). *Hegemony and socialist strategy*. London: Verso.
Lähdesmäki, T. (2011). Contested identity politics: Analysis of the EU Policy Objectives and the local
  reception of the European Capital of Culture Program. *Baltic Journal of European Studies, 1/2*(10),
  134-166.
Langer, S. K. (1951). *Philosophy in a new key: A study in the symbolism of reason, rite and art*. New
  York: Mentor.
Langer, S. K. (1957). *Problems of art*. New York: Scribner's.
Lash, S., & Lury, C. (2007). *Global culture industry: The mediation of things*. Malden MA: Polity.
Lash, S., & Urry, J. (1994). *Economies of signs and space*. London: Sage.
Law no. 5366: Preservation by Renovation and Utilization by Revitalizing of Deteriorated Immovable
  Historical and Cultural Properties. Retrieved from
  http://inuraistanbul2009.files.wordpress.com/2009/06/law-5366-1.pdf
Law, C. M. (1993). *Urban tourism: Attracting visitors to large cities*. London: Mansell.
Leach, N. (Ed.). (2005). *Rethinking architecture: A reader in cultural theory*. New York: Routledge.
Lechte, J. (1994). *Fifty key contemporary thinkers: From* structuralism *to postmodernity*. London:
  Routledge.

Ledrut, R. (1986). Images of the city. In M. Gottdienier, & A. Lagopoulos (Eds.). *The City and the Sign: An Introduction to Urban Semiotics* (pp. 219-240). New York: Columbia University Press.

Lefebvre, H. (1991). *The production of space*. Cambridge MA: Blackwell.

Lefebvre, H. (2003 [1970]). *The urban revolution*. Minneapolis: University of Minnesota Press.

Lehrer, U. (2002). Image production and globalization: City building process at Potsdamer Platz (Unpublished doctoral dissertation). University of California, Los Angeles.

Lewis, B., & Churchill, B. E. (2009). *Islam: The religion and the people*. Indianapolis, IN: Wharton Press.

Ley, D., & Olds, K. (1988). Landscape as spectacle: World fairs and culture of heroic consumption. *Environment and Planning D: Society and Space, 6*(2), 191-212.

López-Varela, A. (2009). The city as e-topia: From intertextuality to intermediality. In A. López-Varela, & M. Nefl (Eds.). *Real And Virtual Cities.Intertextual And Intermedial Mindscapes*, Bucuresti: Editura Univers Enciclopedic.

Lynch, K. (1960). *The image of the city*. Cambridge, London: MIT Press.

MacCannell, D. (1999). *The tourist: A new theory of the leisure class* (2nd ed.). London: Macmillan.

MacCannell, D. (2001). Tourist agency. *Tourist Studies, 1*(1), 23-37.

MacDougall, J. P. (2003). Transnational commodities as local cultural icons: Barbie dolls in Mexico. *The Journal of Popular Culture, 37*(2), 257-275.

Maheshwari, V., Vandewalle, I., & Bamber, D. (2008). Place branding and the Liverpool'08 brand campaign in 'City of Liverpool'. In W. Coudenys (Ed.), WHOSE CULTURE(S)?, *Proceedings of the Second Annual Conference of the University Network of European Capitals of Culture Liverpool*, 16-17 October, UNeECC Forum vol. 1, 119-126.

Maisetti, N., Ökmekler, M. E., & Vion, A. (2012). *working out metropolitan facades: Istanbul and Marseilles as European Capitals of Culture*. 42nd Urban Affairs Association Conference, Panel 85: The Use of Arts and Culture to Reimagine Cities, April 18-21, Pittsburgh. Retrieved from: http://www.sciencespo-aix.fr/media/Okmekler_Maisetti_Pittsburgh_2012.pdf

Maitland, R. (2010). Everyday life as a creative experience in cities. *International Journal of Culture, Tourism And Hospitality Research, 4*(3), 176-185.

Mansel, P. (1996). *Dünyanın arzuladığı şehir Konstantinapolis 1453-1924*. Istanbul: Sabah.

Martins, L. (2006). Bidding for the Olympics: A local affair? Lessons learned from the Paris and Madrid 2012 Olympic Bids. Paper presented at *City Futures: An International Conference on Globalism and Urban Change*, University of Illinois, July 8-10, 2004, Chicago.

Mason, J. (2006). *Qualitative research*. Thousand Oaks, London: Sage.

Massey, D. (2004). Geographies of responsibility. *Geografiska Annaler: Series B, Human Geography, 86*(1), 5–18.

Mathews, G. (2000). *Global culture/individual identity: Searching for home in the cultural supermarket*. London: Routledge.

McAdams, M. (2007). Global cities as centers of cultural influence: A focus on Istanbul, Turkey. *Transtext(e)s Transcultures: Journal of Global Cultural Studies, 3*, 151-165.

McLuhan, M. (1964). *Understanding media*. New York: Mentor.

McMillen, P. (2010). This photo will be an icon of Istanbul forever. Interview by Lalehan Uysal. *Istanbul 2010 – Heritage, Winter* (1), 54-57.

Merriam-Webster's online dictionary (n.d.) *Palimpsest*. Retrieved from http://www.merriam-webster.com/dictionary/palimpsest

Merrin, W. (2005). *Baudrillard and the media*. Cambridge: Polity Press.

Metz, C. (1981). *The imaginary signifier: Psychoanalysis and the cinema*. Bloomington: Indiana University Press.

Miles, M. (2005). Interruptions: Testing the rhetoric of culturally led urban development. *Urban Studies, 42*(5/6), 889–911.

Mirzoeff, N. (Ed.). (1998). *The visual culture reader*. London: Routledge.

Mısırlıoğlu, H. (2010). Now is the time to rediscover. Interview by Lalehan Uysal. *Istanbul 2010: "Heritage", Winter*(01), 58-59.

Moisander, J., & Valtonen, A. (2006). *Qualitative marketing research: A cultural approach*. London: Sage.

Molotch, H. L. (1976). The city as a growth machine. *American Journal of Sociology, 82*, 309-330.

Molotch, H. L. (1996). LA as product: How design works in a regional economy. In A.J. Scott & E. Soja (Eds.). *The city: Los Angeles and urban theory at the end of the twentieth century* (pp. 225-275). Berkeley and Los Angeles: University of California Press.

Morgan, N., Pritchard, A., & Pride, R. (2002). *Destination branding: Creating the unique destination proposition*. Oxford: Butterworth-Heineman.

Mori, G. (2010). *Manifesti: Viaggio in Italia attraverso la pubblicita 1895-1960* [Posters: Traveling around Italy through Advertising 1895-1960]. In A. Villari, D. Cimorelli (Eds.). Milano: Silvana.

Morley, D., & Robins, K. (1995). *Spaces of identity*. London: Routledge.

Mumford, L. (2007). What is a city? In R.T. LeGates, & F. Stout (Eds.). *The City Reader* (4th ed.) (pp. 85-89). London: Routledge.

Nadeau, J., O'Reilly, N., & Heslop, L. (2011). China's Olympic destination: Beijing tourist evaluations of China and the 2008 Games. *International Journal of Culture, Tourism and Hospitality Research, 5*(3), 235 – 246.

Nasar, J. L. (1998). *The evaluative image of the city*. Thousand Oaks, CA: Sage Publications.

Necipoğlu, G. (2010). Konstantinopolis'ten Konstantiniyye'ye: II. Mehmed döneminde yaratılan kozmopolit payitaht ve görsel kültür. *Bizantion'dan Istanbul'a Bir Başkentin 8000 yılı*, Sabancı Üniversitesi Sakıp Sabancı Müzesi, 5 Haziran-4 Eylül.

Newman, P. (2005). Cultural regeneration, tourists and city government. In Küçükçekmece Municipality Publication (Eds.). *Istanbul 2004 International urban regeneration symposium: Workshop of Küçükçekmece District* (pp. 63-69). Istanbul.

Olins, W. (2005). *On brand*. New York: Thames & Hudson.

Ooi, C.-S., & Strandgaard, P. J. (2010). City branding and film festivals: Re-evaluating stakeholder's relations. *Place Branding and Public Diplomacy*, 6(4), 316–332.

Oswald, L. R. (2012). *Marketing semiotics: Signs, strategies, and brand value*. New York: Oxford University Press.

Ousterhout, R. (2010). *Bizans Konstantiopolisi'nden kalan mimari miras, Bizantion'dan Istanbul'a Bir Başkentin 8000 yılı*, Istanbul: Sabancı Üniversitesi Sakıp Sabancı Müzesi, 5 Haziran-4 Eylül.

Oxford English Dictionary (2008a). *Palimpsest*. Oxford: Oxford University Press.

Oxford English Dictionary (2008b). *Opera*. Oxford: Oxford University Press.

Oxford English Dictionary (2008c). *Aria*. Oxford: Oxford University Press.

Öner, O. (2010). Istanbul 2010 European Capital of Culture: Towards a Participatory Culture? In D. Göktürk, L. Soysal, & İ. Tureli (Eds.). *Orienting Istanbul: Cultural Capital of Europe* (pp. 267-278). London; New York: Routledge.

Paddison, R. (1993). City marketing: Image reconstruction and urban regeneration. *Urban Studies, 30*(2), 339–350.

Page, S., & Hall, C. M. (2003). *Managing urban tourism*. Harlow: Prentice Hall.

Palloix, C. (1975). The internationalization of capital and the circuits of social capital. In H. Radice (Ed.). *International Firms and Modern Imperialism*. London: Penguin.

Palmer, R. (2004). European Cities and Capitals of Culture. *Study Prepared for the European Commission Part I*, Brussels, Belgium: Palmer-Rae Associates, International Cultural Advisors.

Palonen, E. (2010). Multi-Level Cultural Policy and Politics of European Capitals of Culture, *Nordisk kulturpolitisk tidskrift, 13*(1), 87-108. Retrieved from http://www.idunn.no/eBook?marketplaceId=2000&languageId=1&method=getPDFVersionFromPro duct&productLogicalTitle=nkt/2010/01/art01

Pamuk, O. (2003). *İstanbul: Hatıralar ve şehir* [Istanbul; Memories and the City]. İstanbul: YKY.

Parkerson, B., & Saunders, J. (2005). City branding: Can goods and services branding models be used to brand cities?, *Place Branding, 1*(3), 242-264.

Parnreiter, C. (2010). Global city formation and the transnationalization of urban spaces: Conceptual considerations and empirical findings. *GaWC Research Bulletin, 336*. Retrieved from http://www.lboro.ac.uk/gawc/rb/rb336.html

Pearce, D. (2007). Capital city tourism: Perspectives from Wellington. *Journal of Travel and Tourism Marketing, 22*(3/4), 7-20.

Peirce, C. S. (1965 [1931]). *Collected papers of Charles Sanders Peirce*. Cambridge: The Belknap Press.

Philo, C., & Kearns, G. (1993). Culture, history, capital: A critical introduction to the selling of places. In G. Kearns & C. Philo (Eds.). *Selling Places: The City as Cultural Capital, Past and Present* (pp.1-32). Oxford: Pergamon.

Doğan

Pickles, J. (2003). *A history of spaces: mapping cartographic reason and the over-coded world*. London: Routledge.

Pierre, J. (2005). Comparative urban governance uncovering complex causalities. *Urban Affairs Review, 40*(4), 446-462.

Pike, B. (1981). *The image of the city in modern literature*. Princeton; Guildford: Princeton University Press.

Pike, S. D. (2009). Destination brand positions of a competitive set of near-home destinations. *Tourism Management, 30*(6), 857-866.

Pine, B. J., & Gilmore, J. H. (1998). Welcome to the experience economy. *Harvard Business Review, July-August*, 97-105.

Pine, B. J., & Gilmore, J. H. (2011). *The experience economy*. Cambridge: Harvard Business School Press.

Pittard, N., Ewing, M., & Jevons, C. (2007). Aesthetic theory and logo design: Examining consumer response to proportion across cultures. *International Marketing Review, 24*(4), 457-473.

Presas, L. M. S. (2005). *Transnational buildings in local environments*. Aldershot, Hants, England: Ashgate.

Prosser, J. (1998). The status of image-based research. In J. Prosser (Ed.). *Image-based Research: A Sourcebook for Qualitative Research* (pp. 97-114). Bristol, PA: Falmer Press, Taylor & Francis Inc.

Quinn, B. (2009). Festivals, events and tourism. In T. Jamal, & M. Robinson (Eds.). *The SAGE Handbook of Tourism Studies* (pp. 483-503). London: Sage.

Raban, J. (1974). *Soft city*. London: Hamish Hamilton.

Radikal (2009, Dec. 4). *'Dünyanın en ilham verici' kentini 'yeniden keşfetme' zamanı*. Retrieved from http://www.radikal.com.tr/kultur/dunyanin-en-ilham-verici-kentini-yeniden-kesfetme-zamani-967525/

Ramo, B. (2007, Oct. 9). *The re-creation of the European city - urban shopping list for secondary cities*. European Urban Knowledge Network. Retrieved from http://www.eukn.org/E_library/Economy_Knowledge_Employment/Urban_Economy/Competitiven ess/Competitiveness/The_re_creation_of_the_European_city_urban_shopping_list_for_secondary_ci ties

Rampton, J., McAteer, N., Mozuraityte, N., Levai, M., & Akcali, S. (2011). *Ex-Post Evaluation of 2010 European Capitals of Culture: Final report for the European Commission Directorate General for Education and Culture*. Ecorys UK Ltd. Retrieved from http://ec.europa.eu/culture/documents/pdf/ecoc/ecoc_2010_final_report.pdf

Rapoport, A. (1990). *The meaning of the built environment: A non-verbal communication approach*. Tucson: University of Arizona Press.

Reid, G. (2006). The politics of city imaging: The MTV Europe Music Awards Edinburgh 03'. *Journal of Events Management: An International Journal, 10*(1), 35-46.

Republic of Turkey Ministry of Culture and Tourism (2005). *İstanbul - Dolmabahçe Palace*. Retrieved from http://www.kultur.gov.tr/EN,31415/istanbul---dolmabahce-palace.html

Rice, L. (2012). The power of image. *Architectural Design, 82*(1), 98-101.

Richards, G. (Ed.) (2001). *Cultural attractions and European tourism*. Wallingford: CABI.

Richards, G., & Wilson, J. (2006). Developing creativity in tourist experience: A solution to the serial reproduction of culture? *Tourism Management, 27*(6), 1209–1223.

Richards, Greg and Wilson, Julie (2004) The Impact of Cultural Events on City Image: Rotterdam, Cultural Capital of Europe 2001, *Urban Studies*, 41 (10), pp. 1931-1951.

Richards, L., & Morse, J. (2007). *User's guide to qualitative methods*. Thousand Oaks, London: Sage.

Ritchie, J. R. B. (1984). Assessing the impacts of hallmark events: Conceptual and research issues. *Journal of Travel Research, 23*(1), 2–11.

Ritchie, J. R. B., & Ritchie, R. J. B. (1998). The branding of tourism destinations: Past achievements and future challenges. *Conference Proceedings of the Annual Congress of the International Association of Scientific Experts in Tourism (AIEST)*.1 September, Marrakesh: Morocco

Ritchie, J. R. B., & Smith, B. H. (1991). The impact of a mega-event on host region awareness: A longitudinal study, *Journal of Travel Research, 30*(1), 3-10.

Ritzer, G. (2000). *The McDonaldization of society*. Thousand Oaks, CA: Pine Forge.

Robins, K., & Aksoy, A. (1995). Istanbul rising: Returning the repressed to urban culture, *European Urban and Regional Studies, 2*(3), 223-235.

Robinson, W. I. (2009). Saskia Sassen and the sociology of globalization: A critical appraisal. *Sociological Analysis, 3*(1), 5-29.

Roche, M. (1992). Mega-events and micro-modernization: On the sociology of the new urban tourism. *British Journal of Sociology, 43*(4), 563-600.

Roche, M. (2000). *Mega-events and modernity: Olympics and expos in the growth of global cultures.* Routledge, London.

Rojek, C., & Urry, J. (1997). *Touring cultures: Transformations of travel and theory.* London: Routledge.

Romanycia, M. H. J., & Pelletier, F. J. (1985). What is a heuristic? *Computational Intelligence, 1,* 47–58. doi: 10.1111/j.1467-8640.1985.tb00058.x

Rose, G. (2001). *Visual methodologies: An introduction to interpreting visual materials.* London: Sage.

Rossi, A. (1984). *The architecture of the city.* Cambridge, MA: MIT Press.

Ryan, R. E. (2002). *Shamanism and the psychology of C.G. Jung: The great circle.* London: Vega.

Said, E. (1989). Representing the colonized: Anthropology's interlocuters. *Critical Inquiry, 15*(2), 205-225.

Samuels, A. (1985). *Jung and the Post-Jungians.* London: Routledge & Regan Paul.

Sassatelli, M. (2006). The Logic of europeanizing cultural policy. In U. Meinhof, & A. Triandafyllidou (Eds.). *Transcultural Europe* (pp. 24-42). London: Palgrave.

Sassatelli, M. (2008). European cultural space in the European Cities of Culture: Europeanization and Cultural Policy, *European Societies, 10*(2), 225-245.

Sassatelli, M. (2009). *Becoming Europeans: Cultural identity and cultural policies.* Basingstoke: Palgrave Macmillan.

Sassatelli, M. (2011). Urban festivals and the cultural public sphere: Cosmopolitanism between ethics and aesthetics. In G. Delanty, L. Giorgi, & Monica Sassatelli (Eds.). *Festivals and the cultural public sphere* (pp. 12-28). London: Routledge.

Sassen, S. (1991). *The global city: New York, London, Tokyo.* New Jersey: Princeton University Press.

Sassen, S. (2000). *Cities in a World economy* (2nd ed.). Thousand Oaks: Pine Forge.

Sassen, S. (2007). *A sociology of globalization.* New York: W.W. Norton.

Sassen, S. (2009). The Immutable intersection of vast Mobilities [PDF] *Istanbul: City of Intersections,* LSE Cities, Urban Age Conference Publication, London. Retrieved from http://lsecities.net/media/objects/articles/the-immutable-intersection-of-vast-mobilities

Savage, M., & Warde, A. (1993). *Urban sociology, capitalism and modernity.* Basingstoke, UK: Macmillan.

Schmitt, B. H. (1999). *Experiential marketing.* New York, Free Press.

Schmitt, O. J. (2011). "Uzun 19. Yüzyılda" Istanbul ve İzmir'de Levantenler: Uluslarüstü bir mezhep oluşumu ve kimliklerin oyunu (Ayşe Dağlı, Trans.), Y. Köse (Ed.), *İstanbul: İmparatorluk Başkentin'den Megakente.* İstanbul: Kitap Yayınevi.

Schneider, A.-K. (2008): Minorities, Margins, Peripheries and the Discourse of Cultural Capital. In W. Coudenys (Ed.) *Whose Culture(s)? Second Annual Conference of the University Network of European Capitals of Culture.* Liverpool, 16-17 October. Pécs: The University Network of European Capitals of Culture, 25–34.

Scholes, R. (1982). *Semiotics and interpretation.* New Heaven & London: Yale University Press.

Schweitzer, J. H., Kim, J. W., & Mackin, J. R. (1999). the impact of the built environment on crime and fear of crime in urban neighbourhoods. *Journal of Urban Technology, 6*(3), 59-73.

Scollon, R., & Scollon, S. W. (2003). *Discourses in place: Language in the material World.* London: Routledge.

Selby, M. (2004). *Understanding urban tourism: Image, culture and experience.* New York: I.B. Tauris.

Sennett, R. (1992). *The conscience of the Eye.* New York: Norton.

Serttaş, T. (2010, Sep. 12). *Diverçity/ Learning From İstanbul.* In Tayfun Serttaş [Blogspot]. Retrieved from http://tayfunserttas.blogspot.rs/2010/09/divercity-learning-from-istanbul.html

Sevin, E. (2010). *Istanbul 2010 - An opportunity for branding.* Retrieved from http://placebranding.ning.com/profiles/blogs/istanbul-2010-an-opportunity

Sheller, M., & Urry, J. (2004). *Tourism mobilities: Places to play, places in play.* Routledge, London.

Short, J. R. (1984). *An introduction to urban geography.* London: Routledge.

Short, J. R. (1999). Urban imagineers: Boosterism and the representation of cities. In A. E.G. Jonas, & D. Wilson (Eds.). *The Urban Growth Machine: Critical Perspectives Two Decades Later* (pp. 37-54). Albany, N.Y.: State University of New York Press.

Short, J. R. (2006). *Alabaster cities: urban U.S. since 1950*, Syracuse. N.Y.: Syracuse University Press.

Short, J. R. (2008). Globalization, cities and the Summer Olympics, *City, 12*(3), 321-340.

Short, J. R. (2012). *Globalization, modernity, and the city*. New York: Routledge.

Shoval, N. (2002). A new phase in the competition for the Olympic Gold: The London and New York Bids for the 2012 Games. *Journal of Urban Affairs, 24*(5), 583-599.

Simmel, G. (1994). Bridge and door. *Theory, Culture & Society. 11*(1), 5-10.

Sirkeci, I. (2013a) *Transnational marketing and transnational consumers.* New York, Heidelberg, London: Springer.

Sirkeci, I. (2013b). Interview by Evinç Doğan on 18.06.2013 at London (UK).

Sirkeci, I. and Cawley, R. (compiled by) (2012). *International marketing.* Harlow: Pearson.

Sklair, L. (2005). The transnational capitalist class and contemporary architecture in globalizing cities. *International Journal of Urban and Regional Research, 29*(3), 485-500.

Sklair, L. (2006). Iconic architecture and capitalist globalization. *City: analysis of urban trends, culture, theory, policy, action. 10*(1), 21-47.

Smith, A. (2005). Conceptualizing city image change: The 're-imaging' of Barcelona. *Tourism Geographies, 7*(4), 398-423.

Smith, M. K. (Ed.) (2007). *Tourism, culture and regeneration.* Cambridge, MA: CABI Publishing.

Soja, E. W. (2000). *Postmetropolis: Critical studies of cities and regions.* Oxford: Blackwell.

Sorkin, M. (Ed.) (1982). *Variations on a theme park: The new American city and the end of public space.* New York: Hill and Wang.

Soysal, L. (2009). World city Berlin and the spectacles of identity: Public events, immigrants and the politics of performance. In A. Icduygu & K. Kirisci (Eds.). *Land of Diverse Migrations: Challenges of Emigration and Immigration in Turkey* (pp. 249-297). Istanbul: Istabul Bilgi University Press.

Soysal, L. (2010). Future(s) of the city: Istanbul for the new century. In D. Göktürk, L. Soysal, & İ.Türeli (Eds.). *Orienting Istanbul: Cultural Capital of Europe?* (pp. 296-312). London: Routledge.

Spink, J., & Bramham, P. (1998). The myth of the 24 hour city. In P. Bramham & W. Murphy (Eds.). *Policy and publics: Leisure, culture and commerce.* University of Brighton/LSA, Publication No. 65: Eastbourne.

Stahl, G. (2009). Urban signs/signs of the urban: Of scenes and streetscapes. *Culture Unbound: Journal of Current Cultural Research, 1*, 249-262.

Stevens, A. (2003). *Archetype revisited: An updated natural history of the self.* Toronto, ON.: Inner City Books.

Stevenson, D. (2003). *Cities and urban cultures (Issues in cultural and media studies).* Buckingham: Open University Press.

Stevenson, N. (1995). *Understanding media cultures.* London: Sage.

Stevenson, N., & Inskip, C. (2010). Seeing the sites: Perceptions of London (Ch.8). In R. Maitland, & B. W. Richie (Eds.). *City tourism: national capital perspectives* (pp.94-109) Wallingford: CABI.

Stoker, G., & Mossberger, K. (1994). Urban regime theory in comparative perspective. *Environment and Planning C: Government and Policy, 12*(2), 195-212.

Stupar, A., & Hamamcıoğlu, C. (2006). Chasing the limelight: Belgrade and Istanbul in the global competition, *Spatium*, 13-14th December, Belgrade, Serbia, 27-33.

Sudjic, D., & Casiroli, F. (2009). The city too big to fail [PDF] *Istanbul: City of Intersections*, LSE Cities, Urban Age Conference Publication, London. Retrieved from http://lsecities.net/media/objects/articles/the-city-too-big-to-fail

Surborg, B., Van Wynsberghe, R., & Wyly, E. (2008). Mapping the Olympic growth machine: Transnational urbanism and the growth machine diaspora, *City, 12*(3), 341-355.

Sutherland, M., Besson, E., Paskaleva, K., & Capp, S. (2006). *Analysis of the mobilising role of the European Capital of Culture Process.* Deliverable 16 of the PICTURE project. Retrieved from http://www.picture-project.com

Şahin, Ş., & Baloğlu, Ş. (2011). Brand personality & destination image of Istanbul. *Anatolia: An International Journal of Tourism and Hospitality Research, 22*(1), 69-88.

Şenay, B. (2009). Remembering the timeless city: Istanbul, music and memory among the Turkish migrants in Sydney. *Journal of Intercultural Studies, 30*(1), 73-87.

Talocci, G. (n.d.). A semiotics of urban voids and their resistance. The case of Istanbul. Conference paper presented at the *Urban Conflicts, Conflict in Cities* programme, Queen's University, Belfast (In press).

Tanyeli, U. (1997). İmge ile gerçek arasındaki uzlaşmaz fark imgelerin istanbul'u, gerçeklerin İstanbul'u, sahte İstanbul, *İstanbul, 21*(April), 82-85.

Taylor, P. J. (2004). *World city network: A global urban analysis*. London: Routledge.

Teckert, C. (2009). *Urban curating*. Retrieved from http://www.ipu.hr/uploads/documents/2032.pdf

Thackeray, F. W., & Findling, J. E. (2002). *Events that changed Great Britain since 1689*. Westport, CT: Greenwood Publishing Group.

The European Parliament and The Council of the European Union (1999). Decision 1419/1999/EC of the European Parliament and of the Council of 25 May 1999 establishing a Community action for the European Capital of Culture event for the years 2005 to 2019, *Official Journal*, OJ L 166, 1/7/1999, pp. 01-05. Retrieved from http://eur-lex.europa.eu/LexUriServ/LexUriServ.do?uri=CELEX:31999D1419:EN:HTML

The European Parliament and The Council of the European Union (2006). Decision no 1622/2006/EC of the European Parliament and of the Council of 24 October 2006 establishing a Community action for the European Capital of Culture event for the years 2007 to 2019, *Official Journal*, OJ L 304, 3/11/2006, pp. 1-6. Retrieved from http://eur-lex.europa.eu/LexUriServ/LexUriServ.do?uri=OJ:L:2006:304:0001:0006:EN:PDF

The Selection Panel for the European Capital of Culture (ECOC) 2010 (2006). *Report of the Selection Meeting for the European Capitals of Culture 2010*, April, Brussels, Belgium. Retrieved from http://ec.europa.eu/culture/pdf/doc674_en.pdf

Thornley, A. (1999). Urban planning and competitive advantage: London, Sydney and Singapore. *London School of Economics and Political Science Discussion Paper*, No. 2, May. Retrieved from http://www2.lse.ac.uk/geographyAndEnvironment/research/london/pdf/lsel_dp2.pdf

TimeOut Istanbul (2011). *Sinan Bökesoy röportajı*. Retrieved from http://www.timeoutistanbul.com/muzik/makale/2245/Sinan-B%C3%B6kesoy-r%C3%B6portaj%C4%B1

Timmers, M.t (1998). *Power of the poster*. London: Victoria & Albert Museum.

Tomlinson, A., & Young, C. (2006). *National identity and global sports events: Culture, politics, and spectacle in the Olympics and the Football World Cup*. Albany, NY: State University of New York Press.

Tomlinson, J. (1991). *Cultural imperialism*. Baltimore, MD: Johns Hopkins University Press.

Torczyner, H. (1977). *Magritte: Ideas and images*. New York: Harry N. Abrams.

Tschumi, B. (1991). Event architecture. In P. Noever (Ed.), *Architecture in Transition: Between Deconstruction and New Modernism* (pp. 125-130). Munich: Prestel.

Tschumi, B. (2004). *Event-Cities 3: Concept vs. context vs. content*. Cambridge, Mass.: MIT Press.

Turner, G. (1992). *British cultural studies: AnIntroduction*. New York: Routledge.

Urry, J. (1995). *Consuming places*. London: Routledge.

Urry, J., & Larsen, J. (2011). *The tourist gaze 3.0*. London: Sage.

Uysal, U. E. (2013). Urban tourism promotion: What makes the difference? *Current Research Journal of Social Sciences, 5*(1), 17-27.

Van Leeuwen, T. (2004). Ten reasons why linguists should pay attention to visual communication. In P. LeVine, & R. Scollon (Eds.). *Discourse and Technology: Multimodal Discourse Analysis* (pp. 7–19). Washington, DC: Georgetown University Press.

Vanolo, A. (2008). The image of the creative city: Some reflections on urban branding in Turin, *Cities, 25*(6), 370–382.

Varbanova, L. (2009). Research mapping. *LabforCulture*. Retrieved from http://www.labforculture.org/en/resources-for-research/contents/research-in-focus/european-capitals-of-culture/research-mapping

Virgo, B., & de Chernatony, L. (2006). Delphic brand visioning to align stakeholder buy-in to the city of Birmingham brand, *Brand Management, 13*(6), 379-392.

Walsh, M. (2006). Reading visual and multimodal texts: how is 'reading' different? *Australian Journal of Language and Literacy, 29*(1), 24-37.

Ward, S. V. (1998). *Selling places: The marketing of towns and cities*. London: Routledge.

Warrack, A. (1993). *Megaproject decision making: Lessons and strategies*. Western Centre for Economic Research, University of Alberta. Retrieved from http://www.business.ualberta.ca/en/Centres/CIBS/Research/~/media/business/Centres/CIBS/Documents/Publications/16.ashx

Weightman, B. (1987). Third World tour landscapes. *Annals of Tourism Research, 14*(2), 227 – 239.

Wetherell, M., Taylor, S., & Yates, S. J. (2001). *Discourse as data: A guide for analysis.* London: Sage.

Whitmont, E. C. (1969). *The symbolic quest: Basic concepts of analytical psychology.* Princeton, NJ: Princeton University Press.

Wigan, M. (2009). *The Visual dictionary of illustration.* Lausanne: AVA Publishing.

Wilk-Woś, Z. (2010). The Role of intercultural dialogue in the EU policy, *Journal of Intercultural Management, 2*(1), 78-88.

Wilk, R. (1995). Learning to be local in Belize: Global systems of common difference. In D. Miller (Ed.) *Worlds Apart: Modernity Through the Prism of the Local* (pp.110-133). London: Routledge.

Wodak, R. (2005). Déjà-vue experiences in applied linguistics, *Applied Linguistics, 15*(2), 240–244.

Wodak, R. (2006). Images in/and news in a globalised world. In I. Lassen, J. Strunck, & T. Vestergaard (Eds.) *Mediating Ideology in Text and Image. Ten Critical Studies,* Amsterdam: Benjamins (DAPSAC Series).

Wong, H. Y., & Merrilees, B. (2007). Multiple roles for branding in international marketing. *International Marketing Review, 24*(4), 384-408.

Wu, J. (2011). Understanding interdiscursivity: A pragmatic model, *Journal of Cambridge Studies, 6*(2-3), 95-115.

Yardımcı, S. (2004). *Meeting in Istanbul: Cultural globalisation and art festivals* (Unpublished doctoral dissertation). University of Lancaster, UK.

Yavuz, Ö. Ö. (2012). Interview by Evinç Doğan on 12.10.2012 at İstanbul İl Kültür ve Turizm Müdürlüğü, Istanbul.

Yazıcı, H. (2010). 2010 is the year in which change begins. Interview by Lalehan Uysal. *Istanbul 2010 – Heritage, Winter*(01), 20-25.

Yerasimos, S. (2000). *Istanbul: Imparatorluklar başkenti.* Istanbul: Turkiye Ekonomik ve Toplumsal Tarih Vakfi.

Yıldırım, S. Ö. (2008). *Kentin anlam haritaları:* Gravürlerde *İstanbul.* İstanbul: Kitabistanbul.

Yüksek, Ö. (2011). İstanbul'un ruhu rüzgari ve iklimleridir, *Istanbul 2010 - Ruh, Winter* (05), 54-57.

Yürekli, İ., & İnceoğlu, A. (2011). Urban characteristics of Istanbul: Problem or potential?, *ITU A/Z, 8*(1), 208-218.

Zizek, Slavoj (1991) Looking Awry: An Introduction To Jacques Lacan Through Popular Culture, Cambridge: MIT Press.

Zukin, S. (1991). *Landscapes of power from Detroit to Disney World.* Berkeley: University of California Press.

Zukin, S. (1995). *The cultures of cities.* Oxford: Blackwell.

Zukin, S. (1996). Cultural strategies of economic development and the hegemony of vision. In A. Merrifield & E. Swyngedouw (Eds.). *The Urbanization of Injustice* (pp. 223–243). London: Lawrence & Wishart.

www.ingramcontent.com/pod-product-compliance
Lightning Source LLC
Chambersburg PA
CBHW021556210326
41599CB00010B/469